WHERE THERE IS NO LEADER...
TAG - YOU'RE IT!

Published by: ADVANTAGE BOOKS™
                   www.advbooks.com

Library of Congress Control Number: 2005927757

Cover Design by Teresa Brierton-Wallace and Jon Syrbe
Carving by Chris Bamber
Photo of Carvings by Carolyn Meadows-Christmann
Photo of Jon Syrbe by Elin Tonheim-Kamara
Interior Layout by Teresa Brierton-Wallace and Jon Syrbe
Editing and Final Design by: Powerful Publishing, LLC . New Orleans, Louisiana
powerful@airmail.net

First Printing: June 2005
09 10 11 12 01 02 03   9 8 7 6 5 4 3 2
Printed in the United States of America

Acknowledgments

Where would this book be without the imparting, blessing, and encouragement of so many?

I am grateful for those who have spoken into my life through word and action and who have also made this project possible: **Christ For the Nations** to **People For Missions**...**Christ Church** to **Christian Family Fellowship International**...**Youth With a Mission (YWAM)** to **Mercy Ships** and **YWAM School of Biblical Studies (SBS), Montana, USA**...my pastors **Randy and Leslie Paige** to **Dennis and Jackie Bambino**...to some of my closest friends like **Eric and Mary Dennie, Joe and Jessica Calabrese** and others worldwide -you know who you are. Major thanks to you!

I am thankful for the experience I gained globally and to SBS Montana, USA; in particular, for without them I would not have come close to accomplishing this goal. To you all, I say, 'God's best' because to simply say 'thank you' would not be sufficient...

Further thanks must be given to a couple more phenomenal people without whom this book would never have gotten this far...even off the ground! First, thank you to my close friend, Teresa Brierton-Wallace, who helped initially by working tirelessly for many a day with me in Africa and Europe creating the layout and design, not to mention teaching me Photoshop and QuarkXpress. 'Teresa, you are amazing.' Next would be my faithful and wise editor with a heart, Elizabeth Foster of Powerful Publishing in New Orleans. This book has far more impact due to her expertise. 'You're a star.' And where would our title of *Where There Is No Leader* be without my friend Steve Wargo from Mercy Ships who helped 'Tag' it with me.

I especially want to thank the Lord for my wife, Seena, and for the many miracles that brought us together. 'Sunshine...you are a great blessing to me. Thanks for helping me to be more like Jesus.'

And the greatest thanks I give to Jesus who drew me out of the pit I found myself in...who took this treasure in the darkness and breathed in life, restoring from self and brokenness, bringing a sense of joy, purpose and freedom.

Finally, I give this book in honor of the **Poor and Needy** to whom I consider myself an ambassador for life, who have shown me how to live an abundant life and a simplicity regarding what is important. They brought me from my selfishness to selflessness and taught me that life is not about me but about restoring value to others' lives. And until the day I leave this earth, I will continue to stand for those of you who cannot stand and speak for those of you who cannot speak. Remember, "You've never been unloved,"...says Daddy God.

TABLE OF CONTENTS

Foreword

As we move into the 21st century, the major shift has been to cut through the cumbersome and just "get it done" in our efforts to touch the world. Jesus Christ immediately broke with religious traditions because He saw them as hindrances to true people-oriented compassion - meeting people's real needs. His ministry exemplified two things: choosing and empowering normal everyday citizens to do the work of the ministry and meet practical needs.

Jon Syrbe has followed this example by encouraging us to "just do it," not waiting for someone else we feel is more called or qualified. We need the humility to admit that this advance of the kingdom is not so much about our humanity but more about our dependence on Jesus - His wisdom coming through His voice and word and His power manifesting when we step out in faith.

One of the first things Jesus did with new trainees was give them power over demons. They came back amazed at what they were able to do in His name. It was almost like Jesus was saying, 'Take note history. It's not about you; it's about my name and power.' In *Isaiah 58* and *Matthew 25*, it is clear that *God* considers meeting practical needs, working for justice, and ending oppression a priority. Jesus not only preached to people but he also fed them. It is high time that we trim the religious fat off of our efforts and get our hands dirty serving tangible needs rather than just discussing doctrine and having lovely conferences.

Jon is my friend. I have seen him practice his writings for many years in some of the most difficult parts of this planet. This is not ivory-tower musings. Jon birthed this book through "blood, sweat, and tears situations" that gave the experience of both disappointment and reward. It is simple and will release hundreds to thrust in the sickle and get what Jesus died for done.

Thy Kingdom Come,
Dean Sherman
International Dean of Christian Ministries
University of the Nations
Salem, Oregon USA

What in the World Am I Doing?

"What in the world am I doing?" must have been the burning question in Moses' mind as he headed for the dry and desolate wilderness with millions of people following his lead. Talk about the ministry of all ministries; the outreach of all outreaches. I sweat just thinking about it. I use to think that leading a team of 15, 30 or more people was a challenge; Moses would have gotten a good laugh.

Moses was not perfect, and he attended the school (as I like to call it) of life experience with two books: sin and weakness. He spent his first 40 years in the world's wealth and wisdom; the next 40 years, he was fleeing the world and being fashioned in the furnace; the final 40 years, he was experiencing the great I AM's supernatural power and provision. Moses was saved, privileged, rejected, angry, and compassionate. He became familiar with solitude and doubt, but it increased his faith, power and strength. He was a shepherd in obscurity who discovered God's love and developed an intimacy with his Creator and Deliverer. He was a humble man, honest with God and comfortable to question Him, and one who interceded for God's nation; a man who partnered with God reluctantly, joyfully, miraculously, angrily, and sorrowfully. Moses was an example of leadership, servant hood, perseverance and struggling obedience. As I often say, "Proper prior prayer, preparation and planning prevents poor performance and pitfalls."

Have you ever wondered why God chose you to go on this wild adventure called Christianity? Whether you are currently in leadership (a role of authority) or practicing for leadership, know one thing: all leaders follow someone else. Even if you were the top-ranking leader in the world, you would still follow the Lord. There is always a higher power. Not everyone who follows is meant to lead, but we all lead in specific areas in the "ministry of life." No one is exempt from influencing another, although those entitled (as leaders) will certainly influence in greater measures. You may wonder, 'What are the exact, specific requirements of life, ministry and outreach? I need to know what rules, policies, and commandments to follow. If not, how am I, as a Christian leader, supposed to set an example in the midst of my circumstances?' Some have said:

"I am the leader, and what I say goes. It is my way or the highway!"

"Gosh, you mean I have to meet with the Tangale man (the spiritual authority in Madagascar) right now?"

"I thought giving was a good thing? So why did they respond negatively?"

"I thought my leaders were to demonstrate Christian life, like Jesus serving."

"I do not believe women should teach or have a position of authority."

"Does the team know we are leading together? Why did they go behind my back and speak to the others?"

"I am not feeling valued as part of the team."

"Why was Jesus approachable but not my leaders?"

"I do not have a clue what to do."

"Why is my leader reacting that way?"

"They did not tell me about this part...how in the world do I approach it?"

"If I am being controlled by my leaders, what do I do?"

"How do I better model Christianity?"

Familiar questions? Concerns? Thoughts? Well, as any brave, courageous leader or follower in ministry would know, it can be overwhelming participating on a team, leading for the first time or, better yet, being an experienced leader who discovers circumstances have changed yet again.

Where There Is No Leader comes from my triumphs and trenches, accuracies and inaccuracies throughout the years. This is a collection of ideas, insights, stories, points, and more from my experience in leading teams and ministering in developed and developing nations, not to mention my varying thoughts and experiences, which I witnessed and gleaned from others whether the good or not-so-good. Many have approached me with questions, concerns, and thoughts, like your own, as I have traveled throughout the world. Through my 17 years of ministry (15 years as a missionary throughout 45 countries), I have served as a youth director and have helped train, serve, teach and lead teams with People For Missions (PFM) and Youth with A Mission [YWAM] schools and bases, including seven years aboard the M/V Anastasis (Mercy Ships). In the last few years, God has birthed a vision in me, a burning passion for training leaders and potential leaders, primarily within developing nations. By providing you with personal "nuggets," this may help to increase your effectiveness and fruitfulness as a Christian, whether you are a leader or a follower in any area of ministry. Some names throughout this book have been changed for respect and security.

The wood carving on the cover, created and photographed by my friends Chris Bamber and Carolyn Christmann, symbolizes how we are all continually being fashioned, refined and transformed into what the Lord intended for us from the beginning of time. *"Be ready, willing and unable,"* says Floyd McClung, one of the pioneering leaders of YWAM. In this posture, God can step in and say, "Finally, I can get started." Before the beginning began, God has always been after your heart. He knew you then because He formed and fashioned you; therefore, lead and minister remembering to keep love the "main thing:" to live preferring others, always looking for the best and purest in them. Choose to see Christ.

When being driven by His love, expect trials. But with love's seed planted in your contrite heart, operating deep within your being, like King David, you will have what it takes to simply pick yourself up, dust yourself off, and carry on without condemnation, hindrances, weights of doubt, fear and drudgery bogging you down. Accept and release grace toward others. To do so is freedom and true liberty. The Apostle Paul's message in Galatians rings loud and clear. Do not bow to the law and legalism, which leads to bondage. "For freedom Christ has set us free..."*(Galatians 5:1)*. With God, there is grace, receiving many times what we do not deserve; it is a gift, and we ought to extend it freely. But we are, at the same time, cautioned not to abuse it.

Life should not stop because people rattle your cage by making life difficult for you. Let the difficulties, which others throw your way, roll down like water off of a duck's back. Do not inhale it, do not subscribe to it, and you will soar to high, unhindered heights. In my walk as a believer in Jesus, I have seen an all too familiar recipe: Christians making chop suey by cutting one another spiritually with words. May we be only known for building up and not tearing down.

In every area of our life and ministry, we need to consider two questions daily, which will enable us to hear the Lord and not our own voice. These are: *"WHY DO I BELIEVE WHAT I BELIEVE? and WHY DO I DO WHAT I DO?"* Some of our former, and possibly current, belief systems may not be Biblical, yet we have been powerfully influenced by them, assuming they were the truth. It is imperative for us to re-examine what we believe is scriptural. God will continually cause you to lean upon Him and not yourself; it is a refining process. For example:

Why have I suppressed women?

Why do I try to control people who are sinning or to keep them from sinning? God, the perfect parent, had His first two children and allowed them to sin, but we have to control "our" people, send spies to watch them, put rules over them, all because we say, 'If "my" people are found sinning, what will people think of me?' This is commonly called legalism, trusting in human efforts and not God's Spirit.

Why do I sit on "my" throne as a pastor, far above and away from others, making myself unapproachable?

Why am I offended if another does not address me as "pastor," "evangelist"?

Why do I have an all night prayer meeting in a village, which disturbs the sleeping villagers? Is that the loving thing to do? Many would be upset to hear the Muslims call to prayer five to six times a day, blasting loudly throughout the streets, yet we are having loud music at Christian meetings…for longer…late into the night.

Try to remember this healthy challenge of continually ask yourselves, 'Why we believe what we believe? and Why do we do what we do?' Do not blindly consume what culture, tradition, and even Christian culture and tradition may feed you. Have you ever eaten while wearing a blindfold? I did not think so. If love is missing from the equation, then your foundation is definitely in question.

My closest friend Eric Dennie M.A., LMHC, NCC, a mental health counselor, whom I admire and learn from greatly, profoundly said sometime ago:

"Love God and love others like Him. Do not accept the belief that any injury or attack from others is more powerful than the sovereignty of God, who is committed to work all things (inclusive of everything and exclusive of absolutely nothing) for the good of those who love Him and who are called according to His purpose (Romans 8:28). It is not as though He causes the evil or wrong, which affects our lives, but it is that He is committed to turn it for the greater good. In that place, there is no room for 'what about…?' Therefore, do not let those who oppose you get the best of you. The goal should be to love God and others well. Occasionally, that means setting boundaries and not overlooking wrongs (not enabling their sin, which ultimately hurts others). Loving them well means confronting (when necessary) with the sensing of the Holy Spirit. It is not by retreating and muttering, 'I just do not feel like rebuking or correcting right now.' It is to be bold and to be meek, whether it is comfortable or not so comfortable."

Where There Is No Leader is not limited to "leaders" but to all in the Body of Christ. We are all "leaders" in a sense, though we may not be given a title. Why? All of us have some degree of influence in our personal world whether it be in the home, work, or socially. How do I know you have influence? Because people are judgmental by nature, always saying, *"I do not or I do want to be like them."* This is why the Christian sphere of influence is so important. Those in authoritative ministry positions cover a broader area of influence, and this book will undoubtedly raise the level of accountability for those leading in various arenas.

If you are a team player, this will shed greater light on a leader's responsibilities, what you should expect from them, and how you should respond. You have received a God-given opportunity to be a blessing to your leaders. You have the potential to make a difference. *Where There Is No Leader* allows faithful followers to comprehend what it might be like in the shoes of a leader, understanding what that leader must endure and hold together while feeding their spirit as well. Allow gratitude and grace to flow through your heart.

My intention is to lower your potential stress level, help you live more effectively, bring you relief, and give you direction through challenging scenarios so you can sit back and enjoy the ride a bit more. I have certainly not "arrived" yet. I am still trying to swim without drowning, run without tripping and bike without wiping out through life's Triathlon. By sharing the wisdom I have gained making and witnessing mistakes, your lives will be challenged and enriched beyond compare if you yield to what God's Spirit has to offer.

During your ministry/outreach together, leaders will find *Where There Is No Leader* helpful for their team, who can continually digest the manual and use it as reference material (most of the scripture quoted is from the NRSV Bible version, unless otherwise noted). It is a companion for those placed in authority or leadership by their headship and who have no one by their side as they leave the "home front." There are decisions to be made. What do you do? Tag - you're it. To have comfort and confidence walking in unfamiliar territories would be fabulous. Let this book enable you to look ahead with grander vision and to avoid possible "hiccups" that can arise. Whether you minister in developing nations, developed nations, or are heading to another nation, I pray that this book will be an asset for you and your ministry, church and teams.

Blessings as you endeavor to demonstrate what many of you consider a dream: to shine brightly in the darkness, to step out and take risks, to always be led by the Holy Spirit, to give greatly of yourself, and to love those who watch, listen and follow you. "God is a Dreamer. Let His dreams come true in you! Know how passionate He is for you. It will drive you to do the unthinkable and outrageous," says my friend Rob Morris, who leads a ministry called *Axiom*. Jesus, the Greatest Leader and the Christ in you, empowered those who wanted to rise and have a taste of transforming the world around them. Express the guts of daily life to the core with the axiom: Jesus!

Outreaching for the King,
Jon Syrbe

CHAPTER ONE

Team Dynamics

Do you think family life is "splendiferous?" Some I know would beg to differ! In your Christian walk, you become part of a family, and, yet, not all families are the same. They each have unique members with distinct characteristics. In Christianity, ministry or the missions' field, families are birthed quite quickly, often times forgoing a nine-month incubation period.

If you are a leader or co-leader, you may have become "parents" in the blink of an eye either by your leader's decision, the purchase of a ticket or the stamp of a passport. Congratulations!

All in the Family

I **do not choose** the word "parents" lightly for, in most cases, it suggests those with a higher propensity to lead and handle greater responsibility. It is a privilege to lead, and, when given that privilege, one should not approach it from a "top down" mentality. Yes, it is a God-given authority and anointing, but I do not see it as unbiblical and authoritarian, as many have unfortunately experienced with leaders who lead by demand and control. Do not give anyone the power to make you jump when they snap their fingers. We are meant to serve one another in love and with desire, not fear, which would be a stark contrast to Jesus' style of leadership. *"For the Son of Man came not to be served, but to serve, and give His life as a ransom for many"* (Mark 10:45). Jesus exercised authority, but He did not lord over people.

Unfortunately, many of you come from challenging family scenarios such as: *'Our father abandoned us...our mother was over protective...our father was over-passive...our parents were drill sergeants; they beat us into submission, dealt harshly with us when we did not meet their expectations, and they yelled at us when they felt threatened (of being wrong).'* Thus when you hear of authority or leaders, you start twitching. You may have heard some say, 'I hear, and you do not; I can see what is best, and you do not; I am right, and you are obviously not; what I say goes, and you have no say; I have been leading for "x" number of years, and you have not.'

If you have been struggling in this area pray and be direct and honest with those you trust as counsel. Often we lead by how we see it modeled. Receive what you can understand from others so that God can teach you and build your character. Question what will make you bitter or better? Trust the Holy Spirit's guidance. *Where There Is No Leader* will disarm negative influences and possibly potential ones not only for you but also for those in your personal circle of influence.

Shall I continue? Dank je wel, plenty-tanky, merci, tak, gracias, jereh-jef, misaotra, spaziba, mu da woasi, thank you - just a little taste of a few languages. It is amazing how one phrase hides deep below the myriad of wonderful flavors, textures, fabrics and personalities colorfully arranged to create God's children. There will be countless factors present when you become part of the family, whether in open-ended ministry or part

of a two-month team. This chapter will target the strains of relationships and miscommunication, offering potential solutions as you endeavor to walk together.

Literal Families

While talking to some friends, they commented on families within the family (team). When you have a literal family, it is important to recognize their mini-team, especially if they are not functioning healthily, because the whole team can be affected. When you have a family (husband, wife, children) as part of a team predominantly of single individuals, consideration needs to be given to the different dynamics.

Key: Help them integrate **yet** enable them to have space within their family.

Even though these are personal issues, create an environment where individuals can express to leaders and/or the team without accidentally leaving room for division and/or a sense of isolation. We are in this walk together but remember to heed wisdom as to what topics are appropriate to share openly with others. I have witnessed people and families healed when certain issues are brought into the open to leaders, those within the team, or other entrusted believers. Seeing others liberated and free drives other team members to bare their sin and struggles and receive healing. This does wonders for the team environment.

One time in the jungle, people were observing how my friend Brenda and I functioned and labored together. We never noticed or suspected people were watching our actions until some couples asked for counsel in their relationships. What a surprise!

How much closer would a team observe their leader's actions? It is inevitable because people need guidance. Often times, they do not even realize they are watching, allowing your dealings to subconsciously influence them. Yet how we interact has more of a far reaching impact than will ever be known to us here on planet earth.

 When you are co-leading, it would be advantageous for you to discuss giftings, strengths and weaknesses to acquire a healthier balance. Define each other's "spheres of influence and authority" to eliminate confusion for the team. This means that both you and the team are fully aware of, say, Jenny, who is an authority on finances. For anything related to finances, you would all run questions and inquiries through her, yet major decisions would be jointly decided between both leaders.

 A safe place to be is inwardly and/or outwardly confessing, *"I do not have perfection in hearing God's voice or having the corner on truth."* Did King David, Gideon, or Deborah? Even if one is revered as the *"senior leader,"* I recommend this highly. Abolish pride from your midst.

 Once you mutually decide upon a leader who will "head up" or have responsibility or "sphere" of authority in that area encourage each other in that responsibility and hold your team to it. If a team member comes to you with a financial question, refer them, politely, to Jenny. Wise, natural parents, shepherds or, better yet, friends do not uproot another's authority. An exception might be if Jenny is not present to make a necessary decision or she has given you the authority to stand in proxy. Not adhering to this principle will almost certainly spur division among the team.

When together, discern whether or not a current circumstance is urgent or can wait.

 Intend (commit) to honor your co-leader (especially) in front of every team member. The team will be affected or infected by your interaction with one another, bringing life or strife.

 It is fine to say, 'Sorry, I cannot give you an answer to that now because I need to discuss it with Jenny.' It is important that the team realizes co-leadership is different and has its own set of principles because they might experience frustration while waiting for an answer. Two cannot co-lead in unity if there is random communication to a select few. So stay in close verbal communication. Trust me; it is a bigger issue than you think.

 Beware of jealousy. If your co-leader or someone on the team has the personality, anointing or gifting that you long for it may annoy you because that person receives more attention than you. Deal with it or the devil will deal through it!

 Make the decision early on never to talk about your co-leader in a negative manner (as in assaulting their character or gossiping). You would lose respect as a leader faster than a speeding bullet!

 What is building them up? "Let us spur one another on," as God edifies us. Look to:

~ Acts 20:32   ~ Psalm 73:26
~ Romans 14:8-9, 15:1-6   ~ Isaiah 40:28-30, 41:10
~ Ephesians 4:25, 5:2   ~ Ezekiel 34:16

 These verses are a helpful reminder to allow grace to go before us as we interact with others, to cancel our pride, and to live for others (not solely for our benefit). We must build with consideration, justice, humility and love. Remember: God only says, does, and responds with the best and highest in mind for everyone.

Avoid the "parent syndrome," which sounds like, '*I did not hear what I wanted from Tom so I will go to Jenny.*' There are some who lived this way while growing up, but you must remain in agreement as leaders. Do not be controlled and manipulated. Being consistent is necessary.

 Agree not to "feed" any problems with a co-leader or with team members. Go directly to the person with whom you are having difficulty **(Matthew 18:15-20; Ephesians 4:15).** In these references, Jesus is confronting our issues or potential issues with people. To deal with others, confront or approach those who are directly involved, not others on the ministry team, the outreach team or the neighbors, but attempt to go directly to the offender or the offended.

If you are comfortable with one leader, this is usually an indication that you should speak to the opposite leader. I say this because, often times, we go to a person we are comfortable with so that we can give our version of the story, possibly directly or indirectly manipulating the situation to make ourselves look good or as the one without fault. This closer person may pat us on the back, making us feel better, but the problem will arise again if not dealt with properly and honestly. It is not about having the outcome your way but God's way. Chuck Swindoll says of some, "I'll do God's will my way." It only lasts for a short time until the floor drops out!

What about female leaders?

 If you are a female leader, become familiar with a country's culture and religious traditions. Do they respect women in leadership? Even in locales, which do not typically accept women in leadership, it still may be okay to function as a leader, yet in other cultures it might not be accepted or tolerated. You may need a mature male to assume "public leadership," leaving you still with the responsibility of decision making while he acts as the mediator in public.

To often, people declare who women are Biblically through a few selective, misinterpreted Bible verses. We are to search throughout scripture, not only about women's roles but also in other belief systems we have possibly held on to incorrectly. Regardless of whatever theological and doctrinal understandings we hold as "truth," they ought to be revisited. For example:

~ **Inductively** = What does the text say? Not what I want it to.

~ **Context** = Scripturally what was the point or issue in that setting?

~ **Widespread** = Is there a continual thread or theme throughout the Word?

~ **Cultural** = Are there cultural considerations (not what my culture says necessarily)?

~ **Purpose** = The writers (especially in the New Testament) were writing to:

* Warn against false teachers and false doctrines
* Encourage
* Challenge
* Address needs and problems

We must recognize if this cultural or Christian tradition affects me:

~ Morally   ~ Physically
~ Biblically ~ Spiritually

...then reconsider what you have been believing, WHO BENEFITS, and WHO is HURT by this or that belief? This will determine the amount of your pride or your humility.

We must realize that the Bible was not written to us but for us, and that is a big difference. Without first observing the needs and problems of the time, we can miss the apostle's intent. Paul was not writing literally to me but to the Ephesians; therefore, I should **observe** the manuscript first, then interpret and finally **apply**. This must be done in this order, otherwise you are putting the roof on a house before building the foundation. Do not be deceived and believe something that God has not intended. Certain comments were not meant for us but for the original audience/readers.

> At a church in South America, I spoke about the value of creation, which I eventually narrowed down to the value of women. I spoke about releasing and blessing women to become and accomplish all that our Loving Father desires. Sadly, I am unsure if I will be invited there again based upon the pastor's response: **"It is written; therefore, we must live it."** Their cultural beliefs, in addition to taking Scripture literally, have postponed their growth.

 Key: Always move out in sensitivity with the right motives.

Jesus and Paul did not crusade for women's liberation, but he and Jesus definitely included women throughout their ministries. Preach the Gospel, exemplify women or humanity, and, when possible and with sensitivity, reveal the truth to the right people in the right situations. This is imperative, as one would not persuade countries and peoples, who have oppressed women for centuries, with abrasiveness. However, if we look closely, we see how radical they were by forcing issues into the light or bringing them to the surface (see Chapter 10 for more).

Did Jesus and Paul speak against slavery? No. Did that make slavery right? Does that make the oppression of women right either? It has taken multiple nations a long time to abolish slavery. Over 2,000 years later, we still step off of the road of brotherly love, which is a commandment by the way. Who are we to say we have arrived at final conclusions in the preceding areas?

As a leader, do not allow yourself to be pulled away from the team too often, being labeled consciously and sub-consciously as the "absent parent." This will also depend on the character of your team as a whole. **Some can function well.**

While ministering in a particular West African country with several complications, I was also bearing the unwanted weight and brunt of authorities. We were the "SL Wannabees" [Sierra Leone Want-to-be's], which became our identity as we were intended to minister there, but this was now impossible for several reasons. Because of the explosion of Rebel activity (civil war) within the country, we remained in a neighboring country to work with refugees. I had to prepare the way for ministry, find and pursue communication (email and phoning), hold several meetings with the United Nations Higher Commissioner for Refugees [UNHCR], local officials, churches, and the leaders of the Mercy Ship, M/V ANASTASIS, all while attempting to be there for the team. Traveling to various meetings would be anywhere from 30 minutes to six hours. I felt divided like a wishbone, being pulled from each side and wishing deep down for the team to pull the bigger piece! They did, though it was not the healthiest environment. I have since learned what is unavoidable and what is not.

 Locate a safe, private place without distractions (if possible) to counsel people and have one-on-ones, which signifies that you respect them. Given the situation, and sometimes the culture, it may be more beneficial to meet man to man and woman to woman (if within the team, discern whether to do so publicly or out of the public eye). And when you do meet for counsel, for protection and accountability, meet in view of others (but not within hearing range) or in an open area (particularly wise with mixed genders). Discern and ask others for wisdom. Unfortunately, many have slipped into temptation trying other methods.

 Team leaders should meet daily/regularly to pray (not only as a team). A friend told me that three weeks into her two-month outreach program, out of the blue, the leader said, "We are not doing anything today. I have not spent any time praying or being with God since we began three weeks ago." This is sad. You give what you have. If you have a muddy well, you muddy others. There is also the other extreme of legalism, claiming they are only effective if they pray every day, before, during and after everything. Yes, dependence on God is acknowledged when praying, but God is in control. Did Jesus pray all of the time? There is always the unexpected to let us see what we know. My life with Jesus is not dependent on one prayer as well. Remember: balance.

Walls have ears. If it is necessary to talk through sticky situations or a team member's needs, be aware of how your conversations carry on the wings of sound to other's ears nearby. Damage comes easy, and reparation is usually more difficult.

Identifying and reviewing team expectations is necessary, and leaders should communicate beforehand, if possible. For example, there are people who misperceive Christianity as a "Christian Utopia," thinking, as my good friend Brenda Hollman, *"I thought people would glow in the dark here, and I found it is not true."* The fact is you will find people who are not "glowing" even in the hypothetically more "spiritual" places. People are people, and they have their days and their ways. The key is our response.

Expectations

As a team, discuss the following expectations:

~ Of one another
~ What the team may be expecting the leader(s) to do and be
~ What the team will *do* and focus on
~ Individually, what they expect from the Lord
~ What you expect from your co-leader, if you have one

Once in place, remind each other as often as necessary and hold each other accountable. When facing challenges, this can be one way of stirring or rekindling unity, and motivation may rise again.

When discussing these expectations, make sure there is a common understanding and agreement. Let everyone be sure that what you commit to is realistic.

Questions are certainly appropriate, but it would be good for you to discuss when and how questions are fitting. Some question for the sake of questioning; others question because of insecurity; others are critical. Sometimes there is no time for questions; the team will have to trust your judgment in a desperate moment. Some questions are better left unasked while others, although helpful and meaningful, would be better asked in private. We should all check our motives.

Continue to stress the need to keep short accounts.

Do not let things fester like an open sore, which can become more infected if not doused with communication, forgiveness, gentle confrontation, etc. If you have a problem or issue with someone, deal with it quickly. Whatever the cost, talk to one another.

Once, while leading a team, we felt it was necessary to discontinue further ministry until all issues, frustrations, and difficulties among team members had been overcome. It was a risk, but one we knew was invaluable. It stirred the motivation to be up-front and clean. We met a few days later to discuss and evaluate each team member's progress and allotted another 30 minutes or so for final clearance. It was awesome. We were excited and encouraged by the results. In the end, ministry was able to continue, unhindered, with God's touch and blessing upon it. The devil's foothold was broken.

How could the team speak messages of love, truth, caring, grace, trust, openness and integrity, if we were not living examples? Their "authority" would not be respected. What I shared with them is this: *"If I let this issue go unattended, then I am allowing you* to walk away with this junk...the unresolved issue of not being real and honest (Mask Living or Mask Ministry), which you will pass on to others." In particular Asian cultures, concealing your true emotions is paramount; one should never let their expression actually "express" their thoughts, so facial expressions are often deceiving. We must be open and speak into each other's life. Many of the world's concerns and needs could be a result of people's fear of openness and feeling vulnerable. One way to muster the courage to speak frankly is to remember that we are meant to speak in love with the question in mind, **"What is the best and highest? To obey God or man" (Ephesians 4:15)**?

In countless homes around the globe, families and workplaces are plagued with the deception that keeping the "peace" is to remain quiet. 'Do not say anything negative to Dad or Mum.' This is a deceptive peace, which leads to undercover tension. Why? Because issues are not handled with honesty, and no one knows what each other is thinking or feeling. In **Matthew 5:9**, Jesus was not addressing those in quiet submission as being "peacemakers." As Pastor Dave Johnson (Church of the Open Door in Minnesota, USA) spoke with conviction, **"Peacemakers are not subject changers. They speak the truth, which usually brings strife (trouble). For example, the Pharisees being called white washed tombs caused some stirring. If you really love, you will tell the truth. Do not use it to humiliate or appease but to bring true peace."**

Take a look in James 3:17-18. You see, if anything is from God, it will be pure and without hypocrisy, yet inclusive of communicating the problem at hand. Action may be necessary for true peace to be resident. Invite peace. Do not be passive. We must let our 'yes' be 'yes' and 'no' be 'no' **(James 5:12, Matthew 5:37)**. This communicates 'I value you enough to let you know that you have spoken in error, hurt me, stepped on my toe, took the wind out of my sails, been incorrect as you to talked to so-and-so about...' We need to discern a passing infraction, and when to speak the truth in love. Again, there is a right time to speak and a right time to be quiet, but fear should not play a part whatsoever.

In situations that need to be corrected, we must speak boldly yet confront others in love. There are two ways to reveal a truth, and they are easier said than done.

Truth spoken harshly (with emotion) hurts, implants rejection, damages, crimps openness and can be manipulative.

Truth spoken in love heals, builds, frees, challenges without fear and breeds hope.

My friend Peter Warren, director of YWAM Denver, CO, USA base, says, "Truth without love is harshness, and love without truth is compromise."

How can it be received (well) when spoken harshly? The motivation of everything we say in life should be through love. Always ask yourself, 'What is the most loving thing to do?' On the other hand, if we are fearful, we ultimately will not speak the truth. We think up such thoughts as, **'God will speak to them; it is not a big deal; I will tell them if it happens again; I will just inform someone else,'** which makes our love not really love and allows compromise in their lives and ours.

Be on Time

It values others. We put "me" first when we stroll in at "our" convenience. One team told me about a time when they arrived to pick up a teammate; the person had not showered, packed and was still playing a game. People are valuable so we must honor our word. Many use irresponsibility as an excuse. People tend to think what they are doing is more important because they themselves are important or so they think. TIME (or "no" time) should be effective wherever you are...to a degree. But if you are with a multi-cultural family, ministry or team, it takes on another form. Decide what is cultural vs. keeping your word. **Find out if time is relevant or significant in this culture?**

When in Mali, West Africa, God spoke to me on a subject that I was about to teach: time management. He said, "Jon, time is not a Western idea; it is my idea. I created the sun to go up and down." Yes, Westerners have created time increments to be more helpful, using hours, minutes, and seconds, but God created time. In some African cultures, stopping to greet someone you know on the street is held in high regard and seen as a sign of respect. However, we must avoid the pitfall of respecting one and accidentally disrespecting another. If you have a prior commitment, the better choice is to honor your first commitment, and, when passing a friend, let them know it is good to see them, but you must be on your way to a previous engagement and would love to set a time to meet with them as well. Judge what is best. And just because others may not honor your time does not mean that you follow suit.

TIME is also connected with your word. If I say I will be somewhere or do something, then I must follow through with my word to the best of my ability (unless there are extenuating or justifiable circumstances which arise). Time management is a form of discipleship that is just as important as self-control, holiness, character, etc., yet it is often avoided because of cultural preferences or pressures.

Some people do not consider TIME valuable. But I ask, "Do people die?" Yes. Well, that is one way of realizing that time is valuable. Often we miss an opportunity that cannot return and is lost forever. Not that all moments in TIME are radically valuable, but this may propel us to reconsider the time we spend unwisely. There is a time for everything (see Ecclesiastes Chapter 3). Remember: balance. There is a TIME for fun and games and relaxing, and there can be value in even one or two seconds. For example:

As I was riding on a motorcycle to Nandhi Hills (India), one rather large Lorry was headed straight toward us in our lane. This truck gave us one of three options: we could hit it, try to stay on the road and avoid it, or swerve off of the road. All three were risky. We kept going with the brake on and attempted to stay on the pavement without wiping out. We made it by one second, and I squeezed my knees inward onto my friend driving. Hey, a few centimeters is significant, too!

My time is not yet, but time has value because God set it in place and because man sinned - bringing death. God's timing is different than ours. Joseph was in prison 20 years. We could go really deep here. We need to reconsider our value (or lack thereof) of our TIME, God's TIME, and others' TIME. And to not do so with excuses: why we could not do 'this' or 'that' or be 'here' or 'there,' when it was in our power to do so. This is a good opportunity to mention again that not everything is the devil. We have responsibilities, which he can use against us depending upon our choices.

When conducting a seminar with leaders in another African country, which began at 8am, I noticed that half of the leaders were on time while the other half entered between 9-9:30am. I said, 'Do you think this could affect UNITY?' I begin the seminar at the time given to honor those who came at the committed time, and, in the first hour, the Lord communicated some significant things and half of the leaders missed it (this is sadly common). If you value time, you may perhaps give a grace period of around 15 minutes, and those who are later than that miss out.

Let us realize that TIME is:
~ Daily and routine or daily and divine
~ Divine and providential

Recognizing Gifts!

Years went by before I discovered my gifts. It takes time and practice with valued and trusted supervision, but there is excitement toward the home stretch when you really begin to gel as the body of Christ or team and see an increase in your effectiveness. Prior investment in this area can help you impact others as individuals and as a team. Some areas we can reflect on with regards to gifts are found in:
~ Romans 12:1-8 (motivational gifts)
~ 1 Corinthians 4:2 and Chapter 12 (spiritual gifts)

- Ephesians 4:11-13 (ministry gifts)
- 1 Timothy 4:14-15 (do not neglect the gifts inside of you and put them into practice)
- 1 Peter 4:911 (be good stewards of His grace and serve with God's strength)
- Hebrews 2:4 (gifts are given by the Holy Spirit and according to His will)

In Romans 12, the motivational gifts are preceded by:

- Be a sacrifice
- Do not think like the world
- Be transformed by the Word (meaning they are moving from who they are into who the Lord created them to be-allow God to be glorified in your life)

Then verse 3ff :

- Do not think of themselves more highly than they ought
- They were assigned the faith given
- They are of or in the same body
- Value
- Compliment each other
- No competition
- Not all have same function
- Gifts given by grace (not earned)

The gifts mentioned here are motivational to bless/touch others. They cannot be commanded because they are gifts. But which ones are for us? Which did the Lord build in us or want to develop in us? And, as with any gifts, they should be used to bring greater health and strength to the Body of Christ and the world. There is no room for superiority, jealousy, or self-preference; all is motivated in love by love.

The "ministry gifts" found in Ephesians 4 are known as the "5-fold ministry gifts." These are roles that equip the Body for greater maturity while protecting people from bizarre, false doctrines and more **(Ephesians 4:12-14).** When we are all working properly within the Body with our gifts, growth is promoted **(v. 16).**

The "gifts of the Spirit," as Paul defines them, are "manifestations of the Spirit"- Spirit led **(1 Corinthians 12:7).** This chapter is enveloped in and around the theme of UNITY...motivated by the best and highest for others, which is LOVE. It is not a bunch of body parts, but IT IS ONE BODY.

** By the way, none of these gifts are selective to any one gender; they are gender inclusive!

Gifts are to build one another. So how do you fulfill that mandate? How do you build up the Body of Christ? How do I exhort, encourage and equip? That is what you need to consider. From the pew to the pastor, all are needed.

* We do not command them. The Holy Spirit gives as He chooses.

* I have walked in many of these gifts, though not "entitled" in them all. There are some who believe one has to be entitled. But the gifts are not only for the select few who are given titles but also for every believer.

* Look to understand people's individual personalities. How do they function best? What hinders or upsets them? What brings them fulfillment? These are some helpful questions that may lead to discovering their gifts. For example, when someone realizes what bothers them, they may find it is connected with a gift they have been given. But it can also be a weakness as well. Another example: I love giving; I know it is a gift, but do I become overly concerned with how others give or judgmental? Am I easily manipulated into giving or is it genuine and Spirit led? Think.

It is unfortunate and detrimental to be told you are too young, too inexperienced, too dumb, too small, too whatever. I have a pal who, albeit professional in her field, is not looked upon as so because of her age. Others believe she does not have the authority to correct and give input. My friends, this should not be. We should recognize and follow scripture. I will not state the obvious in **1 Timothy 4:12** and how God chose and worked powerfully through young people. Help them, encourage them, give them opportunities, walk alongside them. If necessary, come to their aid to free them from intimidation.

Gifts Rejected

I am aware that some of you do not believe the gifts of the Spirit are relevant for today's church. Just consider why God would all of a sudden refrain from exercising His Spirit (power). Why would He limit Himself? The Body of Christ cannot build up one another without His Spirit. He has chosen to work through us. Why would the gifts only be helpful or useful for the New Testament church and not the 20th Century church? If we look closely and in the right context, there was never an indication that they were only meant for the time described within the black and white writing we call "pages of scripture." Some areas, yes, like, "Speak Greek in the assembly" **(Acts 14:1)**.

My friend Joshua from India actually had people praying for him to leave the church. God had spoken to Joshua significant truths for the pastor and the church. The pastor, among others, was offended because he "knew better." After all, Joshua had only been a Christian for two years, and the pastor 20 years. How dare Joshua assume he knew more than the pastor? The pastor severed him from the church. By the way, the Lord fulfilled (to the detail) everything Joshua spoke (in humility). He is one of thousands whose gifts are not welcomed. Will we encourage or discourage gifts to flow? It is the Lord and paramount that we walk alongside people to help them take their beginning steps. They will step out as far as they feel covered and a sense of trust from their peers, colleagues, and, all the more, their leaders. They need a sense of safety, so that if they make a mistake, they know they will not be rejected. They have the assurance of being guided (in love) in the right direction with the purpose of growing.

Too Nice?

Encourage some not to be kind to their own detriment, becoming submissive to everything their leaders do and say. **Sound strange?** Well, there are some who, because of perfectionism or finding their identity and value in what they do and say to others, will make every effort to please and perform. They may even be over protective, wanting to make sure everybody is helped along the way. This keeps others from risking and having opportunities to experience and serve others as well. It also brings tension within a team. Sometimes failure can be healthy. Paul warned the Corinthians to control themselves and stop abusing their spiritual life, yet he never forced them into compliance through manipulation and fear. It was his love and exhortation that compelled them to change their attitude. Just look how cleverly he sandwiched Chapter 13 (the love chapter) in the middle of Chapters 12 and 14.

Keep Them Going to God

It is far healthier to have the team sort out a need, issue or situation with God first, then come to a friend or to you as a leader. There is gain in finding as much solution and resolve directly from God than relying on people, **an all-too-often pitfall in the church.** Think of how many leaders are burning out because of this scenario. They are bombarded so much with people being co-dependent on their leader(s). Your (their) upreach needs to exceed your (their) outreach (like looking up a tree) or their upreach needs to exceed your inreach. They need to know that God hears and responds to them or can if they give Him an opportunity. May they learn to depend, first and foremost, on Jesus. Those in leadership should desire to lead by example, but, alas, that is why I feel there are so many Christians still being "potty trained." They spill out on others and keep going around and around-instead of going to God or they become co-dependent on people to give them answers and direction, thus growing in faith can be delayed. What a word for the church at large.

Provide A Supportive Environment

As a leader, be a part of what the team is doing. Be there. Support them. Encourage them. I know some fellowships where you walk away so uplifted that it skyrockets your faith. While some others? Hmmm...

You are there for them. Remember, their perception of leadership is painted or tainted from your modeling and standards (ah, no pressure!). Look continually for ways to surprise them.

~ How about a night out with them or an individual
~ A pat on the back
~ A gift or token of appreciation
~ Cook or clean
~ Pray for them
~ Thank them/honor them in creative ways
~ Say what you appreciate about them or write it to them
~ Spend time with them

We are on this journey together. Did Jesus separate Himself (in a negative sense) or elevate Himself? Be approachable. Show interest in them. Perhaps take the team away for a weekend, as we did when we were living in the jungle. We did not tell them where we were headed. Only the person responsible for "hospitality" conveyed what the Jungle Jumpers should take along (this was in the middle of a two-month outreach). It was refreshing for them to get away and regain perspective. We did not have to do this for them, but, in the long run, their strength was renewed to tackle more ministry/work.

Again, knowing your team can give you an idea of what is best, but you must KNOW your team - not just their names but their personalities. Each one has a different way of responding to stress and so on. The above example may not be best for every team, but true leaders know how to handle their team accordingly because they care.

Protect One Another

Exploiting or harassing people should never be tolerated. I have vowed not to tolerate the harassment of anyone, but I keep a special watch over the women. Do not allow ladies to be subjected to very uncomfortable circumstances, whenever possible. Make sure women are not putting themselves in risky or unwise situations, within reason. In some countries and locations, if a woman needs to speak with a man, it would be wise and best to do so in the presence of others. If, at any time, something happens, they ought to be quick to let you know. I have had to be firm and strong in some cases. Supportive environments aid this process.

In addition, I also have had to speak to women about how men generally think. This is not easy. Be sensitive in what you say. Perhaps discuss it with other leaders and/or men of maturity before approaching the ladies on this subject. They will feel so much more appreciated, valued and secure. It is not meant to instill fear but to bring awareness and protection. Sometimes women may be naive and cannot see the potential dangers or uncomfortable circumstances. Man is attracted by appearance, smells, touch, and prolonged time spent with them. Do not be paranoid nor be foolish. By no means am I singling out women. The men have need of protection in the same fashion. Both men and women have motives that are, at times, governed by the (ungodly) flesh, in addition to motives they discover in a ministry/evangelistic/work setting.

Reacting vs. Responding

As I see it, reacting is barking at the individual or team in frustration. This usually happens when we react out of emotion without taking the time to think. Rashly reacting and not giving consideration to consequences is dangerous, and the outcome may include a bit of a mess to  clean up. Look to Proverbs 12:18, 13:3, 19:2, 20:3, which may give advice on how the tongue can be an instrument of healing or a problem expander.

When you respond, you withdraw to think, process, pray, and then return clear-headed without the burst of emotions, which leaves a "**lessa messa**" and is clearly the more favorable course of action. Withdrawing could be anywhere from a minute to a day or so. Depending on the person and the severity of a circumstance, it may be best to say: *"I am feeling overwhelmed and hurt at the moment; therefore, I think it best to leave this for now. We will talk later"* or *"Could you give me a minute because I might react in a way with my words or actions that could be hurtful or not the best way for us?"* It is easier to swallow your potentially hurtful words than to eat them!

James 1:19 talks about being quick to listen, slow to speak and slow to anger. Why? Because it shows the other person that you value them. **Proverbs 12:15** explains that fools think their own way is right, but the wise listen to advice. Perhaps you are thinking of **Ephesians 4:26** where it says do not let the sun go down on your anger. This implies that we ought to deal with the problem, not feed it with unnecessary, extended time, giving the devil a foothold.

Watch Out...the Devil Is There

Do not be unaware of the devil's schemes. The devil certainly tried stopping Jesus from exemplifying humility in **Matthew 4:1-11**. The devil is there and quite aware of your activities. He may attempt to keep you from reaching your potential. Although he does not push us off of the cliff, he convinces us it would be better to jump...and we may believe him. Jesus spoke God's word right back to him and moved ahead. I was reminded by my Dutch friend Marcial Eilers: *"As your outreach, ministry, and Christian walk begins, there is excitement brewing in the air; nothing of bother may be coming your way - so you think. The devil, sleek as he is, inaugurates his mission, a surprise. He goes for weak points...a crack in the wall."* Unity, usually, is not an issue at the starting gate; therefore, he will try to affect emotions, cause self-centeredness, divert compassion, plant doubt, fatigue, busyness, gossip, and twist the truth. Half of the battle is being aware; the other half is being active when you sense him stirring something.

Teach the team to keep their spiritual antennas up. Be aware of the temptation to deny what is going on in the spirit realm as you cross the street to McDonald's where some may think witchcraft does not exist "over there." It may not be evident but do not have the mindset of going to McDonald's or shopping center as a means of "escaping the enemy." The battle continues. The enemy and our flesh will rise in selective, inopportune yet opportune times and deceptive ways that seem "good." After all, the devil disguises himself as an angel of light **(2 Corinthians 11:14).** Even what seems to be "good" can be the enemy.

If all seems to be going steadily, do not take it for granted because then- wham - unity is challenged, people become critical of circumstances, decisions, the leaders and others. We all have blind spots, so look for them. One sign is if we quickly become defensive. It takes humility to recognize the possibility 'I could be wrong.' Often, we are quick to believe it is the other person.

> **"He irritates me by the way he cooks." "Why does she have to get ready for bed like that?" "How come they get upset with those jokes?" "That is not for me. I will not do that." "I do not feel like going there now." "I do not believe we should do this (that way)." "Would you believe that leader said...? I do not agree with that!" "What do you think about him/her leading?" "They are not very good at..." "Those people are never going to change so why bother."**

What about strong personalities?

There are introverts and extroverts so be aware of those who are dominant types and those who need some time to express ideas and/or feelings. For example, at a meeting there may be some extroverts who spill out all the ideas while the introverts are quietly processing internally. Be sensitive of this and help facilitate responses and inclusiveness. Maybe have a one-on-one time and ask what is best for them in a meeting. Gangrene spreads ever so quickly as it demands its position within the body, eventually bringing death if not removed or not having the situation "changed." So it is with those from the team who talk behind the leader's back (and about others). This is another plight that chips away at unity. Gauge this upon 'Would I say what I am saying in the presence of that person?' And think of being the victim.

Observe and count how often people gossip behind others' backs while using their names. It tarnishes your relationship with the victim. I would challenge the team to be bold enough, yet with gentleness, to ask the gossiper, "I do not mean to interrupt but is it necessary to talk about them like that, to even use their name? Could you pray for them instead?" You can tell them you would rather not know even if the other had been clearly wrong. Encourage them to go to the right source.

I also might add a word of caution for those who may have a mother tongue different than the team. If you often speak in your own language, it insinuates exclusivity, paving room for doubt. It causes those left out to think they are being discussed negatively. On a smaller scale, there was a woman on one of my teams who I preferred to talk to in Spanish. It was not her fault but mine. There was no hidden agenda. I just enjoy Spanish and the practice of it. But I realized my co-leader and others felt uncomfortable. In the end, I ascertained that I needed to be more mindful of when I was speaking with her in Spanish and avoid it when surrounded by others. On a larger scale with three or more teammates (who speak in their own language together), disunity could weave its way in quite nicely.

Watch out for sarcasm and humor that excludes others or pokes fun at them. Dominating personalities and those who are part of a nationality greater in number than others may suffer with pride. The recipients of this kind of humor may feel they have to outwardly or inwardly defend themselves. Additionally, with different languages and cultures, they may feel alone because they cannot comprehend your thoughts or humor. So be inclusive of others. Be patient enough to explain what you said. *"If there is a problem then someone is thinking more highly than they ought to, and someone is thinking more lowly than they ought to, functioning in superior or inferior pride,"* as Dean Sherman (Dean of the University of Nations) points out from **Romans 12:3.** Superior pride is thinking of myself more than I really am. Inferior pride is the opposite. For example, one who listened to Loreto play the drums was amazed and tells him. Yet Loreto responds, "Ah, no it was not me, it was the Lord." But the one listening says, "Funny, I thought I saw you playing!" This can be considered false humility. Loreto should thank the person for recognizing his gift and that he worked hard to play so well, then he can praise the Lord for His goodness and blessing later.

Superior Pride: elevating yourself to be more than you are. Example: how some talk about their country too much (USA, for one).

Inferior Pride: seeing yourself lower than you really are. Example: inability to receive compliments by responding, *"Thank you, but it is Jesus, not me." But in actuality, God inspired them.*

Read Ephesians 5:8-14, Romans 13:11-14, 1 John 1:5-10, 2:7-11 to see more of what the Lord says about exposing darkness, not operating in pride or the flesh, and living and walking in the light and in truth.

One evening, I was having dinner with Dave and Barb Witbeck. Being from the ANASTASIS, a common topic that arises is cockroaches. In the dimmed light, Barb saw something on the menu resembling a roach and gasped. Dave said, *"The light's torture for the roaches,"* and I thought to myself, *"That is right. The flesh and the roach are similar because they both run from the light."* Always ask the Lord to bring everything into the light that causes the flesh to fail. Let your love for the light be greater than your flesh.

CONFLICT RESOLUTION

"As you slide down the banister of life, may the splinters never point the wrong way"
-Irish Blessing

Are the Kangas hugging or fighting? Sometimes we forget that we are on the same side. When our character and place is threatened, out come the boxing gloves and claws. My grandmother, "Be-Be," used to have this cat we called the "Thisser." Her name for it was "Mow-da-mow." Anyone would have thought it entered the world and was going to leave the same - with an attitude. The only things it liked on this earth were mice, food, and maybe my grandmother. My younger brother was still working on his pronunciation skills, thus adding further humor to the name...guess?! But this cat, like some, abruptly and without warning would start "thissing" and spring up the claws. As did Thisser, there are others who have an eruptive attitude about everything. It is imperative for the problem and truth to be spoken in the right way to the right people at the right time.

Steve Brien, friend & former Chief Operations Officer aboard the ANASTA-SIS, once began his teaching on confrontation with the foundational reasoning of why we should want to joyfully confront issues with one another. *"Adam was the first to blow it in the garden with Eve. He was not the one being deceived (1 Timothy 2:14 tells us Eve was also deceived), yet he said nothing. Ouch! He forgot his image; He forgot who he was and Who created him.*

As it was in the Beginning and now, God speaks into the chaos, darkness and void and sees the potential beauty and order of His Universe. If we saw the value, then why we should confront will be more understandable with further steps to promote action toward resolution. Adam botched it. He did not communicate with Eve and confront her. I trust you will find some encouragement and courage as you look at Joseph's astonishing response in Genesis 45 and Chapter 50:15-21 after the atrocities that broad-sided him as his brothers abandoned him, threw him into a pit, and sold him!" Bottom line: when you value a person the way God does, you confront in love to promote their growth as well as your own.

 PRAY - God's perspective is always a better view. In the 81 questions that God asked Job (**Chapter 38**), He demonstrates that He was in the beginning - the Father knows best.

 Be willing to address hard situations. Not many people find unending, pleasurable joy in confronting. If this is you, like me, you are not alone; however, without reservation, it will secure the preservation of your team/member/friend. And if it is something you have done, be willing to receive and listen without becoming defensive. Pride comes on the scene when we become defensive. It is one of the greatest tragedies in the church. How many believers refuse reconciliation and fellowship? Everybody is right and nobody is wrong.

 Be aware and sensitive to each other's differences yet be aware of justifying someone who is confrontational habitually.

 Gather facts. Do not assume. There is more than one side of the story. We need to maintain a level of trust until we have pursued the facts and witnesses, if possible (with initially going to the others involved). Jesus instructed us to confront each other in love, not gossip and damage the other's name.

 Self-control is a needed discipline and a precious fruit that is not often picked or taught.

 Ask (for them and you) if this matter is really worth the strife.

 Hold your tongue if it is not something you can express in a way that builds up, brings light, shows respect, helps and cures (**Matthew 5:21-26, 18:15-20** or even till the end of the chapter).

When *"two or more gather in Jesus' name, He is there."* But He is there when we are alone as well, right? 'So what is the point,' you ask? I believe it is His strong desire to see people forgiving, reconciling and living in unity (you cannot have unity by yourself). If believers cannot do it, who can?

~ "By this everyone will know you are My disciples, if you have love for one another"**(John 13:35)**.

~ Love can be messy. If it were easy, more of us would walk it continuously. So, the challenge...carry our cross.

~ **Look at Luke 17:1-4.** He addresses the offenders, then being offended or sinned against. Also, **John 18:25-27** shows Peter not willing to confront truth. In **Galatians 6:1-5,** Paul shows us that when a transgression is present, we must work through it gently. Wow! Imagine that! This is a wake up call for us not to be self-righteous, as though we are perfect because, after all, we are not exempt from falling. It is a continual call for humility and carrying burdens. In **James 5:19-20,** helping to restore a brother or sister is the goal, not only looking at yourself. In **Numbers 16,** we see Korah's rebellion and how Moses responded. Is he patient? To a point. What was his first response to their accusations **(16:4)**? How long was he on his face? What was he doing? Is this our first response? Or do we scream or add to the fire by reacting? Moses was willing to be wrong. Later, Moses did become angry **(v.15)**. Was it justified? We ought to be careful how far we take our words, actions and emotions. Let them be weighed rightly, objectively, and with accountability. Watch for extremes.

What else can be learned through their conflict? In **Matthew 7:1-5,** we see one of the oldest, most recognized, yet discarded commands of Jesus! "Do not judge…" In context, it is referring to hypocritical judging, and, oh, how we love to "help" or rather knock others down (consciously or sub-consciously). Is it because of our lack of security? Jealousy? Or is it because we simply see in others what we do not like in our own character or lives? We often cannot see what is wrong or lacking in our own life. Be aware...Jesus knows when we are wrongfully judgmental of others. Take responsibility for the speck in your own eye. What in me may be wrong?

"Repent and ask forgiveness where you have sinned against another. Forgiveness is an act, not a feeling" - Dennis Bambino, my home church Pastor of CFFI - Christian Family Fellowship, International

**We are to take initiative - not wait for the other to come around.

 Think before speaking. Will what I am about to say hurt or heal, strengthen or weaken, mend or tear, encourage or discourage, fuel the fire or put out the fire, bring relief or disbelief, unify or disband, honor or dishonor, respect or disrespect, help or hamper, fulfill or regret, satisfy or dissatisfy.

I **met a family** in India whose daughter had an accident, which caused my friend Stephen Chary and I to rush her to the hospital. I began counseling them about their internal conflicts. One time, while discussing Biblical principles, I realized, as their emotions were flaring, they kept interrupting each other. This was an opportunity to address something practical. Not only did the light bulb go on in their minds, but, in the days to come, I knew it had helped. When you interrupt:
~ I am not concerned about what you have to say.
~ I am not listening.
~ I have only been thinking of what I wanted to say.

Translation: I am not listening because I am demonstrating, whether consciously or subconsciously, that I am more valuable than you, and what I have to say is of more importance.

A**lso, do not react** like your instigator expects, negatively speaking. This will speak volumes to the listeners. If someone yells, simply do not yell back. If someone hits, do not hit back. This is where we are the salt and light of Jesus.

Romans 12:14-21 radiates challenge. I used to scratch my head questioning, *"Why in the world would I want to bless them? How will they see they were wrong?"* But I decided that God must know best. Ask the Lord what specific ways you can bless that person. You may not feel the warm fuzzies; you may be kicking and screaming on the inside, but, if you persevere, God will work with the situation, even though His priority is to work primarily on you. Do not worry. Nothing passes by God's eyes. Take a look at **Proverbs 10:12, 17:9-10, 1 Corinthians 13, and Galatians 5:13-15** to reflect on what loving another does. True love shakes people. It is like walking around a corner and being caught by surprise. Love (blessing an offender) brings a shocking surprise, which counteracts the offenders.

Mary, a former Jungle Jumper, said her Pastor challenged people with two wonderful choices: *"You can rehearse it or release it."* Whatever happens (and a lot happens), you can choose to hold on to it or let it go; you are the one imprisoned by it. Dean Sherman spoke of one of his father's most remarkable character traits, which inspired him - the astonishing ability to let things go. Just letting go. It is not worth it. And may we be protected from those who have the "ministry of discouragement," which infected Job, Jeremiah, Paul and others. The people around these men of God attempted to discourage them and cause them to walk a lonely road. Job's so-called friends condemned him; God welcomed Jeremiah into ministry by declaring that the people would not listen to him and would eventually turn on him while Paul, in **2 Corinthians,** had to defend his ministry and character as well as toward the end of his life in his last letter **(2 Timothy)** where we see how many people abandoned him **(2 Timothy 1:15, 4:10, 16).** Let us not discourage others, hold grudges, stay bitter or remain resentful.

There are two kinds of pain: one leads to freedom; the other further bondage.

Bondage = Holding on to and nursing the pain, which prohibits freedom.

Freedom = Letting go by swallowing pride or anything keeping you back. It could be painful allowing old issues to surface, but it brings freedom.

"**If you leave it alone**, it will go away." Ever hear that while growing up? Well, nine out of ten times it will not leave. Deal with the issue at hand. Do not wait for the "big bang." Be open to confrontation. It does not have to be a scary thing as long as you are balanced in your mind. Balance is not easy at times. I am a professional tree climber, and sometimes it is easy to balance while other times I find myself slipping or slamming against the trunk, usually due to unforeseen, adverse circum-  stances, like weather. So it is when we make decisions.

How much compassion do you have for a friend/teammate/colleague? When issues are flaring, when the team is in cohesive, what is best for the relationship/team? The greater good? Make sure you allow time and space for the rest of the team and do not get out of balance with too much emphasis on one individual. You must eyeball it, so to speak. It is sometimes a challenge to know which branches to cut, where to cut them, how to balance the weight of each limb, but ya gotta do it. Balance the team's needs while leaning on the Lord.

Processing

When we experience life, ministry and teams, situations arise where it may be necessary or helpful to process with one another for a healthier outlet. In what the team individually and corporately experiences, processing is a paramount feature of a healthy team. That being said, it should be monitored. I have been on teams where they processed too much and other teams who did not process enough. If there is an over abundance of processing circumstances, there is a tendency to become withdrawn with too much navel gazing (looking inward at themselves, like a belly button). Following a crisis on another team, I purposely, but reluctantly, sent them out to minister throughout the village; I felt it was healthier than them sitting around idle and becoming too withdrawn. Infections begin when they are processing too much or depending on how they are processing. You know what happens to film that is "over processed!" It spoils the prints and can spoil the team as well.

Regret: One of the Greatest Weapons of Defeat!

Regret plagues many around the world, like a mosquito that continues buzzing by your ear or as a 35 ft. (12m) Anaconda of the Pantanal holds on to its prey. And what is regret? Regret is the longing, resentment, and discontentment of not taking more risks. It is the reminders of your stained life that spin through your mind. **The would have, could have, should haves** could fill the globe's bodies of water. Let those waters recede by following through with obedience, fruits of the Spirit, preference of others (instead of indifference), and dependence on the Lord. Do not allow the enemy to dirty your mind with one more stain.

Yet Christians make chop suey out of their fellow brothers and sisters, many times without hesitation, through vocalizations, disputes and actions. For the smallest thing, they become so critical, like chewing people out for poor driving or an incorrect perception of someone's facial expression. As horrifying as this sounds, I was driving through South America, and a gunman, driving along side of me, pointed a big, shiny pistol at my head (at 90kmh), then raised the gun, fired two shots in the air and sped away. Some of us cannot fathom killing a fellow human, but we are quick to assault and murder another with our words. So, live your life without regret; a life that takes advantage of opportunities and does not speak out against another. It would be awesome to hear God say, "You could have reacted poorly, yet you chose to let Me be your outlet. Thank you. You have just given people a chance to see Me."

One more point, live as though it may be your last day. Carpe Diem: live for the moment. Act when Jesus tells you. Pray the prayer of faith. Speak the Word of life. Touch the untouchables. While journeying to Boukran's Bridge in South Africa (216 meters/648 ft.), the World's Highest Bungee Jump, the jump coordinator, with great confidence spoke out:

"Fear is temporary, but regret is permanent."

How profound! Fear definitely fed me with doubts about jumping, but I jumped. In most cases, our fear lasts but a moment whereas regret is more lasting. Think of it: "I wished I had obeyed God's prompting to speak that Word to them" or "If only I had expressed forgiveness to her." God's grace and forgiveness is available to let us jump, but He is faithful to hold on to the bungee cord. How do you spell R.E.L.I.E.F.?

CHAPTER TWO

Ouch!

W**hat can assure you of defeat** is condemning those around you, especially if others are present. When in South Africa, a baboon (nicknamed Clyde) had jumped through our car window, which caused those of us in the back of the Land Rover to start squirming! Similarly, when you soil a person's character in front of others, one thing is for sure...someone is in for a surprise! I have made mistakes, and, recently, made more in this area. It is sad and alarming for Jesus says in **John 3:17** (right after the most spoken and memorized verse in all of creation), **"God did not send the Son into the world to condemn the world, but in order that the world might be saved through Him;"** yet, we cannot wait to condemn...anxious even to condemn Christians. Imagine that?! I have more (and have heard more) problems with Christians than unbelievers. The very mention of that statement is contradictory to true Christianity. Unfortunate, but true.

I once had a "secret condemner" who put notes on my door. I can assure you, they were not love notes! And, with further manipulation, they used scripture, which was misinterpreted and out of context. **Even if they had been right, we should be addressing one another face-to-face.** You do not find Jesus hiding and dodging the people he had to confront. If we are all in the family, we should be careful with one another. If we are careless with people's hearts then we are actually careless with God; it is God we are condemning. Scary thought.

Words That Tear

Some time ago, a neighboring team came to visit. I was a bit stressed and tired because of several things taking place at once (no excuse). Where we were had a grand size of 30 in populace; our team increased the population by half of the village. Meanwhile, one of my team members had done what I assumed was wrong, and I gave her my two cents, letting her know how 'smart' I was. I ended up eating my words and asking for forgiveness, but I also had to ask the visiting team's forgiveness, as some heard how and what I said in haste.

Message?

~ Think first
~ If necessary, take time away from the situation
~ Correct in private (when applicable)
~ Do not assume; find out the facts
~ Ask what happened before conclusions are drawn
~ Be willing to admit being wrong
~ Own you perception instead of passively indicting others, i.e. you entered a room with an attitude

Our words may be forgiven when we ask, nonetheless, they are like feathers in a pillow. Imagine you are on a speeding train and you poke a hole in the pillow, allowing the feathers to blow out of the window into the wind. Here is the catch - try to retrieve every lost feather! A difficult and sometimes impossible task, aye? It is better not to cut into the pillow. If it happens, God can heal the wounds, but, in reality, scars can also remain. Hurtful memories can be avoided if we are more careful. Scars are reminders to avoid painful situations, but they are also evidence that we are being healed or even that the pain is already gone. Much like Christ when he appeared to Thomas, the scars no longer hurt, and He was not bitter for having gone through the experience. *"Scars are like snapshots of the past that we wish not to repeat."*- Eric Dennie

To Condemn-

To judge against/to damn = no way out. In harshness, love is not evident. Often, with the devil, there is no specific area pointed out, and he causes us to feel isolated with no hope. Focus is on the past/retribution with a pain attachment saying, *"You blew the whole trip for us!"* instead of saying, *"It seems we have lost some of our credibility."*

To Convict-

To convince/tell a fault = leads to change of action. It is a process where God can bring change. Love is evident, and there is a specific area pointed out. The Holy Spirit is not vague. He will be clear in convicting wit peace and hope. Focus is on the future/teaching saying, *"Sam, when you left my equipment out it got wet and that made me angry"* instead of saying, *"Sam, you never think! You make me so angry!"*

CONDEMNATION VS. CONVICTION

Condemnation

A general broad sweeping, negative statement that is elusive to correct. It is without manageable or measurable goals toward change.

Offers no hope and no way out; invites despair and depression.

Attacks your individuality and self-worth; you feel like a failure.

Brings accusation and judgment. The focus is on what you have done rather than your ability to change, yet it is significant to see how devastating it has been to the offended. Separate what is the offended vs. offender. If focus is on the offender, keep that direction. Do not try to excuse it or attach strings and point fingers. Just accept it.

Guilt and shame enter your heart. God seems distant as though you are cast out of His presence and separated from Him. You feel so wicked. You are weighed down with burdens.

An obstacle is wedged between you and that which you long for, leaving a sense of hopelessness and a fear of failure.

Conviction

Specific, concrete. We can respond to it.

Offers a way out through repentance (changing your mind).

Aimed at a specific part of your character that God desires to change into His likeness.

Our value in God's eyes does not change, and this should be evidenced by the convictor's intentions. God loves; therefore, He chastens, otherwise we would be illegitimate and not His sons. It is God's love and our love for God that brings conviction. The focus is on God, not on the offended or the offender.

God extends mercy to us. Do you feel guilty for what you have done? Or is it because of how God feels? If only pain is caused another, that is Humanism. He is waiting to forgive when we repent. It is through Him that we see the pain we have caused others and more so to Him.

Conviction makes us aware of His presence. His love reaches out and responds to our call for help. There is a connection without barriers between you and God. You are full of hope and long for change.

RIGHTEOUS AND UNRIGHTEOUS JUDGMENT

Three verbs used in the Greek language:
1.) Dokimazo - to examine, test and prove
2.) Anakrino - to ask questions
3.) Diakrino - to weigh thoroughly each part

The Righteous Judge, who discerns, will:
A) Evaluate self first
(*1 Corinthians 11:28* - dokimazo - "examine self")
B) Check the accuracy of all the facts
(*1 Corinthians 2:15, 1 Thessalonians 5:21* -anakrino)
C) Deal with the issue as privately as possible

Whereas the Unrighteous Judge, who cannot discern, will:
A) Sentence, condemn and conclude pre-maturely (krino).
B) Judge and condemn others for visible problems but fail to realize that they have the same problem *(Romans 2:1)* - used with permission by Peter Warren.

During my Christian journey, it has been appalling to hear and recollect horrendous judgments people have made, put upon, and spoken against each another. Christians have been known, shamefully, to wound our own - often times, no different then those who do not know the Lord. The exception: we just tag God's name on it! In India, a female friend of mine had completed an international organization's two training schools and had also been a committed staff person. But because of having an attraction to someone of the opposite sex, they forced her to re-do the primary six month training course (with a bit of humiliation sprinkled on top). I realize there were cultural issues involved, but no immoral actions occurred. The legalism was so strong. Well, she is now in another organization and happily married to that very same man. As my Pastor Dennis warns, **"They [the church] are His precious little sheep, not lambchops!"**

Remember why and with what motives we are judging others (and how often we internally judge). Judge (wrongfully) and you (and I) will be judged *(Matthew 7:1-5)*. *"I use being judged to test my response to grace. In my judging, I am taking the place of The Judge. And the Pharisees never delivered anyone; they only judged people (condemned)."* - Pastor Bryan Coelho of India. They even judged and condemned Jesus, The Judge, face to face. Yikes. The Pharisees prided themselves in knowing the Law (truth), yet it is clear to see how far they had fallen. In judging, they shed light on where they were missing the mark scripturally, and it is shocking how many Christians and leaders, who believe the Words of Christ, are not far from their shadow!

Dealing with Others
The Danger in not Being Open

Openness or lack of openness within yourself or others can determine what pleasures and dangers may exist in the immediate ministry environment. Tension and division (disunity) within the team could invite deception and/or denial. If I am continually denying conviction from the Holy Spirit or exhortations, encouragements or corrections from others, I am allowing the devil to come in and sow division. The more I deny my need for change, especially when my life or actions may be witnessed by several others, I can begin to slip into a spiral of deception. It may be little by little - not happening all at once. You believe a lie, then another, and another, and, after some time, you become convinced that your lifestyle, attitude or actions are fine. This will then affect or infect team members, which could then affect ministry outreach.

Blessings as you step into this arena. One could imagine laying by a swimming pool as a splendid alternative to this type of confrontation. As a leader, you may not come to a comfortable or favorable outcome initially. The reality is that people have free will and may not choose to look into God's mirror. Our prayer, of course, is that they will. Be steadfast, knowing God is fully aware of what is happening. We are not to automatically take on a burden of failure (condemnation - remember?) should there be no clear resolution. I remind myself not to put God in a box or these albeit unpleasant situations for that matter.

Scenarios are somewhat unique. It may take prayer one time, confrontation another time, while another set of circumstances may lead to God dealing with them after the fact - in conjunction to their openness. Below are some indicators of this process. By these comparatives, you may be more apt to detect when someone could potentially be walking in denial or deception, how to define what you have been observing, and what to speak into their life.

* Negative Rebellion: Willingly or deceptively turning against directives, commands or advice given by the Lord or others responsible for you; considering your own preferences on how to live, where to go, and what to do because you "know better" than others and choose to be the decision-maker.

However, there are rebellions in history, which were necessary for the preservation of life and principle, i.e. William Wallace of Scotland was considered a rebellious man for fighting against the tyrannous English Empire. His agenda was freedom from their control, manipulation and abuse and to have their families, land and sovereignty regained as a nation.

There is little provision for the rebellious (Psalm 68:6) even though God is ready to forgive. The rebellious must see the light to repent.

They become a threat or danger wherever they are placed or with whomever they are laboring (Psalm 5:9-12).

It is most difficult when one is not seeing or denying their need or struggle. It takes courage for one to admit their problem while other times they simply chose not to acknowledge it.

Have the courage to address them. It is not easy, but it is unavoidable if you desire to help. Loving someone is the willingness to confront or speak the truth, no matter how difficult. I have a friend who was deceived into believing she was loving her relative (who was involved in immoral and illegal activity) by helping him, when actually it was hurting him and her as well.

Pray. God in His mercy can (and has done in the past) bring awareness hopefully sooner than later. At times, because of His love for us, He allows people to get caught in their acts against Him. People think contrary to **Numbers 32:23**, assuming they can get away with what they *do* and are deceived thinking that God has blinked and missed what they have said or done. Our sin will search us out. God is not unaware. Furthermore, in **Hebrews 12:5ff,** we see that God's heart is to discipline in love. Our Father knows best!

Depending on the level of rebellion, steps may need to be taken:

1- Attempt the following notes (definitions) on rebellion.
2- Walk them through potential regrets, i.e. what this could mean in the future if they choose not to repent or change.
3- Discuss options with co-leader(s).
4- Involve leaders who cover you.
5- If no change is apparent after much consideration, possibly release the person from ministry/duties.
6- A final option may be removal from the team (a benefit for all).
7- Discuss/inform the team if necessary, perhaps sharing the steps that formed your decision.
8- If repentance occurs, consider including them on the team again. Why? Because God gives people like Peter and us second chances!

"The Bible clearly reveals a propensity of the human heart toward deceitfulness. It is like an automobile out of alignment, which pulls

away from a straight course. Our hearts, like all automobiles, need periodic outside intervention to keep us aligned to truth, integrity and the simplicity of devotion to Christ. For each disciple, it is not a matter of "if" but "when" we need the correction and exhortation of another to realign our hearts. We all have blind spots and a deceitful heart ready to cooperate with our sinful nature to keep us blind. As we acknowledge this truth, we become more committed to being both an enthusiastic recipient and deliverer of reproof and encouragement. My passion for Christ is demonstrated as I welcome any confrontation from others that will help me serve him more purely. I demonstrate my love and commitment for others as I, with a spirit of meekness, bring questions, correction and edification, which serve to realign a heart that is a bit misdirected." - Eric Dennie

As Eric mentioned, we ought not allow rebellion to run its course. I confront when I see early signs of deceptiveness or rebellion, thereby minimizing the potential of greater stress, conflict and division. It is an unfortunate necessity at times to do the uncomfortable. Jesus was not afraid to confront others.

"A dead and resurrected church prevails against the gates of hell. Without confronting people who are trapped, manipulated, used, or oppressed by demonic influences, these spirits of depression, jealousy, fear, lust, etc. will continue to operate in the church. Any flesh that is not on the cross is used for demonic activity. How big of a pebble in your shoe will it take to destroy your race or theirs? A $10 leaking seal destroyed the $2.8 billion space shuttle Challenger at launch, killing its entire crew, including the first woman to go into orbit, and setting the program back by two years. Fear, pride and rebellion are the primary leaks that cause destruction. A little is all it takes (like rebellion against authority) for the devil to destroy. Humility is key. If you cannot be wrong, you cannot repent." - Pastor Dennis Bambino

The Deception Spiral

The Deception Spiral

1. *Openness*

Living in the light (Ephesians 5:3-14 and 1 John 1:6-10 - recognizing I have sinned, then can be forgiven)
Humility (Philippians 2:3-4)
Honesty
Natural victory
Interdependence-having place in body of Christ
Corporate Unity

One of the five walks, in Ephesians Chapters 4 and 5, is "walking in light." In 5:3-14, we see this is again part of spiritual warfare. How I walk (live) affects the spiritual realm. I can feed or starve the devil by how I walk or live. Exposing works of darkness and bringing something in my life into the light is ammunition to defeat the devil. But if I keep it out of the light, I become a vessel for destruction, which affects others as well. By walking in the light, I am transparent, inside and out, and giving people the opportunity to see my dirt. Trust is essential in order to "expose" myself.

Keep in mind that, according to Paul, we have some responsibility. That is what "walking" or "living" implies. In Philippians 2:3-4, we should consider others better than us and place their interests higher than our own, which should transmit more openness.

1. *Lack of Openness*

Pride - holding up a front
Secretiveness - doing your own thing
Super spiritual/spiritual pride - false
Independence leading to disunity

Often, we are blind to certain realities, like pride.
"I know better than you," we say, becoming quick
to point the finger and make excuses, and, at times,
becoming defensive (like a raccoon pinned in the
corner). Sometimes we even use humor as a cover-up.
Everybody else is wrong.

The Deception Spiral

2. Submission

Protection (1 Samuel 15:23; James 4:7)
Authority
Spiritual Warfare
Secure

In Samuel, God defines King Saul's rebellion as "witchcraft." It appears to be with demonic implications, which, if you trace his life, you can see how deceived he had become (not without jealousy, rage and even denial of his own actions). He was plagued with insecurity. Also, in James 4:7, when we submit to God, we are allowing Him to rule and reign in us. This includes submitting to those of authority in our lives. If we are submitting (to God and His appointed man), we resist the devil. So if one is not submitting, as these two references show, there can be a lack of protection. which should transmit more openness.

2. Rebellion

No Protection
Unwilling to submit to authority
Vulnerable
Insecure
Dangerous

See above. Functioning this way (running), I become vulnerable to isolation and harassment by the devil. This also affects and, at times, infects the lives of others around me.

The Deception Spiral

3. Open to Truth

John 14:21 - truth is realized when the correct
steps are taken.
Revelation
Confident of hearing God's voice
Obedience becomes easy
Freedom

Jesus is the Truth. Yes, He speaks to us; because,
there comes a time that we may be blinded
whereas we become dependent on others that
the Lord may use to speak Truth to us-in love
of course. But if we are open to the Truth, then we
are following the right course of action to receive aid.

3. Unteachable

Deception
Confusion - all kinds of voices
Disobedience becomes easy
Bondage

When we refuse instruction, we come to a standstill. We have probably begun listening to lies from different voices. Remember, there are four voices we hear: God's, the devil's, others, and our self. Obeying the wrong voice causes confusion, even misreading or misinterpreting what others may be telling us. We find ourselves following the "courses of the world" more than God.

The Deception Spiral

4. *Victory*

Life everlasting (Proverbs 22:41)

Humility brings life. You can never go wrong being who you [really] are and letting faults and weaknesses be known (within a healthy setting). Then issues can be dealt with and victory and life come!

4. *Death*

(Proverbs 16:18)

Pride brings death (destruction of self and possibly others) and a sense of isolation. You become cut off from God's ability to work through you. The end of the rebellious road is spiritual oppression and bankruptcy, maybe never considering "could I be wrong?"

Rebellion is not worth holding on to a little pride. In light of eternity, is it really that important? You may think you feel better, but, in actuality you lose and may unfortunately cause others to lose. Remember: God knows the thoughts and intentions of the heart (Psalms 44:21 and Hebrews 4:12-13). We may run, but we cannot hide.

CHAPTER THREE

Developing Team Vision

Unity

What's the big deal about unity?

It is God's design that we care for and prefer one another. Anything of lasting value and significance embarks on the road of love, which flows from God's heart. Unity expresses itself through love, and love expresses itself in unity through humility.

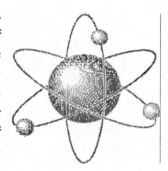

Unity is much like an atom. Atoms are the most powerful elements in the universe. The creation of the world is housed in them. God's Word keeps the world together and could finish it at the snap of a finger. God is amazingly precise. Unity is like an atom's potential power. Life comes from it. Death and/or defeat comes from the lack of it. If a team is void of unity, their effectiveness, power and fruit will greatly be hindered, wasted, and possibly non-existent.

How is unity found? How do you get it? How do you keep it?

Is it by shooting up a prayer and waiting for instantaneous results to fall from the sky? God commands a blessing from it as mentioned in *Psalm 133*. The psalmist exclaims how very good and pleasant it is when people can live and function in unity. If people could get along, God can and will do something through it! And we see it is possible because Jesus prayed for it *(John 17:11, 21-23)*. How many know Jesus' prayers get answered?!

God, in His infinite wisdom, is remarkably and strategically abreast of humanity's major issues; after all, He created us. As the aroma of a freshly baked pie, the splash of a whale breaching 10 meters ahead, a child's laughter, and the joyous emotional scream of a newly engaged woman cannot go by without notice, so it is with God's view all the more. Through His foreknowledge, He inspired people with His principals for living and bound them together in books we call the Bible.

Themes of unity are woven throughout Bible books like Romans and Philippians (I learned this from the School of Biblical Studies [SBS] of Youth with A Mission [YWAM]).

The Book of Romans is God's answer for racism and unity.

In 49 AD, Jewish believers were expelled from Rome. In the five-year period following, the Gentile church began to grow, but when the Jewish believers were allowed to return, major tensions arose. The Jewish and Gentile believers were not meeting together, thus great divisions occurred. One group had been declaring (arrogantly) that they were superior to the other. In this light, Paul addresses the Jews and Gentiles separately and then both together. He drives the reality home that they are in the same family and are all capable of sin **(3:23)**.

"In our world today, what is one of the most major issues? RACISM! When a person of a different color, race, tribe, family, or country walks into the room, what emotions rise in you? If you have an uncomfortable or sick feeling inside, you are having a problem with racism." - Ron Smith, co-founder of the School of Biblical Suffering...I mean Studies (where you study through the Bible book-by-book in nine months...intense)

The Book of Philippians shows humility as the key to unity.

For a moment, focus on Philippians where Paul uses himself, Jesus, Timothy and Epaphroditus as humble examples who produced unity. It is THE way. Humility is one of Jesus' greatest fruits, if not the greatest besides "love." But humility is more than being honest about who you are or a correct estimate of self. If I let people know I live with a bad attitude, that I am miserable, and that I respond harshly, that is not being humble - that is telling the truth about what others already know.

Song of Songs demonstrates how warped, cheap and devalued love has become in the world, as God addresses pure and intimate love (which is possible). In Galatians, false teachers have been clever in devising ways to bind people who were once free through Christ's liberty, reverting them back to the familiar ground of "the law" (as in letter - not relationship), thereby causing the legalistic thought, 'Jesus plus "something" equals salvation.' How you long and loud do you pray? How many meetings do you attend? How do you dress? Do not be concerned with how well people follow rules. This comes as a result of being insecure in God's ability to sanctify others and keep them. Many attempt, solely or collectively, to stamp unrealistic or unbiblical rules on people. It is called playing the Holy Spirit! They believe God is big enough to save them but not big enough to keep them, so God must need their help.

"...but in humility, consider others better than yourself" (2:3).

Now, Paul is not interested in stardom; his concern is not being the star evangelist. He does not care who preaches as long as the message is correct. He does not grasp the spotlight. He counts the Philippians better than himself and lives to be their servant. He provides conclusive descriptions of humility: do not be selfish, being interested in and concerned about yourself but count others better than you. The word "but" is a small yet powerful word. Looking after #1 is a full time occupation for some. Giving up your rights is also part of humility *(Chapter 2: 7-8)*.

A girl I know cleverly shifted a worship song's lyrics from, *"It is all about You, Jesus"* to *"It is all about me; it is not about You"* to prove a point, which is the truth at times, huh? But it should be about the giving of self, renouncing pride, arrogance, and the demands of stature. Always being right is not always the right

thing, although it may be difficult at times. True humility produces gratitude not pride. Jesus, who had all and could *do* as He desired, chose to give up the need for the cause. God serving man, man serving God and man serving man. What an unheard of, ridiculous, scandalous statement! I can be humble because I understand my security is in Jesus (one of two main messages in *Ephesians 1-3).* Of course, expressing my weakness is also a form of humility.

Why does Peter say in *1 Peter 5:5, "Be clothed in humility?"* Dr. Gary Parker (Chief Surgeon and CEO of the ANASTASIS) and my pastor, Randy Paige, are the most amazing examples of humility. They are hard acts to follow, but I know they do not wake up every morning with their humility switch turned on, although I am sure that a certain level is internally and externally maintained. But for all of us, it is attainable and maintainable. "What will I clothe myself in today," they may ask. It is a choice they make each day. It only takes a little crack for the flesh to run for it. It is painless to be humbled around Don Stephens (President of Mercy Ships), but it is harder around those we rub elbows with on a regular basis. We have many chances to evaluate ourselves more highly than we ought *(Romans 12: 3)*.

When each part tries to do its "own" thing, problems and breakdowns occur. We need to lay down pride, desires, and preference and function in love. It cannot be, "I will do it my way." The goal is to be of one mind and spirit, constantly search for the greater purpose: the benefit of all through the Gospel. Ever wonder why some ministries do not experience the power of God? Is it because they hold back women? Have flaky doctrines? Are they ignoring the attributes of unity in attitude, heart and spirit? People need to know when to speak up, what to say, and when to be quiet.

We were created for relationships, to relate and depend upon one another. God may move despite our lack of unity at times (as we see in the Old Testament), but we really will not be truly blessed because we have not truly made His Spirit welcome. Unity will help the Christian community overcome its opponents *(Philippians 1: 27-28)*. Paul describes unity with these statements. His followers are not only to live worthy while he is present, but also in his absence, and, furthermore, they are not to be intimidated by the opposition of others. The mission of the Church is successful when we all work together. Partnership is mentioned six times in *Philippians (1:5, 7, 2:1, 3:10, 4:14, 15)*.

FOUR NATURAL STAGES OF TRANSITION

The Dreaded "Quadruple H"

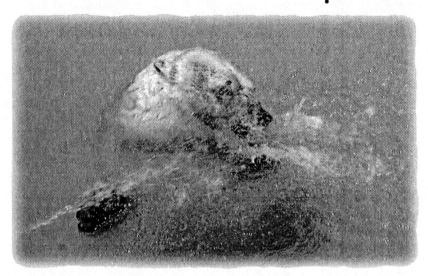

The following may be helpful and not limited to any particular ministry, as "ministry" is indeed a change from the norm of everyday life for many. It is more intensive, of course, within a team who consistently works together outside of their known "home territory." In the beginning, getting the team unified may take some time and effort. For most people, this will be a new experience, so kid gloves may be necessary. Perhaps you have experienced such descriptive emotions as you will see collected below. What you once thought would be fulfilling may suddenly, quickly become drudgery and seep in through varying circumstances. You may feel shipwrecked, side-swiped by an oncoming car or womped by a passing freight train...thus, the dreaded four stages of transition, known for their element of surprise. How you, as a leader, and your team deal with each stage is imperative, and, at the risk of seeming repetitive, anticipation is golden. Keep your alert buttons on when possible. There may be one, a few, or several team members who may be facing these possible transitions. You might want to talk them through the following list of emotions, thoughts, and expectations (whether false or not):

Honeymoon

~ So glad to be here (remember how you first felt when accepted or knew about your ministry/work opportunity?)
~ Excitement - nothing bothers them
~ On the clouds
~ Overwhelmed by the expanse of ministry
~ Thrilled about being a part of fulfilling the Great Commission (reaching the world)
~ Ready for another culture's tastes, smells and experiences
~ Fulfillment of a dream; answered prayer

Hostility

~ Begin to see all the mistakes
~ Little things start upsetting them
~ Negativity tries to set in
~ The job seems too big
~ Doubts about God's will
~ Bad attitudes and selfishness
~ Finds schedule frustrating
~ Sees flaws in leadership
~ Insecurities creep in
~ Gives ear to rumors and gossip
~ Verbal stoning of post distress (internal distress released upon others)
~ Starts to compare how things are done at home or in other ministries
~ Food, food lines and the menu are a problem (either not enough or do not like food)
~ Little, insignificant issues begin to irritate them that normally would not

~ "We are not really impacting the world like I first thought we were!" syndrome
~ Begin to think the Great Commission is not so great If they do not pass through this stage, they will leave bitter and frustrated with God (do your best not to let this happen).

Humor

~ Pulls them out of the previous stage
~ Begin to accept circumstances
~ Little things can now appear amusing
~ Go with the flow and become more content
~ Making room for others
~ Some things still bug them but their attitude changes

~ Gain well rounded perspective
~ More willing to go to people and ask forgiveness
~ Applying God's Word helps their perspective shift

Ask them:
***How many of you this week have:
        - Asked for forgiveness?
        - Put right an exaggeration?
        - Corrected a bad attitude?

~ Checked your attitude when confronted?
~ Were willing to confront? **Proverbs 6:23** - "The corrections of discipline are the way of life." (NIV version)

Home

~ Where they live and work becomes home (scary?!)
~ Begin communicating this unaware in **conversation**
~ Circumstances are never perfect, but they become **comfortable**
~ People and places feel right, acceptable
~ They have finally learned how to be effective in a new culture
~ No need to strive; it becomes natural

In the end, if not the beginning, they can rise above the circumstances with a bird's eye view and gain a clearer perspective.

When shifts of the "norm" come, emotions rise and confusion rears its ungodly head. Rational thinking can become subjectively altered. One may be blinded in how they are processing and exaggerating the circumstances. Try not to deny what they are feeling but get them to:

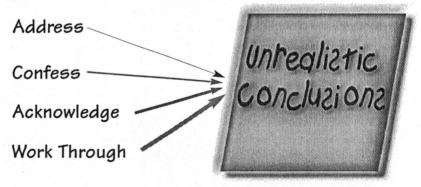

Address

Confess

Acknowledge

Work Through

Unrealistic Conclusions

Address: Address the need or difficulty and bring to light the struggles. 'I have realized by how I have been reacting that there is a need.'

Confess: 'This is what I am going through.'

Acknowledge: 'I acknowledge that I do not have the vision to see. I acknowledge my need for you. Help me process my struggles, frustrations and doubts.'

Work Through: 'I commit, in humility, to work through my need. By confessing and acknowledging the problem, I make myself accountable to resolve and deal with this issue. I realize that there is protection for me while being accountable.'

In **heeding the above** advice, unrealistic conclusions are washed away. Your team member's are given new sight, protection and liberty for the Lord to work for them, with them, and through them. Their thoughts and concerns should never automatically be dismissed. In most scenarios, ask the Lord if there is any truth in what the "seemingly irrational" have stated. Following this developmental advice will solidify the team as individuals and as a group and also open the door for team vision.

Developing A Team Vision

No **vision,** no purpose; no excitement, no impact = no team or certainly a diminished and weakened one. It is of utmost importance for the team to have vision. What are the goals, strategies, ideas, and drives that signify purpose and fulfillment? Is the team part of the decision making process? Do they find joy in their activities because they are within their abilities and strengths?

"Without vision the people perish" - Proverbs 29:18 (KJV).

Life comes from having vision; purpose is a close second. I find they are connected. Inseparable. You need one to have the other. Does your team really feel or really believe there are possibilities for them to participate with God on something that has NEVER been thought of before, NEVER been spoken before, NEVER taught before and NEVER enacted before in the history of the world? What a radical and pinnacle view into vision! Believe it first for yourself, then speak and prophesy the vision over each team member. God has NEVER run out of ideas, thoughts, dreams, pictures, or visions.

Organize prayer times to seek the Lord's heart for the particular outreach, meeting, ministry, program, day, and week, even for adults and children. [Suggestion: if you are on an outreach team, do not jump into ministry upon arrival on location. Again, this depends on how long your outreach is. Regardless of the time frame, it is still good to spend time together formulating a decent foundation. Doing so before arrival has it pluses, but being in the midst of the sights, smells and sounds could be more advantageous, accelerating the team's preparation. You then have something substantial with strength to build upon for outward ministry. Leaping too quickly into ministry could have an effect contrary to your liking, yet it is significant that they mingle with the people soon after arrival. Buying supplies is a grand opportunity to interface with locals. Language Acquisition Made Practical [LAMP] is a good method to exercise (learning words and phrases in the local language). If there is no concrete plan or purpose for the first couple of days, it could be easy for the team to lose sight of why they are there. Some could become withdrawn, unmotivated and move into themselves].

At some point, we all need to exit our comfort zones and be stretched - but within reason and not just for the sake of saying, "Well, it has always been done that way." Ask the Lord to give you vision for each one on the team, encouraging their potential and helping them along. Sometimes it is necessary for love that pushes them into the unknown.

"Release team members. Prepare the ground for them to discover, learn and walk in their giftings. Facilitate as much as you can as a leader for them to develop their own ministry while experiencing, at the same time, the Body of Christ."
                    -Judith Straub - former Discipleship Training
                    School (DTS) leader from Switzerland

I **have discovered,** "You do, and they watch. Then they do, and you watch. Finally, they do, and trust is fulfilled." A leader should never want an individual's dreams to go unsatisfied, not having space to develop a ministry with their own unique gift and calling. Of course this is contingent on the team's size and the time frame. It is not a realistic goal for a 7-10 day team, like it would be for a two month team. An unfortunate reality is that many never aspire to or find their vision, ministry "place" or "outlet" in the Body of Christ in regard to giftings.

W**ill you then** streamline the team's vision? Some trends have ended in a dead end. Why? Because what may have looked tasty from afar may have underwent a grand transformation (psychologically anyway), just like when grandma's beautiful fruit arrangement made your mouth water until you realized it was plastic. Watch for yield signs to see if there should be a collective, simple or unified team vision. Do we do what we first thought? Do we only work as a corporate team? Do we work corporately yet individually or by two's and three's in our particular desires, strengths, and giftings? [Note: this may not work if people are too independent and want their own way, forgetting the (potential) team benefits, expectations expressed and the commitments that followed.]

Revisit expectations!

What If?

What if God could not take the time to bless us today because we could not take the time to thank Him for yesterday?

What if God decided to stop leading us tomorrow because we did not follow Him today?

What if we never saw another flower bloom because we grumbled when God sent the rain?

What if God did not walk with us today because we failed to recognize it as His day?

What if God took away the Bible tomorrow because we would not read it today?

What if God took away His message because we failed to listen to the messenger?

What if God did not send His only begotten Son because He wanted us to be prepared to pay the price for sin?

What if the door of the Church was closed because we did not open the door to our heart?

What if God stopped loving us today because we failed to love and care for others?

What if God would not hear us today because we would not listen to Him yesterday?

What if God answered our prayers the way we answer His call to service?

What if God met our needs the way we give Him our lives?

Are you not glad God loved us first! -Author Unknown

This is an exercise of humility, commitment and accountability. It will be tested. Will everyone keep their word? This is a great way to see what people's motives and words are worth. Integrity will be present or absent. The "Mercy Pact" (an idea I received from Mercy Ship) has been a good team challenge, yet people have challenged it. The merciful may not be so full of mercy after a few nights. In the daily grind, some might need a reminder and a refresher. It does not take long before you find yourself about 10 mercies behind. Everyone should have a copy of this and go at their convenience to speak to each teammate, and the recipient can sign it.

1. Mercy (Matthew 5:7)

"Blessed are the merciful, for they will be shown mercy."
No matter what is going to happen, I am supporting you, even if I disagree with something you are doing. I am on your side. I want to see you with God's eyes. I want to be willing to talk with you and to listen.

2. Openness (Ephesians 4:12)

"In your anger do not sin. Do not let the sun go down while you are still angry." If there is something between the two of us, I will come and talk to you. No wall shall be built between us. I promise to come to you if I feel that there is something between us and to come to you before anyone else.

3. Forgiveness (Ephesians 4:32)

"Be kind and compassionate to one another, forgiving each other, just as in Christ, God forgave you." I commit to forgive you, even if I do not feel like doing so.

The Most Loving Thing (Philippians 2:3)

"Do nothing out of selfish ambition or vain conceit, but in humility consider others better than yourselves."
I want to look for the most loving thing for your life. I do not want to be an obstacle in your way with God. I always want what is the best for you.

Team Building

Building and shaping the unknown is a great challenge to conquer. Intricately weaving lives together is no small task; it is a great adventure headed by the Father. When opportunities are given to dig deeper, it is invigorating to discover what makes new "family" members tick. As you begin this project, it will enable you to understand what bothers, excites, disappoints, challenges, and hinders each other. What makes them soar as eagles? What are their likes and dislikes? What is their background?

The following are thoughts and ideas to reflect upon as a team. At times, when thoughts are given, they trigger a myriad of creative roads to travel down. Among the team, you should be able to expand to further levels. Ask them or have them ask one another the relevant questions.

- Develop prayer partners

- Find ways to bless each other. Investigate what someone else enjoys or prefers.

- "Face the Music" - Gather everyone and pick one person to be in the middle. Ask those around him/her to speak out what characteristics of Jesus they see in that person (and/or other topics). Is it true that we do not encourage enough? Learn the difference between flattery and exhortation.

- Serving moments

- Testimonies - Be creative in how they could express their testimony to the team, even in preparing to share it at a public meeting.

- Bible Hunt - Search for particular portions of scripture.

- Secret Angel - Everyone pulls a name from a hat. Unbeknownst to them, you would make, buy, write, draw, create, make a song, write what you prayed for them, etc...and have it delivered to them. This could be for a day, week or longer.

- Meditate on something you see, something of creation that exemplifies God's character.

- Write a poem to Jesus. Once in a while have someone share what they wrote.

- Have them bring an item that shows part of their personality, i.e. a jacket, hat, or flower - to explain more of what they are like.

- Make or pickup a funny prize for each of the team that, as leaders, you would give them, i.e. a rope that everyone signs, which you give to Trevor, the transport guy, who has been diligently tying down and strapping everything.

- Hold a special event. It shows the team that you appreciate and value them.

- Talk about strengths and weaknesses. "What do you feel like when you make a mistake?"

- What do you find valuable?

- How do you process?

- What are your interests?

- Considering culture and location, what is your favorite part of that culture? What do you appreciate about it?

- Who is the person you greatly admire and respect? Why?

- What would be the perfect day?

- What is one thing that you feel ashamed of in your past?

- Did you ever deliberately lie about a serious matter to anyone (close to you)?

- What is one of your "pet peeves?" - something that really annoys you?

- What do you regard as your best personality trait? Worst?

- What are two things that you really like about yourself?

- Is there a feature of your personality that you would like to change? What is it?

- Split in two's or bigger groups. Find out what you think each group's place in the body (of Christ) is? Are they a kidney? A foot? Why? Discuss it and pray for them.

- What emotions do you find difficult to control?

- What are you most reluctant to discuss right now?

- What is the most difficult concept or truth of God for you to understand or fully believe? How does this affect you?

- Who are two people that have influenced you the most (besides Jesus and parents)? How?

- What animal best describes your personality?

- What do you see yourself doing in 10 years? Where would you be living?

- What would you like to be doing in 10 years' time? Why?

- What do you think the person to your right will be doing in 10 years?

- Choose three words to describe the person next to you?

So, let us fill our mouths and give opportunity for one another to express what is happening in our lives, as this man in Ripley's Museum in Hong Kong is exemplifying in this photo.

CHAPTER FOUR

Start Your Engines

Flexibility is the key. "Blessed are the flexible for they shall not break!" Or as some friends (the Okuleys, Hans Christian Anderson, and Peter Hughes) put into a song, "Blessed are the flexible, but this is just detestable!"

There is no particular formula!

From mistakes in the past, and there were a few, I have found and been instructed that it is best to over communicate. Communication does not have to be all of the particulars, but communicate what you can, not unnecessarily withholding information (some like that power). Vital communication, whether it is five minutes or 50 minutes for up-to-date understanding, is critical for the team's unity. Leaders, always put your words somewhere in writing so they cannot say, *'I did not hear that.'* This is for you as well as them. Take a look at this example:

In a 24-hour period, I taught the New Testament, talked through wedding plans, arranged evacuation for someone near death (who eventually died) and then sorted through funeral arrangements, pulled off a community dinner (requiring the death of 12 live chickens), celebrated the house owner's birthday where we resided, and orchestrated the farewell meeting of six villages! Whoa! Much decision, planning, arranging (with sensitivity in communicating), and addressing various needs was necessary within the team and outside of it - so maintain flexibility. Try the following:

 Have a notice board with as many details as possible, yet the team should expect plans to change. Daily schedules, work duties, ideas, prayer goals, and what God has been answering are good lists to post.

"And yet do not plan so much that you plan God right out of it"

- a good point made by my friend Brian Blackburn.

Set up guidelines/rules. Perhaps ask the team to decide so that they will take ownership of it and include consequences. I am not a great fan of unnecessary rules, but, at times, some are necessary and of benefit for all. I do agree with Steve Brien who expressed, "It would be great not to have signs like 'One Per Person,' 'Clean Up After,' 'Do Not Slam,' and just have one sign that would be stuck on our fingers, eyes, feet: *'Love One Another As I Have Loved You - Love One Another As Yourself'* (John 13:34, Matthew 22:37-40). *Here, we see Jesus squeezing the whole Bible into two concepts: love God - love neighbor! It was meant to be simple, yet we make it so complex. If you love God, you WILL love your neighbor and consider him/her as you do what you do or say what you say. Just think: if we only did these two things, nearly ALL the heartaches and problems in the world could be eliminated! Steve also remarked that revival is defined as loving your neighbor. How poignant!*

 Let them know days in advance of their schedule so they can plan their lives. Some have greater flexibility than others and can move in a moment while others need mental preparation.

 Send team members to organize ministry opportunities while you oversee or even train someone before the outreach and let them meet with leaders and contacts. In my leading adventures, this activity is the most time consuming. As a leader, you should handle specific and closely related contacts, yet not all are necessary for your involvement. Grooming another to lead is a trust test for you.

 There are many **"visual types"** who need to see things written down, as mentioned earlier.

Communicate everything within reason, even tentative schedules, and keep communication lines open. It helps everyone grasp the bigger picture and understand where they are and where they are headed as a team. It also gives them the opportunity and responsibility to pray.

 It may be good and stress relieving to have a set 'quiet hour' each day or every other day.

 Included within the schedule, ministry preparation and team member responsibilities would be a good suggestion when feasible. Though you cannot assess everything at the onset, it could be the start of a team schedule. Do your best to model real life missions. What would be normal for someone in it for the long haul? Know your aim, focus and philosophy. If you are only together for a short time this would differ, as you will want to take advantage of the week, like a blitz in a sporting game. If it is quick and short, you can put in all your effort for that moment of time, but you need to consider long-term missionaries who consider this their life. Do not burn them out either.

Lifestyle Marathon Missions

Consider what is best for the team in regards to ministry. Avoid rushing the team and adding unnecessary stress upon others. Think of the team's welfare; they should always come before ministry as a higher priority. People are not projects; we use things not people. There are well-oiled machines (churches), yet at the expense of its people. Often, Pastor's kids (PKs) grow up not knowing their parents or their love because, as pastoral parents, they were consumed with ministry. I also know of countless women who would not want to marry a

pastor because he so often gets consumed and taken in ministry that his family life comes second. Yet, on another note, whatever you do, do not be overly motivated and controlled by local ministries. Do not allow projects or others outside of your team to dictate your life and schedule.

Miscommunication

There was a miscommunication once when my team decided to do separate Bible studies with the men and women of the area. The ladies on our team had not been ready when these women emerged from the jungle waiting to study. Thus our ladies were caught off guard and were unprepared. The study started with a precious woman named Malandra pursuing prayer for her baby who had been quite sick. I asked Malandra to wait just a of couple minutes till I sorted out the team. But I forgot to tell my co-leader. Then my co-leader, on the spur of the moment, joined the study without knowing the woman's need for prayer. I took full responsibility. Unfortunate misunderstandings caused hurt and brought guilt upon others. This could have been avoided if there had been better planning and a touch of 'slow down.'

Take the Time to...
Think,
Communicate,
Etc...

On the first day

Why did you choose to come here?
Join this team?

What are your expectations?

What makes a successful outreach?

Prayer time for direction and vision

Orientation-perhaps invite some local leaders,
learn some local songs

Talk about potential or current fears; help them
walk through these

When ministry is over, what do you do?

How much can you help people?

Do you continue providing help?

How long are you responsible?

Afternoon time may be required to accomplish laundry and other personal needs during daylight hours, especially if you are in the Bushe/Jungle or without machines.

Remember time off is a wise necessity. For example, perhaps 1/3 of the day should be free, plus one or two days a week off (when possible) to rest, spend time with God, and be on their own. Others may want to be out and about with some people they have befriended. Everyone is re-charged in different ways. Sundays are usually ministry so these days are not usually considered a day off (if they are ministering - a thought?)

Once again, remember flexibility.

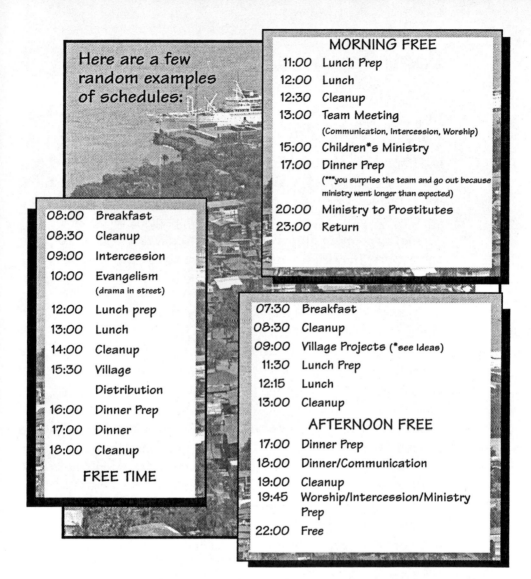

Here are a few random examples of schedules:

MORNING FREE

11:00	Lunch Prep
12:00	Lunch
12:30	Cleanup
13:00	Team Meeting
	(Communication, Intercession, Worship)
15:00	Children*s Ministry
17:00	Dinner Prep
	(***you surprise the team and go out because ministry went longer than expected)
20:00	Ministry to Prostitutes
23:00	Return

08:00	Breakfast
08:30	Cleanup
09:00	Intercession
10:00	Evangelism
	(drama in street)
12:00	Lunch prep
13:00	Lunch
14:00	Cleanup
15:30	Village Distribution
16:00	Dinner Prep
17:00	Dinner
18:00	Cleanup
	FREE TIME

07:30	Breakfast
08:30	Cleanup
09:00	Village Projects (*see Ideas)
11:30	Lunch Prep
12:15	Lunch
13:00	Cleanup
	AFTERNOON FREE
17:00	Dinner Prep
18:00	Dinner/Communication
19:00	Cleanup
19:45	Worship/Intercession/Ministry Prep
22:00	Free

Journal! Regret comes if the team is not encouraged to write down their experiences. Usually when they realize, it is too late. Encourage them with a good regret story (of not journaling). We all have one. A journal is an invaluable, *'never-possible-to-recover-again'* jewel. Recording a team journal is also not a bad idea. It can be a tremendous source of challenge and encouragement when the team or ministry is going through difficult times. **They need to be reminded of what God has been doing.**

Long Term vs. Short Term Race

At this time, it would be meaningful to address short and long term mission agendas for the needs are greatly different. One of the greatest debilitations for long-term potential candidates is that too many leaders and teams run a two-week or two-month outreach like a rabbit out of control. They run people into the ground, zapping all of their strength and more. Their baggage practically drags them to the airport. They want to go home where things are 'normal.'

What you want to impress on others is normal life. Missions or being a missionary is someone you are, not something you do; it is a lifestyle just like Christianity. You do not "do" Christianity, although some try. You are - then doing flows naturally. It is the same with missions and ministry. It is impossible for most to function at a crazy pace, which conveys a negative feeling or bad taste in their mouth about missions; they assume this is "missions' life." If schedules and plans are nuts from time to time, it needs to be communicated that this is not the norm (or should not be) for most missionaries. It is not really God's way. It is more of Mr. Performance's way. You are not the full answer for the needs and the lost of the world. There will always be a far greater need than you can fulfill; therefore, let God be God and follow as He prompts.

I was part of another team who had challenges facing them, which brought me to the base more often than I had liked. Upon arrival I dreaded comments like, **"Jon, how are you? I thought you were on Outreach?"** I would respond as lovingly as possible, **"Wherever these two feet go is Outreach."** I mention this because there are, I believe, religious types who think you are not 'ministering' or 'doing' God's call when you are not where they expected you to be. Again, it is helpful for them to be reminded: "You see me as I am, but God knows where I have been. And wherever I go are ministry possibilities or at least openness for them."

GOD'S WILL ON OUTREACH

"Knowing God's will is the greatest treasure. Doing God's will is the greatest privilege."
-Gareth Evans,
former Chaplain on the M/V Anastasis

"Surprises are never a surprise to God. It is part of discipleship to depend on Him as we live our life, live our part."
- Swiss queen of outreach,
Judith Straub

Take note of where and when people become disappointed or disillusioned. Like the time we had a set up with Hans Christian Anderson in West Africa. He met the president of a Beach Club. We were going to be on television. There were about 2,000 people present. We were prayed up, stored up, preached up and ready to roll! We had dramas planned that were powerful, testimonies, and songs prepared. We were to be the main focus that afternoon. Then the whammy came. There was a power failure, among several other hiccups. There went "the opportunity?" Several questions popped up as if on cue from the team:

What do we do? Could we have planned better? Do we miss it sometimes? Was this God? The devil? Were we not recognizing or hearing God's voice?

An arrangement was made for us to return that very week, but there were far less people. Yet we were able to do everything, and there were several incredible conversations that night. The key is trusting that God is going to be there. Do what you sense is right. Be careful not to be overly governed by others. Listen to counsel but do not turn off your relationship button with God and His Word. Getting a Word from Jesus adds confidence.

Sometimes, in more serious circumstances, the brunt of the decision(s) will not fall upon you but those over you. That frees you from the responsibility. It would be smart for leaders to trust people like Hans who set up ministry opportunities. Encourage them yet follow up to see if help is needed and details are worked through, which perhaps could have been overlooked.

Another episode, where it is suitable to mention God's will, was when I was part of the "Sierra Leone [SL] Wannabees." We wanted to be (believed we were going to be) in Sierra Leone. This all changed. The Rebels came into Freetown, Sierra Leone, and wrought further havoc, which was utterly atrocious, demonic and beyond human. Without warning, these Rebels would come into villages and cities destroying everything within their path. It was "come and kill, steal and destroy or stay and be killed." They would line up their fellow citizens and inquire if they would prefer long sleeve or short sleeve cuts? Shorts or trouser length cuts? Then proceed to butcher and amputate them (according to size preference), like my friend Victor. They would also pour melted plastic in the eyes of their own blood-kinsmen. Lighting houses on fire, beating, shooting and raping was part of their common daily diet; laughter was for dessert. So getting a Word from Jesus was absolutely necessary.

We went to live in a refugee camp and were removed. Then a couple guys were arrested in town, followed by myself and some others being escorted by the military to our compound and falling under house arrest for some hours while being given one hour to pack all of our belongings after they had already done a full search. We were escorted out of town, not to return. Nothing like a "de-welcoming!" Now what? What was that all about?! The SL Wannabees were making an incredible impact. Was it God's will? Talk about a high hurdle for the team to jump. Yet God's ways and means are high above the six billion minds around this celestial ball put together. It is good to know that God loves His children. He is Just. So we can even rest in a bed of questions.

Cliches: Guess It Is Not God's Will

There are those who are quick to utter Christian clichés, which are often not from God or not Biblical, at least in some contexts. Continuing with our journey in SL, we were bombarded by well-meaning friends who patted us on the back, not without presumption, saying, **"It must not be God's will for you to be there, to be here, to be doing that..."** It almost seemed as though several people got together and planned to announce that particular statement. It was difficult to swallow and not say anything. Instead we would smile and express thanks for the lack of encouragement we

were given so generously. Nevertheless, I need to point out at the start of this challenging section that I do agree with the statement, **'It must not have been God's will,'** but with proper discernment.

Why the song and dance? Why this section? I pray you do not have to face what I have faced or worse...that of others who had to endure far more than I ever imagined, making my adventures seem like pre-school! I would like to pose this question:

Is everything expressed and experienced on earth GOD'S WILL?

Would all the stories the Media portrays (at times embellishes) be directly related to or even be a distant cousin of God's will? Does God work through many of these pitiful, through sorrowful accounts and lives? Yes, without question. Some of today's events, in my life and yours, are the result of a fallen world, our mistakes, the mistakes of others, our fears, and being controlled by what others say, which can cause temporary paralysis, keeping us neutral, complacent, quiet, and not doing what we know or believe to be right. Do not settle for comfortable. Could this fear of change be part of a belief system that has been enforced and lodged in our brain, clogging the filter between soul and spirit. *How many have said because circumstances are difficult and hard, it must not be God's will.* Thus, the easy route is best for some. Actually, I am concerned that the vast majority of creation wishes this to be the "truth."

Were the Disciples on the easy route? Look how they died. Were they in God's will? Paul even told the **Philippians**, in **Chapter 1:12**, that his suffering (imprisonment) has actually helped the spreading of the Gospel. Hmm...puts a monkey wrench in people's ideals and stereotype of God.

Is death natural?

Death is as unnatural as a year-old child against Michael Jordan in a one-on-one basketball game, or a person's body without water. Whenever we see a death, we should be angry at sin, as we are reminded of its results. During life, sin also results in spiritual death for its wages are death **(Romans**

6:23). Yet the paradox: when death comes, there is life. It was not through Jesus' miracles, works, or words, but it was through His suffering and death that brought Life. What a mind-blowing mystery!

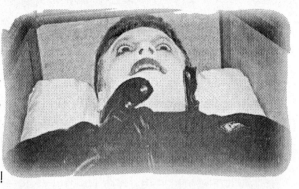

As I stated before, I do not believe everything that happens is the will of God. Is He in control? Absolutely. Anyone who bets against that fact would lose every cent in the twinkling of an eye. Regardless of your role, there may come a time where you will be asked to speak about, answer and give your understanding of God's will. For some bizarre reason, God has chosen to work through us in a big way (bigger rather than comfortable for you and I at times)! One incredibly encouraging revelation is that every person, who seeks first His kingdom, reduces the amount of suffering, selfishness, greed, corruption, illness, and more in this world. That is exciting. With every birth, there is another opportunity to perfect this world (as in one becoming so God fearing that they make a radical difference). Ongoing tragedies are, in large part, due to the Church's lack of being present, speaking up and praying, as well as people and areas being void of God's Spirit (missionaries).

We cannot shove God into a box (as if we could) and count everything as His will. Furthermore, let us not declare, "Because this was difficult or easy, it must be God's will." Through the centuries, we have complicated God's intention for simplicity. The reason for suffering and all the yuck we are bombarded with on a continual basis is simple yet profound. We have forgotten to 'love the Lord our God with all our heart, mind soul and strength... and love our neighbor as ourselves' **(Matthew 22:34-40).** The year 2000 approached unstopped, and yet, in these 2,000 years, we still have not heard the command. But as long as we have breath, there is hope, and that is something to consider. Remember, at the beginning, middle, and end of the day, the Lover of your soul is after your heart; therefore, there should be zero fear of God's will as long as we are connected to Him with openness and a willingness to obey with genuine motives.

THE SILENCE OF GOD

While I was praying with a team headed for the Ukraine for two months, this continual nudging about Russia kept coming to my mind, yet I did not understand what we would do there. My sensing was confirmed by what I saw on the cover of a *Newsweek* magazine laying on my bed, the words jumping brightly off its page proclaiming, *"MOSCOW NOW."* Our team continued to pray (and through our time in the Ukraine). There were only enough morsels given initially to spring up the vision within - or so I thought. Nothing seen in the natural caused us to believe we would go to Russia 'with love.' We interceded and interceded in prayer. Nothing came to us (really) as we were praying to confirm our hopes. I had thought it was the Lord. Russia had first come to my heart early in October.

December 5, 1997. It was 2:59 p.m. Friday. One hour and 46 minutes before the Russian Embassy shuts its doors for the weekend; one hour and 46 painstaking minutes before all hope is gone. After all, we were to fly out of Kiev for a debriefing in England on Thursday, the 12th. Monday would be too late.

Hours of prayer; more than $200USD spent on communication to and from Russia; invitations provided by a contact in Moscow were $325USD; train tickets that had already been purchased came to $350USD; and hours spent on computers trying to relay information (while being disconnected by phone/fax) about the team. We would not have gotten nearly this far without the incredible ingenuity of my good friend and teammate Keith McPherson from South Africa. All the while, our ears simply heard *God's profound silence.*

It was a chase through Kiev's snow-filled streets. Traffic was heavy, as people were anticipating the close of their week. And here we were, racing the clock, praying for a storm that would top any downfall of snow...'God, please move on our behalf!' Officials had previously removed us from the Embassy on one occasion, and on another denied our visas (somewhere in between discussing (rather demanding) that the visas would be granted for $100USD and then changing the price to $250USD)!

At the tone, the time will be 3:01 p.m. Friday, December 5th . The long awaited answer comes. The **Silence of God** became the sound of God (but what is the difference?) It is official. The visas were not only less than previously stated but were also sitting now within our grasp. HALLELUJAH!

However, there is a catch..., and this is where most Christians would decide they did not hear God's voice. But listen. Half the team and I were off that night to Moscow. Since September 27, there had been another ban on Christian and missionary work. Marie, who is from France, had (apparently) the wrong number on her visa (their passports have two different numbers). The military was speaking strongly against my passport's validity because I had 24 pages added to the already full-book at the U.S. Embassy in Amsterdam. They tried to frighten us yelling, **"Where are the rest of those on your team?"**

The rest of the team is in Kiev," I said. That was not the answer these (large) men (with guns and Russia behind them) wanted to hear since I had been responsible for all of our visas through the Ukraine Embassy. I thought it best to get a double entry visa (to add to my list of faith steps). And so they only saw half of us on the train coming from Russia. Yikes! It was looking a bit dismal and shaky. [Side note: There had been several people removed from our train already. Were we next to be deported?!]

Suddenly, I heard one of the most soothing, beautiful, relieving sounds in my life up to that point, the "chah-ching, chah-ching" of the stamp okaying our passports! There were a few more hurdles throughout this journey while in Russia. While in a school for four hours, an irate female teacher reported us to the police. Lee, pushing two meters in height and well...many kilos, was accosted by the

police. As they were taking him away, a few girls from the team happened to take notice and yelled for him, "Lee, what is happening?" At this point the police, with great amazement to Lee, released him.

There were miraculous events all along the way for us while walking in God's silence: 11 students and a teacher wanted to begin life with Jesus. They began to meet together, even continuing to meet more than two years later. Even in the silence, we somehow heard the sound of God, which squeaked us through these pressure-cooking adventures.

Hence, go with what you hear and be surprised at the hand of God in His apparent silence. I theorize that one of God's greatest ways to bring health and trust to the Body of Christ and the on-looking world is to gain trust in what and who they cannot see and not trusting in situations, as they are not always as they appear. We could have bailed out because of the obstacles, believing God did not want us to go to Russia, but, through it all, God was faithful, glorified and right there with us. Wow...God trusting us in His silence...deep. If that is not mind blowing, I do not know what is.

What can we learn of God's will?

His Revealed will:
~ *Genesis 50:20*...He overrides the desire of the wicked.
~ *Proverbs 19:20*...Listen to advice.
~ *Micah 6:8*...To do justice, love kindness and walk humbly...
~ *Matthew 6:10, 1 John 5:14*...To pray and depend on Him.
~ *Luke 9:5, Acts 13:50-51*...Sometimes to leave an area.

~ *John 3:17, Matthew 18:14*...That people do not perish.

~ *Acts 1:26*...Drawing lots to decide, though not all of the time.

~ *Acts 13:48*...He destines people for eternal life.

~ *Acts 18:20-21, 1 Corinthians 4:19*...Sometimes He keeps us back.

~ *Romans 9:11-18, Psalm 37:1-7*...He does as He chooses.

~ *Ephesians 1:9,11-12*...You can know the mystery of His will.

~ *Ephesians 5:15-24*...Build up and be filled with the Spirit.

~ *1 Thessalonians 5:12-22*...Thankfulness, test everything...and more.

~ *Hebrews 12:5-11*...Trials and discipline can come from God.

~ *James 1:22-27*...Have pure religion; truth in action.

~ *1 Peter 2:15*...Do right and silence the foolish.

~ *1 Peter 3:13-17, 4:19, Acts 14:22*...May include suffering.

~ *1 John 2:15-17*...Do not love the world: having pride and lust of eyes, flesh.

~ *1 John 3:6*...Do not live in sin (context: continually bent on sinning).

~ *1 John 3:16-24*...To lay our lives down; love in action.

~ *1 John 4:18*...No fear; know His character.

There is much we do know about His will. This trust, while experiencing hardship in other, unknown areas, will keep you relatively safe. Safe in the sense that Jesus is in control. There are times when scripture will confirm thoughts you have had. If you find yourself wondering whether or not you are in God's will...rest. Do not strive with fear. Have faith *(Hebrews 11:6)*. It is quite consoling to have the revelation that God holds no stone in His hands as said in *Matthew 7:9-11* where Jesus warmly tells us that there ought not to be doubt and fear; that if we are asking and seeking in His name, desiring with right motives for His will and purposes, He will lovingly re-direct us if need be. Too many are afraid of missing God's will. I think He loves us too much. If we are genuine and real, I believe we can rest with peace.

CHAPTER FIVE

Ideas for Ministry

reas for **potential** ministry should be bathed in prayer to gain Jesus' perspective and enlightenment. When asking the Lord (and ourselves) what is best for that particular people, place, and time, let love be the forerunner. What I have concluded is this: loving is not just crying over people from a distance; love is entering the lives of others. Compassion means feeling-with action-into the life of another. *1 John 3:17-20* seems to confirm that real love is with action. If we see a person in need and refuse to help, what we have is meaningless. "...let us love, not in word or speech, but in truth and action..." *(v. 18)*. The late musician Rich Mullins, poignantly sang, "Faith without works is like a screen door on a submarine" (sometimes it can be preaching and teaching without works is less than the best). The ideas to come are simply to spur on vision.

Let Love Be the Forerunner

Town/Village/Jungle Setting

Projects for Objects of Love

1 - Praying hut to hut
2 - Cleaning huts
3 - Removing cow dung, emphasis on health and sanitation
4 - Building steps to the river
5 - Water catching systems
6 - Latrines
7 - CHE (Community Health Education - worms, diarrhea, Malaria, where diseases come from - this is also a form of spiritual warfare)!
8 - Repairing porches, roofs, and other domestics
9 - Planting, weeding
10 - Community meals
11 - Cleaning around village
12 - Ask what the church needs - not your wants
13 - Ask what the village needs
14 - Cleaning and sewing clothes
15 - Bringing people for surgery
16 - Involving children/locals
17 - Building/starting small business
18 - Awareness of people's needs
19 - Child care
20 - Help to feed prisoners

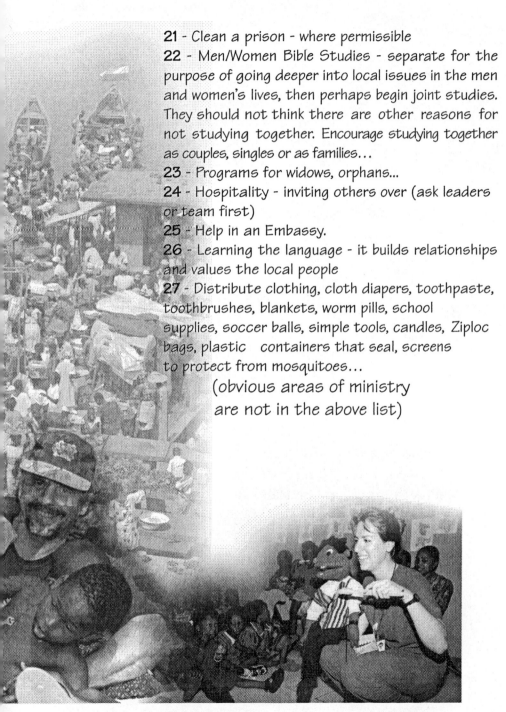

21 - Clean a prison - where permissible

22 - Men/Women Bible Studies - separate for the purpose of going deeper into local issues in the men and women's lives, then perhaps begin joint studies. They should not think there are other reasons for not studying together. Encourage studying together as couples, singles or as families...

23 - Programs for widows, orphans...

24 - Hospitality - inviting others over (ask leaders or team first)

25 - Help in an Embassy.

26 - Learning the language - it builds relationships and values the local people

27 - Distribute clothing, cloth diapers, toothpaste, toothbrushes, blankets, worm pills, school supplies, soccer balls, simple tools, candles, Ziploc bags, plastic   containers that seal, screens to protect from mosquitoes...

(obvious areas of ministry are not in the above list)

Surgical Help from the Jungle

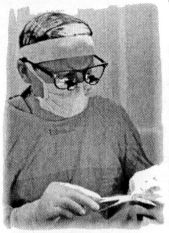

You can aid by bringing surgical help, plus being aware of opportunities makes a huge difference. In one country, we helped three people from the Jungle to have life-changing, village-changing surgeries. One such surgery was for Savaka's cleft lip (his very name meant 'hair lip' or 'rejected one'). The shocking part is that it only cost us $20USD (hope this makes you appreciate a $20 bill from here on out)! This had a major impact on the region. We were able to talk with his family and ask if they would pray with us and consider changing his name. They were thrilled at the idea. We gathered together after some time had elapsed and discussed a name, which we believed God desired for him since the Lord confirmed it through our prayer. It was Jonathan. He received a new name and a new beginning, a gift from God. His name was no longer a reflection of the past, his birth defect or rejection from the world, but now his name reminds him that he is a gift and a treasure. The young man is forever changed physically and now spiritually because of God's love through people.

See the need and work with God in fulfilling it. Love is seeing the need and doing something about it. True Christianity is practical Christianity.

Ministry in an Embassy

For us it was a total blessing from the Ambassador to the people as we brought aid to the Refugees stranded within the Embassy, listened to their traumas, prayed, taught health education, fed them, etc. However, not all places and people will embrace your efforts. Go as God leads. Move out carefully and with caution, yet creatively and with openness.

What You Want and Need

What you implement could be fruitful or forgettable. If you come to do just what you want, there is a high probability that it will not generate much life. You must have a life-giving spirit because they need to see vision, value, and purpose in their own lives. It has to meet their current need.

Teaching While Illustrating

People will benefit more if we express why we 'do what we do' followed, perhaps, with why we 'believe what we believe.' "We are giving these items because..." More people receive understanding when we illustrate what we are teaching with objects, paintings, drawings, photos, video clips, and, of course, storytelling. Also, involve the people. BE CREATIVE! We only remember 10% of what we hear, which should tell us that if we want our efforts to go deeper and further (more than just moving our lips), we must utilize the different senses (taste, touch, smell, sight and sound). Take advantage of everyone's different learning style. After I taught on Women in Missions, Bible School Director Jennifer Creamer told me that because of my humor throughout the presentation on a controversial and challenging teaching, it really let people's guard down and caused greater receptivity. There are times for preaching and teaching to be serious, yes; however, let us not be known for condemning people. There are some parishioners AND pastors in West Africa who tell me (confirming what I already have experienced) many leave evangelistic crusades and church services feeling like they want to commit suicide because they were screamed at and condemned week after week.

N‍ext, make sure that what you are teaching is practical. All too often people teach, 'You should pray, walk in obedience to God's Word, love one another!' BUT they do not give practical everyday ideas on HOW they can practically walk these truths. HOW do I PRAY? HOW do I really OBEY? HOW do I LOVE?

Some ideas for teaching could be the following:

Giving

Fatalism

Belief Systems
(as well as: why I believe what I believe and why do I do what I do)

Value of the Created
Value of Life
(land, creation, animals, humanity, men, women, and children)

Value of EVERY Individual

What Is Freedom?
(freedom from sin but in contrast to legalism)

Old Testament/New Testament Overview

Sin - Why Is Life Like This?

Love of God = the Cross

Lack of Initiative/Laziness
(usually when I do not understand value)

Family Life and Values
(be specific with issues that are relevant; ask for insight)

What is Your Word Worth?
(being real, integral, excellence, trust)

Christianity Lifestyle in Every Part of Life
(not living several different lives - one way at church; another when conducting business)

***Perhaps some areas within this book may give further ideas on teaching practically

Ideas for Ministry in the West

1- Carrying a coffin through the streets (part of a drama)

2- Carrying a 10 ft. (3m) cross through the streets

3- Roses for prostitutes, going to window girls, etc...

4- Sidewalk Sunday school

5- Prayer stations. Set up somewhere in town and be available to pray with anyone who would like prayer. Perhaps have a table, banner and literature so when people walk by, they will understand - Nick Savoka (YWAM - NY).

6- Going to discos. In the Canary Isles, we went along the Strips talking with people leaving the establishments. It was more fruitful than we initially thought.

7- Cleaning up streets

8— Hospitality. Invite others to be a part

9- Look to assist in the neighborhood

10- Shopping and bringing food for those bedridden in the area

11- Language; it builds relationships and values the local people

12- Do surveys, which can raise the "God" question, asking what they feel about life. Do they believe in the after life? What is important to them? What famous figures they respect and why?

13 - Hang out with the treasure of the streets with no agenda (even sleep on the street with them).

14- Offer free services such as car washes, maintenance, etc...

15- Torch run throughout cities or coastlines for the nation or reconciliation

16- Just have fun and get to know people

   * This is not a complete list; there are more obvious venues
   of ministry not mentioned.

WHY YOU DO WHAT YOU DO

Success Is Being Faithful

As a leader, you will have your own ideas or projects that you will want to accomplish. Say you want to build a latrine, but your team is either slacking off or they continue to focus on other projects. You may think, *'I do not understand why they will not follow through with this; the need is so clear.'* This could cost you unnecessary wasted time, materials and strength. Be careful. If the team does not want what you had wanted in your heart, you could be subjected to disappointment, all the while the band (team) is playing "out of tune" behind you. So it may be helpful to discuss vision, intentions and purposes for what you might desire to do. Make sure the team is in unison or strategize together. Minimize potential disunity by making your and their expectations known. There may be a respect issue, as well. Simply take a personal inventory to see where you stand. I have had to remind myself that respect is not demanded or commanded but earned.

How have I been in communicating with the team in regard to time specific issues? It is a different story if you communicated clearly what would take place. Although, it could be possible that you misunderstood God or realized that it may not be the best project for that time or people. Be open to listen. The issue could possibly be the team as well. It is normal for there to be durations waiting on the Lord. Ever hear of the "hurry up and wait" syndrome? Of course you have, and it is true. So do not hurry so much. They need to see value and take ownership.

What **do you do** when members feel like they are not making a difference on a team? They seem to be lacking in successful responses. What about the "not busy enough" or "not doing enough" plight? It is imperative that they live their lives daily under God's definition of success. What if the "masses," who you or your team dreamed of reaching, never materialized? Reassure the team that God's idea of success is not man's idea. I know of some missionaries who had their support suspended and were forced back to their home front because they did not have "fruit." Where were the hundreds of salvations? Were the masses discipled?

Man **could not see** the changes that had taken place in the Spirit; therefore, they deemed it an unsuccessful effort. They failed to see the missionaries' incredible commitment to the people and region. Do as you are called and leave the results to God. Naturally, we should evaluate if there is fruit in what we are doing, but some of us may need to reconsider what we have believed fruit and success are. *What I have learned from Paul's example is: success is being faithful.*

When **studying Paul's letters,** I began to weep and was gripped by Paul's words to Timothy in his 2nd letter. This was most likely his last letter before being beheaded by the Roman Emperor in the late 60s AD. Why such a response? Look what he endured, as *2 Corinthians 11:23-28* describes his beatings, imprisonments, etc. In addition, he turns the world upside down with the Gospel, writes 13 letters of 27 in the New Testament, yet he tells Timothy how many deserted him, showing his ability to be hurt. In *2 Timothy 1:15,* he tells that all of Asia turned on him (though the household of Onesiphorus often refreshed him). Later in *4:10, 11,* we find Demas, Crescens, and Titus left. Finally in *4:16,* Paul tells that all deserted him at his first defense. Yet through the blood, sweat and tears through the years, he remained faithful until the end. How sad that some of us, because of a simple disagreement, walk away, divide, and become disgruntled.

Unfulfilled Expectations

Expectations are not wrong in and of themselves, but what we do with them that counts.

The following is used by permission of Jack Hill, former Chaplain for Mercy Ships.

1 **Accept** the fact that we all have expectations.

2 **Learn** to recognize what your expectations are.

3 **If an expectation** goes unfulfilled, find out why you are disappointed.

4 **Evaluate** your expectations.
A.) Are they realistic? Reasonable?
B.) How much emphasis do you place on them?
C.) Are they based on reality or fantasy?

5 **Allow** people to be people. They will change their minds and will make mistakes.

6 **Allow** God to be God.
"Come now, you who say, 'Today or tomorrow we will go to such and such a city, spend a year there, buy and sell, and make a profit,' whereas you do not know what will happen tomorrow."
James 4:13 and *14b (NKJV)*.

Are your expectations flexible enough for God to adjust your comfort zone?

Pay **close attention** to the number of times you experience disappointment over the next day or two, which will help you realize how many expectations you have on a regular basis. Then evaluate them with points two and three above.

Catch a glimpse of what Jack targets above in regards to reality vs. fantasy. He says elsewhere in another teaching that you will not find God in fantasy. Why? Because He is not there. He only lives in reality. Fantasy is embellishing your life based upon who you want to be, which can seem attractive but actually becomes deceptive.

Be There

It is necessary to understand that the team will possibly have high expectations of you, as a leader, to be involved and present during ministry. A friend of mine was on a team with a leader who did his own thing (who would often be gone), which greatly affected the team's unity, enthusiasm and movement. (Here is a thought: there are characteristics and qualifications for leaders mentioned specifically in *1 Timothy 3, Titus 2*, and elsewhere. How are these qualities to be known and modeled if the leader(s) are not available or there?)

As I see it, the best coach is the one who played...and still plays the game...not just the one who observes it from afar (hmm...like Jesus, Esther, Paul, Miriam, Peter, John?). This is certainly not God's example as He was, is, and always will be the best coach; He's always involved. Experiencing the easiest route is not always right, best or good. Some leaders are accomplished at being too still. Leadership is more than a title; it is a style, a life-style.

Involve the Team in Decision-Making

At times, you may do well involving the team in decision-making. They can more readily grasp the outreach and ministry as their own. It is their outreach and ministry too, not just your own, so move out accordingly. Ownership is necessary to fuel unity and forge motivation.

My friends Dan Eastep and Joe Valenzuela, two directors of the YWAM-SBS in Bangalore and Mysore, India, involved others in decision making, and myself and those involved appreciated that the two had not tried to control everything but instead offered an ear to what others had to say. When necessary, they made the final decision, but at least they asked for other's input and involvement. I feel it aids integrity and respect, not only keeping the leaders in safer positions, but also enabling their disciples to learn more about decision making, processing, and working through various scenarios. If you keep others at bay, how can they grow? [this may differ depending on the kind of team you have, i.e. a team of leaders within a church ministry would be more involved in decision-making then say a youth team.]

Hospitality and Welcoming

Hospitality goes a long way when touching the lost and those in need. Endeavor to be a team with hospitality. Welcome others. Unwelcoming teams are unpleasant. Please do not let that happen. If it does, work through it quickly with your team or the other team. You may actually have to speak directly to the leader(s) of that team. If a team comes with a need, prioritize their need as much as it is reasonable. If someone you know has just trekked a long way for hours with a need, help them hospitably. **The last thing we want is to taint relationships with those who have opened doors for us.** *Remember: God is the Divine Helper in time of need.*

When I was leading the drama evangelism team "Crosstide" (sometimes mis-named "Crossed-Eyes or Crossfire"), the hosting Pastor in Capetown, South Africa, disclosed to me his concern regarding a former team that he had set up. He was mortified because the team continually squabbled about who was going to speak. *'I am not giving a testimony; you do it.'* 'No, you do it.' At his house, they asked him to leave his back room because they were deciding if they were even going to stay with him or not. This is not quality behavior. Needless to say, it left a terrible taste in the hosting Pastor's mouth, and he soured at the thought of entertaining future teams. Then we show up on his doorstep - surprise!

He had some uncertainties, but I was able to reassure him that we were respectful. In the weeks ahead, his church experienced a revival. Lesson: be alert because you do not know who has paved the way before you, whether good or bad.

From extending hospitality to strangers (widows to prophets), we see God continually exhorts us into the area of hospitality (especially leaders). The following verse and **2 and 3 John** are for further study regarding hospitality God's style. Think creatively what you can do in providing hospitality: a meal, bed, full spread with items like biscuits, toothpaste, welcome card and/or token of appreciation. There have been people who have even given me their bed while they chose to sleep on the couch or floor - dirt floor. "In everything, do to others as you would have them do to you…" *(Matthew 7:12a)*. What would make you feel special?

Hospitality is:

~ Part of discipleship

~ Crossing social barriers

~ Commanded by God

~Christians opening their homes

~ Spreading the Gospel and being supportive

Use discernment regarding false teachings *(2nd and 3rd John)*. If someone is known to be teaching falsely (against what is clear in the doctrines of Christianity), they should not be extended hospitality (welcoming them to stay or to come into your home). There are many false religions all around us. Beware. If you believe their agenda is only to confuse, divide, and to push their beliefs on you, then hospitality is not to be extended, as it gives an acceptance to what they are doing; some, who are not strong enough spiritually, could be persuaded and confused. We do not just throw the door open for anyone. Use discernment. Do not worry about people pleasing. If they seem open to your beliefs, that COULD be something to reconsider BUT with caution. Yes, we are called to reach out to people and witness but not when others are not interested in what we believe or have to say and, instead, only have a desire to push their deceptions on us. Furthermore, be aware of some who may have split from the church, trying to persuade you to follow their parade.

Entrusted Guardian

You **might find** it helpful to have an entrusted guardian, when possible, to watch the house while you are ministering (where appropriate). At times, it is a difficult balance. If you are in a village setting, you would want the guardian (a local or team member) to participate when possible. Try to compensate by bringing home some spiritual food for them. On one particular outreach, we made the mistake of realizing too late in the game that one of us had to always remain in the house, especially because we were living with no locks on the doors or even the ability to have any. Never place your team or anyone in your direct reach at risk. **Duty helpers, please contact the canoe!**

If **there is a need** in a remote setting, it would be a blessing to hire some locals that could get you situated in your new environment. Often, they are willing to extend help for nothing in return. But be prepared to bless them in any way, whether financially, spiritually, or possibly helping in return. What an opportunity for you. Again, know when to give and when to let the helpers rely on God. Sometimes we can short circuit the blessing of a one-way giving by giving also. It may be healthy to let the helpers just do it out of their heart without expectation of something in return. You may want to ask your contact who is integral in the area.

Translators

I have found it advantageous to have a personal translator as a leader. For a team of 15, perhaps three translators could work. The more translators you have, the greater your opportunities, depending on your leadership functions. For some leaders, a translator may not be necessary, as their gift may be more behind the scenes focusing on/within the team. Others' gifts and strengths may be working directly with local leaders or people of influence, building them up or following up in situations that arise, etc. This usually requires a

Helpful *Go-Go* Gadgets to Bring

leader with vigor and wisdom in communicating.
Buy supplies from a local city, town or village
when possible, as it aids the local economy.
~ Headlamps
~ Ear plugs (for those early cock-a-doodle-doos)
~ String/rope/clothespins
~ Ziploc bags, big and small, and garbage bags
~ Wet wipes/toilet paper
~ Strainers, filters, funnels
~ Pocket knives, sharp knives
~ Repellent for bugs/bug killer/fly strips
  (for an outside latrine), water repellent spray —
  spraying items before going is a good idea
~ Soccer balls/pump/needles
~ Rat kill or a friendly snake (ha, ha)
~ Buckets
~ Shovel/hammer/nails/machete
~ Sewing materials
~ Do not bring large air mattresses - (space, weight,
  less flexibility)
~ Permanent marker
~ Super glue/duct tape/masking tape
~ Lanterns/candles/matches
~ Pots/potholders/ladles
~ Containers that seal from bugs, rats...
~ Rain jackets
~ Light gloves
~ Just bring 2-3 outfits (suggestion)
~ Sandals that fasten

These are helpful, simple living suggestions (not a complete list since
I omitted obvious items). When entering a village with all of your
belongings, it could be tempting and overwhelming for the locals of
the area. Furthermore, keep your items from being seen in the open.
This helps you and them from feeling uncomfortable and prevents
problems. Bringing less is better!

Ideas and Strategies for Ministry

Now after taking into account the culture and the appropriate interactions acceptable between the genders...
"Ask the Lord for a reason to enter into the lives of others." -Sharlene
(for neighbors and/or while walking around different areas)

1. Keep eyes and heart open to discern/see needs as you proceed with your day.
2. Like the broken zipper in my wallet, I walked by a house with a sewing machine and asked for help, which began a ministry with some families. Pray for God to use [sometimes frustrating] moments to be God moments.
3. Cook for them.
4. Bless them with a bag of groceries left at their doorstep.
5. Cut their grass.
6. Ask them directions or input for something good to do in their area/city/country.
7. Ask if there is anything you can pray for (without forcing, coercing or preaching at them...be casual).
8. Do a survey. Perhaps ask some of the following:

    a. What is important to you?

    b. What is the most significant thing that has happened in your life (and even to pass on to others)?

    c. What bothers you?

    d. What do you think is the answer for the selfishness/tragedies or_____in life?

    e. What is the perfect day for you? What would it look like (as in what would you do or would like to happen in that 'perfect day')?

    f. What advice would you give someone struggling with _____ or who wants to know or needs to know _____?

    g. Is there value in life? If so, where do you think value comes from?

    h. What do you enjoy doing?

    i. When you die, where do you think you will go or what will happen?

j. What is the meaning of life to you?

k. What would you like to see happen in your neighborhood or _____?

9. Speak up when you see something wrong, i.e. when someone is being beaten, like a child being beaten beyond emotional or physical boundaries, somebody throwing rubbish on the road (I am a bit more radical, always asking them if they like a dirty country or I just pick it up and let them be challenged by my proper actions), or when they are playing loud music at 2am…gently talk with them about it and why there may be a better compromise - like a do unto others what you would want them to do to you.

10. Pay for a parents night out and watch their kids.

11. Ask if you could borrow something of theirs.

12. Ask for a ride.

13. Organize or teach about a "Neighborhood Watch" concept. This can give more of an opportunity for care/concern/accountability/unity in the neighborhood.

14. Show them your photos. This brings incredible opportunities for communicating, like my photos of helping at Mother Teresa's in Kolkata, saving a refugee, being attacked by a baboon, cliff jumping, etc.

15. Taking spontaneous digital photos where they can see themselves right away. It brings laughs, lower walls, etc. I even surprise people at times and print some for them. Or offer to do family photos. Be creative. This has been one of my greatest tools for reaching into peoples hearts and lives, among other acts of compassion, especially in developing countries.

16. Collective gift for each neighbor with a card that greets them, and gives an idea of who you are, written skillfully, cautiously and sensitively and only what is necessary that may draw them in and/or may give them a sense of reassurance that you might be there for them should they need you.

17. Ask them random advice. You have a situation…you need some input, so you [humble yourself] ask them…listen to them. This can have a significant impact.

18. Ask/inquire about their culture/history/what they believe, not to argue and defend what you believe, but just to genuinely listen and show them respect. Perhaps later you can talk more about what you believe.

19. Clean the streets.

20. Ask local authorities if there is anything you can do for them (this depends upon where you are and if you are known to be 'allowed' in the country).

21. Block Party or kids party. Often I have sensed from the Lord that if you reach the heart of the children, you will reach the heart of the parent. Invite neighbors to your house or on the street. Block it off to cars if there is a general acceptance to do so or if there is another way of entrance/exit/or thoroughfare. Be creative with games/storytimes/drama/spontaneous stuff/food/contests...

22. Keep a Base Log of the happenings with neighbors/neighborhood so that others can know where to build from, make further bridges, or to avoid the neighbors feeling neither left out nor bombarded.

23. Look for opportunities to build trust.

24. Appreciate them when you see them doing something you valued or thought was nice, whether big or small, even if you do not know them or know them well, and even when they might not have known that you were watching!

25. Unfortunately, to state the obvious, smile and acknowledge the neighbor/clerks or whomever you frequent as they pass.

26. Ask them to translate a letter for you.

27. Ask them to teach you some phrases in their local language.

28. Ask for or borrow recipes, books, games, a movie or offer one to them, i.e. they seem to watch movies a lot. Then chat about it after.

29. Find points of interest and build on it. If it is something they are interested in, become interested in it for their sake.

30. Night watch. Friday night prayer vigils/walking/reading scripture, etc. through the night/day and fasting for neighbors through the night in shifts of 2-3 people every 1 hour or 2 hours.

31. Or you can have a contest of who can come up with the best excuse for not reaching out to their neighbors...ah, #31 is only a joke.

But remember the words of Dr. Gary Parker of the M/V Anastasis:

"Do you love them so you can preach the Gospel [at them] or do you preach the Gospel because you love them."

People will know/sense if you are genuine or not, so let motives be pure and real. *So let us go love our neighbor as we [would or should] love ourselves. And never cease to be amazed at what can be around the corner while you are being a Prayerfully Practical Person of God!!*

CHAPTER SIX

What Happens When...?

In this section, you will find helpful hints and answers for your "how to, what if" questions in preparing to communicate with your ministry team and perhaps increase your effectiveness and flow. Sometimes equipment failure is a God thing. Ooops! Time for Plan B. Be open to change. Try to keep in step with Him. I usually keep going until I see a red flag or light. Be sensitive and aware, always listening for what His Spirit is saying; however, I realize it is much easier to write this than to live it.

As I have said, plan B can be a God thing so it is vital to ascertain what is a God thing vs. a good thing. **At the end of the day, technique and performance matters not.** It is all about love and how faithful we have been to live it. Do not allow sloppiness, whether physical or spiritual, to be poured out. Many ministries or Christians excuse their poor appearance, preparation or quality with the mind set, *'We are just doing this for Jesus, and it does not have to be like...'* But I beg to differ. If it is for the King, all the more reason for it to be the best we can offer. In *Colossians 3:22-24* we see Paul's exhortation for the slaves to do whatever they do not because they are seen, or half-heartedly, but the best to their ability since it is for the Lord. Ah, if this is for slaves, how much more us? And we are slaves/servants to Christ as well-no?! Leave the results and what is beyond us to Him. And whether we are ministering in developed or developing nations, favoritism should not be apparent, as in with the mentality that we can do it half-heartedly, and with little excellence, or quality if we are in a developing world setting. Yet only excellence should be our aim and desire. Like my mom instilled within us as children, "If you are going to do something-do it right...if not do not do it at all!" She has a point aye?!

The following is a traveling ministry checklist for leaders and their teams to utilize; however, you may be in a country where they would chew you up and spit you out before you had a chance to say *John 3:16* in their native language on the street! Not all parts of the world will give you the opportunity of expression within the general public. Use discernment and wisdom, and She [wisdom] will protect you!

1 When setting up a public meeting, discuss with your contact what is best and fitting to do, where is best, and how long of a program he/she would recommend or prefer, rather than just deciding yourself, though they may ask your opinion.

2 Find the best area for performing, usually where the most people will congregate. Try not to have the crowd face the sun, if outdoors. On average a sufficient stage is about five paces wide and five paces deep. When setting up in churches, be sensitive to where you sit, perform, and with what you need. Ask before you use any of their equipment.

3   Make a checklist for equipment to ensure all (necessary) equipment is brought.

4   Bring a torch (flashlight). You never know!

5   Have certain people responsible for carrying (traveling) with different items (the same item to and from).

6   If you have a puppet stage, tuck it away when not in use, and avoid taking it down during meetings. It is distracting.

7   Have CDs/cassette tapes ready or rewound before the meeting (cassettes - a half turn before music would start).

8   Have an MC (one who introduces your team and each drama, etc...) responsible for the "flow" of the meeting, avoiding confusion and gaps and too much talking between songs.

9   Pay attention. Some talk and goofing around is fine but be sensitive. Perhaps locals are watching you being silly during a testimony or another serious moment, giving them the impression, *'If it is not important for them, maybe it is not for me.'* Again, be aware and keep a healthy balance in all that you do for the Lord and the people you are there to bless.

10 Try not to cause distractions. If possible, talk to the person(s) after the meeting.

11 Intercede during the meeting (while someone is telling their testimony, preaching, doing dramas, etc.).

12 Keep personal belongings together and out of the way.

13 Tuck wires and cables away (or tape down) for the safety of all. Watch where you step and what is around you while performing.

14 Street programs are best around 20 minutes. Afterward, talk to the onlookers. Honor the time allotted for you to speak and the team to minister. Then maybe perform the enactment a second time.

15 Project your voice; it is only good if they can hear you. People eventually realize they can do this, but, because they feel insecure, they do not concentrate on projection but on their subject matter. This is one reminder that many need. Keep reminding them that, whether they are singing, talking, acting, they are not ministering only to those in the front but for those who

are perhaps up to 20 meters or more away. Keep all people inclusive by sight and sound.

16 Avoid squelching with the microphone by turning the volume down before speaking then raise the volume afterward. Do not play with it. This always needs reminding because of my last point.

17 When sharing testimonies, it helps (especially on the street) to say, *'Before the next drama'* or *'We will have more drama or puppets in a few minutes, but I would like to take a minute to tell you…'* People will linger around longer. **See Appendix for more on giving testimonies.**

18 When there is a problem with locals during a performance (a drunk comes on to the stage), above all, alert the locals and/or your contacts to take care of it. **Next,** guys-to-guys and girls-to-girls intervene, when possible. Your **final** option is whoever on your team is available to help, but preferably those not involved in the drama, etc. Be gentle and only use the force necessary for the situation, otherwise you could lose respect from the onlookers. Avoid a scene as best you can. It is best to avoid touching, pulling, or pushing. Try gently talking with them, with your arm around them (where permissible), guiding them to the side. If it is an explosive situation, you may want to pause the meeting, deal with it, then resume. But if so, communicate with the crowd. The enemy's tactic is to destroy all involved.

19 Avoid the 'us' and 'them' mentality. Beware of the temptation to stay with your 'own.' Talk with the people. Involve yourself in their lives.

20 Draw people in by asking questions. Mention them during your speaking, perhaps what you appreciate in their village/town/culture, such as the dances, the dress, demeanor.

21 If you make a mistake in drama/puppets…fake it. Remember, they do not know the scripts.

22 Crowd control. Be gentle but firm (remember that all eyes are on you as the example). Before the meeting, establish good boundaries, otherwise it is too late.

23 Some areas have been out of control with chaos, deterring your desired influence. It may be common in a village setting where they will all (in enthusiasm) want to be near the front. But the viewing area can be impaired when the crowd is too close. Not to mention, it is dangerous and uncomfortable to minister while tripping over people. We have used sand lines or ropes (with little posts) to define the area. Local contacts oversee the crowd and help maintain order. But, depending on where you are, the locals can be controlling and harsh, using too much of the stick. My opinion is not to beat someone because they are getting too close while we are proclaiming, *"God loves you."* If possible, express your disinterest in that method politely.

24 Keep equipment clean and neat, and be careful when packing cables and puppets. This will ensure longer life. Be a good steward of what you have been given; treat it as your own. Many lack this fine principle.

25 Wear proper clothing to avoid embarrassment and distractions. It makes a difference when you look good as well, i.e. tucking in shirts. Make sure each gender is dressed in a way that would not cause eyes to go where they ought not to go. Be culturally sensitive. Often while working, guys tend to take their shirts off or have their trousers/shorts droop low, exposing more than need be. Locals may feel uncomfortable but will not say anything, even if you ask them if it is okay. One safety: how do you see them dressing? Do their men wear shorts or not? Do the ladies expose their shoulders? Do the guys take off their shirts? Do the Christians do differently?

26 Be wise and sensitive when you respond to new things or surroundings (also be aware of body language for it speaks a message all its own), i.e. *'Oh, that smell,' 'That tastes horrible,'* or *'Well, in my country,' 'Wow, that is cheap! It is nothing compared to my country.'*

27 In some cultures, it is best for guys-and-guys and girls-and-girls to stick together (unless within a group), as it frees everyone from uncomfortable situations and especially cultural offenses. Cultural norms are different; they could think you are interested in them and want to make a marriage!

28 Discuss with your team the proper handling of the laying on of hands. Ask the person you are praying with before laying your hands on them...*anywhere*, especially on the head. In several countries, it could be offensive. Express why you might be doing so for the benefit of those unfamiliar with this practice, explaining to them that it is not your power but Christ's and a symbol of your faith in His ability. Take caution with unfamiliar people and places.

29 Sometimes, it is wise to pray with your eyes open, especially in unfamiliar surroundings or when you are unsure of people's condition. Pastor Dennis Bambino taught me to keep my eyes open. During a meeting, we prayed for this large man, and I had my eyes closed. Pastor Dennis tapped me and said to keep them open. Sure enough, it took five or six men to hold him, as he had a demonic manifestation. So be wise! Besides, where in the Bible does it command, "Pray with your eyes open or closed?

30 Ask the Lord "who" you should to go to during a meeting to counsel or talk, thus avoiding wasted time (could be the flesh or the devil distracting).

31 Arguing (when expressing your beliefs) is not the best bridge-builder, so avoid it. Be a listener. Ask them about their beliefs. Respect them. You probably do not want to slam their gods or beliefs verbally. God knows where they are; that is why He chose you. So be sensitive and wait for the time/opportunity (see if they ask you what you think). Paul did argue, reason and persuade, yet with wisdom and sensitivity. How? He would never blaspheme their gods **(Acts 17:3; 19:8; 37)**. Be inquisitive and genuine in seeing what and how they believe.

32 Remember, you are in a culture that is not your own, so ask your contacts what is best for the people.

33 When ministering in an Islamic area, do not put or throw your Bible on the ground. It is a Holy Book to them. They will lose their already limited trust and respect toward you if you have written in it, dropped it or displayed other ways of disrespect (in their eyes). Place your Bible down (but not on the floor). Other religions have observances, so inquire and observe. Within whatever culture or religious areas you find yourself in, keep your eyes searching for potential bridges to avoid valleys or setbacks.

34 Have ministry opportunities for the entire team. Avoid too many team members sitting around passive because they are not included. Occasionally, it is okay. It gives them a break. Step back and observe if everyone is being utilized and fulfilled consistently.

35 Bring the right tools for the right job/project. Me Mum always said, **"If you are going to do something, do it right."**

36 Proper Prior Prayer Planning & Preparation Prevents Poor Performance & Pitfalls!

37 As mentioned earlier, it is advisable to travel with a translator. There is a good chance I would not have written this book if we had not had a translator with us on our way to and from Moscow. In brief, as you are familiar with this saga, we were harassed by military/police while in the midst of an 18-hour train ride. Problems occurred both ways. It made their day to instill fear in some foreigners - so it seemed. A friend's father and his comrade had been arrested and deported back to Russia because of refusing to pay a bribe of $500USD; he did not know the language and neither did we. But for the grace of God...we had a translator. [By the way, my friend's father and comrade got away by jumping out of the bathroom window and miraculously found a trustworthy taxi driver who got them past the border]. So, translator or the window - your choice. I am kidding. Do what God tells you, not what your circumstances dictate or even what seems good for others, unless it is His call and game plan. Travel with your team as much as possible.

Is there a difference between **foolish** and calculated risks? Hmm.... Just a thought to ponder. Some argue that taking risking is foolish. Though that is true, let us not forget that there are risks that are Spirit motivated; Spirit led that are calculated.

Some have thought I take "foolish" risks. Why should I have gone to Russia…why work within a refugee camp…why fly to India when there is a potential war? I go because I am called. I am committed to God and the people…not CNN and safety.

Before moving on, I feel compelled to burst what I refer to as the "Christian Bubble Mentality." When I was talking again with Rob Morris, Director of Axiom, he enacted a common Christian mentality to missions and/or ministry. *"Okay. Is everybody ready? We are going 'OUT THERE' for two hours. I know it is wicked 'OUT THERE,' but you can do it."* Then they return after two hours of public exposure with 'the sinners,' withdraw to their safe-haven, and blurt out to one another, 'Whew, we made it. Man, that was tough being 'OUT THERE.' 'What did you feel about being 'OUT THERE?'*

We are to rise above that "bubble mentality" and mature in Christ. It is not us and those 'out there.' Do not separate yourself from the masses. Always remember where you were when the Lord smiled upon you!

Christianeze? This is another area of concern. We have developed our own language called **Christianeze.**

We do not talk; we share with people.
We do not write in a diary; we journal.
We do not listen; we preach at people.
We say, "Thus sayeth the Lord" (KJV).
We "go forth," not "forward".
We say "unto you," not "to you."
We say, "Praise the Lord, Hallelujah, Glory to God, Amen" after every sentence we or someone else says.

Like this:*"Wow. I was sharing with a heathen going to hell when he was slain by the Holy Spirit. Now I am so blessed that he is experiencing sanctification, having been justified. He was lost, but Jesus, the Lamb of God and Lion of Judah, saved his life, which was full of transgressions. Glory, Hallelujah, Praise the Lord. So I told him 'PTL.' Sorry, that is: 'Praise the Lord, brother.' Have you ever experienced grace in the eternal secu-*

rity of the Almighty God? Amen. You know, being born again? Praise the Lord. Well, that devil's a tricky fellow, and he's got your number. Amen. He wants to take you to hell. Do you know, hallelujah, what it is like to be filled with the Holy Ghost and delivered by the Blood of Jesus Christ, the Son of God? Hallelujah. And you just have to get His anointing. Oh, yeah. I can feel it. Can you? Amen."

Meanwhile, the other guy is saying (while scratching his head), "I know he is human, but he is talking like an alien. I do not have a clue what he is saying. I know he has got something exciting to share, or so he thinks, and I sure do not have it...but do I even want it? Filled with the Holy what? Blood? Anointing? He sure says 'Hallelujah' a bunch! And that 'Amen?' I wonder why he said it when he said that the Devil had my number? Whose side is he on?!"

This may not be the most effective way to communicate on the streets or anywhere for that matter. Our challenge is to remain and maintain relevancy in a language that unbelievers can comprehend. Be real, not distant and super spiritual.

"Fill My empty arms, bringing back my lost treasures." - GOD
-Rob Morris describing God's heart

CHAPTER SEVEN

Challenges and Joys of Giving

I thought Giving was biblical?
-A well received act of love?
-Demonstrating God's love?

"The response to giving is amazing!"

"I will not give up anything?"

"How do I give? Who do I give to?"

"Why do I give?"

Why Giving "Up" Is So Hard to Do

Giving could have an incredibly wonderful or a hurtful and regressing effect on its recipient(s) and the giver, depending on the fabric of their beliefs.

For instance: Amida gives a family a much needed blanket, and the family receives it with great joy. Then they notice that their neighbor was given two blankets or something else of interest so they continue to ask for other items. And so the story goes.

Principles of Giving

I have found it necessary and significant to use opportunities like above to disciple - no matter what culture. And one of the greatest ways to break a "spirit of greed" is by learning (teaching) the principles of giving. The same goes for jealousy. Bless those who have received. **It is a principle of sowing and reaping.**

In our communication, we have stressed the importance of false expectations when the locals deal with another team, should another team come. It could be hurtful and disconcerting for them and for the new team, who has their own ideas. We discussed the importance of giving the new team the freedom to work as God leads them with the village and church leaders. We also expressed the dangers of having a "get" mindset and not to expect to receive but to welcome whatever that next team may have to offer, even if it would mean only teaching. But what an invaluable gift!

There is also a need to teach as gifts are given (the why's, how's). A gift is not to be "commanded" but comes from God and His leading. The giver has the freedom to give how and what He gives. Sadly, it is true that some really do not want to listen; they simply covet what you have. It is imperative to pray about and discern when, how, where, who, and what to give. I have come to realize the significance and timing of giving. It would not have had a powerful and positive effect had I given material goods the first week(s) of meeting new people. The same goes in every day society.

Distribution

Before distributing blankets and other items, we requested a list of family names. One-by-one we called out names. Upon hearing their name, they would approach one of us to receive what we had for them. *It is a favorable approach in a small village setting, and no one felt as though they were second or left out. And, at the end of our stay, we gave away many of our personal belongings, in addition to team equipment (pots, spoons, water jugs, etc.) We did this FAIRLY after dark on the last night, putting items in nine piles (number of huts) in front of each hut. This lessened the probability of strife, jealousy, and greed (as there are some villagers who pass by frequently or from another village). No one saw anything in broad daylight that could potentially give them credence to question, **"Why is that person getting....?"** At any given time, it could be best to go within the recipient's house and, once inside, take out the gift as opposed to outdoors for the world to see. *** It is strongly recommended to draw upon these God-given opportunities to speak God's principles into their lives.

It is one of the most precious and rewarding blessings to have an opportunity to give, but remember to allow the Lord to pour out more than just material gifts. Do not allow your giving to be simply a "receiving" something without an explanation or teaching because greed and jealousy will swoop down like a vulture and ultimately keep the recipient from really being blessed. They are not blessed even though they receive because they are not content...always wanting more and more. **"It is more blessed to give than to receive" (Acts 20:35)** is a precious truth to behold. How true is it? Valid? Even for the poor? Well, just recall the poor widow who gave *(Luke 6:38, 21:1-4)*?

Does He care who gives and what they give?

Matthew 6:1-4 will help you check your motives. In the middle of the service, Jesus calls over His disciples and asks them who was giving more: the widow or the rich man. This means Jesus was watching. How many of us hide what we give? Are we ashamed (at what we do not give)? Did those in the synagogue hear Him? If we feel ashamed in what we are giving or not giving, we ought to check our heart and motives. I find it difficult for anyone to claim intimacy with Jesus without being a giver. There is no condemnation or shame in our giving if we are led by what the Lord leads us to give. Whether $1USD or $1,000. Yet it seems that we often allow the Lord to touch our character without allowing Him to touch our wallet! In my experience, it is often those who have less who give more, and the smaller churches give more as well.

Have you been in a large service where the secret feeling is, "I do not need to give that much because there are so many people around me." Here is a brilliant example. Carman, who is a well known American Christian Musician, offers free concerts as to not to hinder anyone from coming. At his Madison Square Garden concert in New York City, he announced that in 20 years there has never been a concert that was fully paid for through a free-will offering. Thus we give perhaps not from the leading of the Holy Spirit, but our giving is influenced by the 20,000+ people we are surrounded by at the concert.

Mark 12:41-44   Acts 2:43-47
2 Corinthians 8-9, especially 8:2-12 and 9:6-9
3 John 7-8   Deuteronomy 15:7-11

The scriptures above are good challenges on giving. Whether it is supplying the needs of one another in the early church or giving even when we are in a place of need ourselves or even like **3 John 7-8** where we give to God's fellow workers, we are now in a position to become His workers as well.

Are we known in Heaven and earth for being a giver? Generous? Do we give until It hurts or only when it feels good?!

Help those keep what they are given

 When helping someone continually who is living in shaky national (or corruptive) conditions, equipping them with a secret pocket within their clothing or investing in a waist wallet could be helpful. If checked and frisked by corrupt military or the police, they would not leave "lighter" than before harassment. Komba, a precious friend and a refugee from Sierra Leone, has been beaten and left with his life threatened on more than four occasions. Each time, the officers/military stole whatever money he had. Since then, I have taught him how to practice further safety measures.

 Make your gift known to people close to the recipient so there is an accountability factor (basically those close to the person or within the family). If the money is not accounted for within the family, then we can trace who had the money. For example, if nobody within the family knows you are helping them (and had given money to one of kin) then the temptation is far greater to spoil the money.

Trusting another person with a responsibility is also a gift. By giving people opportunities to be upright, you build trust. Test and trust = trust and release. With some, beginning on a level of trust may be better.

 Depending upon the culture, you could hurt someone by giving to them once, then the next day giving to a different beggar/needy one, like at traffic lights you frequent. They may misunderstand your intentions and the good you have done has now become hurtful. It may be more beneficial to have the person(s) work for what they are given. It raises the value of what they receive, their dignity increases, and they often have greater appreciation.

One Final Compelling Note

I have experienced several villages, towns and peoples who have demonstrated to me "true giving." From the impoverished areas of Mexico and Guatemala to a village church in Ghana, West Africa, to struggling towns of the Ukraine, I have learned much about sacrifice. "Sacrifice is the giving of one's life need - not out of their surplus (extra)." So I do want to honor those who are givers. I believe that one cannot claim to be intimate with God without being a giver. And do not assume it has anything to do with monetary wealth - how little you have to give or how much you could give. I can name too many Christians and churches that know little about giving. No one in all Creation can out-give God, yet He calls us to be like Him. Unfortunately, the wallet is probably one of the last things to be "given" to God-if at all.

How much does one hold onto or give away, especially if you are responsible for the budget as a leader. If you have a budget of $300USD or $15000USD for two months, which comprises of food, housing, local transport, etc., do you give away $50USD or $2000USD or more or less? You must be open, sensitive, and always pray for wisdom, which God gives liberally to all who ask. I have also encouraged team members to give of their own means. There have been times where we have corporately given up to $1500USD (within the budget of $15000USD) to particular ministries who have served faithfully and who have obvious needs.

Giving vs. Frugality

Weigh the worth of saving a penny. Do not be a tight-wad or a penny pincher. Be observant with your antennas up. See the need. While in the jungle of Madagascar, there were three people who needed surgeries. I saw the need and responded by asking my co-leader. In turn, we brought it to the team. Prayer turned into action. And it became an example, a testimony, which sparked the villagers to begin helping one another.

What I have heard before:
> "We have already spent so much money getting here. Why do we need to give more?"
>
> "That is what our budget is for, so I do not need to give from my own pocket."

Selfish hearts echo these sentiments, not giving ones. When is the last time any of us gave our all or even close, like that of the poor widow? Is it 90% for me and 10% for God? Or is all of it God's, and He's given me the responsibility to bless others with it? Given to give? I am glad God did not give only 10% of Himself. There are many who function within a certain parameter regarding tithes and offerings. In doing so, the commonly understanding is 10%. But as Ron Smith, co-founder of the YWAM and SBS, pointed out from the Old Testament, the people were actually giving more like 33%.

Since we are living in the New Testament era, do the figures remain the same? The New Testament interprets the Old Testament so, to gain further clarity, we should look at what the New Testament has to say in light of the Old Testament. For example, do we really see exhortations in the New Testament about tithing? Or is it more as we see in 2 Corinthians 8-9 about giving not under compulsion but from a generous, Spirit-led heart (this particular exhortation had to do with those who were poor also). They gave out of their need! You really know someone's heart and priorities by how they give. After all, it is God's money anyway.

In *Luke 6:38*, it states, "Give, and it will be given to you. A good measure, pressed down, shaken together, running over will be put into your lap; for the measure you give, will be the measure you get back." And, in *Matthew 6:21*, "For where your treasure is, there your heart will be also."

Giving to the Local Economy

A fabulous aspect is that we are automatically giving or buying into their local economy for supplies and food, but this is not a reason for not giving. I encourage local buying. There are ministries who spend thousands to ship and post items of need whereas more aid (of certain items) could be dispersed if purchased locally. When individuals or teams travel into poorer countries, this would be my recommendation. Many enjoy picking out clothing, food, toys, etc. because it is more hands-on. They tend to trust more in items being sent then money. I agree to an extent. However, people tend to give more of their junk or things they just do not want than actually giving a sacrifice.

Overwhelmed at the Needs?

"Maybe you have driven through a city, and, when you stop at a traffic signal, the onslaught of the needy approach you. Whom do you choose? They come with their hands cut off, tumors, with their sad faces and dirt-covered children and those blind with their guides. Should you help all? What is the answer for them? Before the green light rescues you, with guilt you reach into your pocket and give to maybe one or two, then role up your window, shaking your head, trying to indicate you cannot give any more, but which really indicates you WILL NOT give. In reality, you could give more if you wanted - more times than not." - Dr Gary Parker, CEO of M/V Anastasis

I've realized that there are myriads of world needs that I cannot fulfill single-handedly. Often, I would feel paralyzed or neutralized, and walk along guilt-ridden (guilty for what I have, guilty of what I do not do, guilty that I do not give enough). After all, my wallet can define my priorities and what is important to me. So I admitted my weaknesses and confessed to God my concerns and sorrows saying, "God, I cannot do it all, but I thank you for seeing that. Now what and where and to whom and when do I give?" Make it simple. Ask the Lord the who, what, why, when and where's of giving. That freed me. I had given the responsibility back to God, and I now carry an appropriate, God-given burden. He does say that His yoke is easy and His burden is light, does He not? Furthermore, if I continue to feel guilty for what I have, I spurn God's blessing; therefore, I am not really thankful. The key is 'what am I doing with what I have been given?'

Give to All Who Beg?

Are we to give to all who beg and ask of us? What a question with complexity! Jesus said to do so in **Matthew 5:42**. We also see a similar command in **Deuteronomy 15:7-11**. However, at the same time, is it saying we are to be a doormat for the ever-asking? Could our giving to a particular person or entity be feeding or increasing their need?

We must activate our discernment. We all have the God-given ability to judge a situation. But we tend to give out of guilt and fear, instead of love. Another way of looking at it is lust. In part, lust is self-fulfillment and self-gratification. In this context, I instantly feel gratified or relief when I give to someone needy, and, in many cases, it is the easy way out. Love is looking to and being a part of fulfilling what is the best and highest for the other person. Sometimes giving money is the least loving you could show to the person in need.
Perhaps they need:

A hug	Money	A drive somewhere
A kind word	Job	Responsibility
A sweater	Education opportunity	A friend
A meal	A friend to listen/talk to	A prayer-Word from the Lord

Maybe take them into my home.

The problem is that real love can be and is often times messy, time consuming, uncomfortable and more. Giving a beggar or someone in need a few coins is the easy part. It eases my conscience for the moment…then I move on.

And often, people can have wrong motives. I remember testing a man in Brazil. I said no, tried to talk with him, and he became very irritable. So I chose not to help him. However, had his countenance remained as one in need or sorrow, I would have chosen to help him. What someone sows, they reap. There was another poor man who was selling sandwiches. When he turned away, I ran up and threw a $10USD in his box and scooted away. He was blessed and never knew how and from where. Other times I have (like many) tried to take the person for a meal, and their true colors come out. There are yet others who have been maimed by their parents so that there will be more pity for them, thus greater earnings to the family. There is still yet another family who send their precious little children (eight of them all under 12 years of age) from 6am to 10pm begging in the streets and are beaten if they do not return with sufficient money. There are even those who make more money begging than by earning a regular living.

Am I just feeding their poverty by giving in to their begging? If I choose not to give, will it lessen their chances for walking in a new life or enhance that chance?

The line is a hard one to draw…how far to go, where to stop, who to give to and who not to. Jesus did say to give to those who ask. But does it mean give blindly without checking motives? Or is He questioning our motives? Our heart? Sometimes I challenge people that they will be judged and held responsible from God with what they are given and their motives (and God does work through our wrong motives as well as theirs). Be open to the Spirit's leading. Remember, at times He may inspire us to say, do, or respond in a way that may seem foolish to us, unreasonable and strange. If necessary, be accountable to someone else to be sure or to be safe.

CHAPTER EIGHT

Protocol with Local Leaders and Authorities

It is inevitable that you will come across, rub elbows with, greet, discuss, strategize, plan, agree (and think you agreed), disagree, laugh, cry, shake hands, misunderstand, pray with/for, address, prefer, avoid and want not to avoid, run from, run to, learn from, disciple, or walk along side local leaders. They may be Pastors, Ambassadors, Tangalemena (spiritual head of a village), Chiefs, Mayors, Directors, Church Hierarchy, Muslim Imams and Marabous, Priests, Government Officials and more. Interaction with these leaders can be an aid or a hindrance to your intended ministry, especially with some leaders, so it would be highly beneficial for you and your team to learn local protocol.

Why, Ah, Hello Mr. Ambassador

Always ask questions, repeatedly if necessary, to gain insight on the best procedures, the sooner the better, for you! In many locations, like in a Western city, this may be unnecessary, as you may have already contacted the local ministry where the officials have either invited you personally or have zero cares regarding your presence. But in West Africa and other developing nations (closed nations), you would take as many necessary precautions as pertinent for that given situation. No cause for alarm…many precautions are simply for honoring or respecting local customs and formalities.

Typical Questions You May Have
~ How do I greet the Chief?
~ How do I introduce who we are?
~ What do I say?
~ When should I meet with that leader?
~ Should it be before our herd of 15 or 50 people arrive?
~ How much detail is necessary to communicate?
~ What should I avoid saying? Revealing?
~ How direct ought I be? How firm?
~ "Why have you come?" they may ask.
~ How to respect and honor yet disagree without arguing?
~ Should I meet the leader alone or with the team?
~ How much about "Jesus" should I mention?
   Or should I wait?
~ When they ask what our motives are or purpose is
   for being here, what should I say?

My, my…what are the answers? I have discovered that it is like working on a crossword puzzle (how comforting, ha, ha). You ask questions, figure out one word or answer, find out the next word from the word before; it is a process. It is your well planned questions that search out the answers, realize the needs, spark thoughts, bring back memories, give awareness…so you are on a good start. Go for it!

Well, I will say this. Do not be [too] religious. Religious in the sense that you feel you need to use Christian words or expressions. Use discernment. There are times when I mention in the beginning of conversations that I am a Christian believer. Other times, I wait until I think it is necessary, as it could hinder a potential open door. For example, when going to a Hindu school or other public school, I show pictures that speak a thousand words. These may be humorous photos or perhaps of those you have touched through poverty situations, etc. I may choose to talk about principles for life and weave in Jesus without causing offence or mentioning Him so much that it abuses their open door or makes them feel I am manipulating them. There was one school in the Ukraine where we are allowed in to do drama and speak **BUT** were to only say the name of Jesus or God once during our program. Big challenge. But we did it!

Be "as wise as serpants and innocent as doves"- Matthew 10:16.
Use this wisdom.

It really depends on the situation, and who you are standing or sitting before and where:
   ~ What is the setting?
   ~ Why are you meeting? What is the intention?
      The purpose?
   ~ Who initiated the meeting? Had they called for you?
   ~ Is it formal?
   ~ Is it informal?
   ~ Is it official business? Or government? Or local?
   ~ Are there known conflicts in the area with Christians
      or against Christianity?
   ~ What leaders/authorities are you with? Are they legal,
      i.e. will they have an affect on your potential for being
      in their country, state, or region? Or returning?

* Obvious caution is needed when entering into a security conscious nation.
* At times you may consider only giving information, which is required and unavoidable. Yet, even so, be sensitive how you communicate who you are. There may be ways to communicate that can still give you favor.
* At times you may want to emphasize development, relief, or other practical implementations. For example, what practical benefit will you be for their people, etc.

I am **not suggesting** diluting or watering down the Truth, but be wise not to close a potential door prematurely.

To Bribe or Not to Bribe

Bribery **does exist** and is a tricky thing. In many countries, their nation and local public offices come to a complete standstill without it. If you want action, something taken care of...and quickly...simply slip in an extra sum of money and, VOILA - quicker than e-mail downloaded at 115,000 kb speed, the answer from a stern "NO" becomes "Why, YES!"

The question is: **do you subscribe to these pits?** Decide if you are not going to feed the angry monster of "corruption" by giving a bribe. I have chosen not to as best I can. There have been times where my drivers and close colleagues have found it an absolute necessity. I specify to them that this is money for them, and no more will be paid for bribes or they lose out. One time this driver of ours threw himself down on his knees, grabbing the feet of a military official at a checkpoint. Crying, he pleaded with the official to let him go. Sadly, I know of worse situations. Life slows down when you refuse to give into bribes.

I **could write another book** on bribery experiences alone. A man, who rented us a house, had not paid his water bills. He took us to the road, having bought something to "get" the water going. It was illegal, clearly wrong.. It bypassed the "watah-meetah"(water meter), as our local friend declared. I had some of the team present, 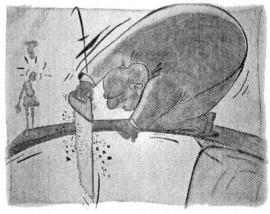 along with the guardians of the house and the architect's assistants. It was a golden opportunity to discuss why we could not be a part of scooting around laws. I asked him to please hold off on his procedure, as tempting as it was to have running water in West African heat! We would wait. This meant not having water for three days (we did have drinking water out of a well) while he sorted out what was needed. But it was worth the favorable outcome. God so touched them through this, and I am truly convinced that God uses all things.

Grace through the Difficult

One valuable tidbit while negotiating, disagreeing, or being in the midst of a seriously threatening discussion is to ask the Lord to enable you with the grace to withstand the blows. Control your emotions as best you can and keep a level head. Yes, it can be difficult. I can attest to this as I have had guns (and machine guns) to my head and also pointed in my direction. My "number" could have come up prematurely had I let loose what I had been feeling on the inside. Instead, I asked the Lord to help me control my emotions and tongue.

Yet there have been other times when the "adventure" intensified as I expressed myself about the situation with perhaps too much emotion and raising of my voice (during incidents of corruption and injustice, in particular). Be wise on how and when to speak in a sticky predicament. God has given me the grace to fulfill my life's purpose and calling. Before I had understanding, I would get wrapped up (not necessarily self-intended) in these questionable, cliffhanger moments, from situations involving driving to questionable scenarios with authorities.

Whatever the Lord has for me, I do not want to miss - I think? Some experiences are anything but enjoyable, yet they are necessary. As a result of one of these particularly intense experiences, God penned these words within my heart, which became a song in the honor of the Kingsleys, fellow Sierra Leonians, and countless others who have been lost *In The Sea of Nothingness*, having been struck by the arm of injustice and corruption, thus becoming refugees:

In the Sea of Nothingness

Where are they that cry?
Who are those who cry?
Can you hear their cry?
Or is it deafened by power, corruption and greed?
Will you hear their cry?
Or is it too far away? Away from your eyes?
Will you turn the page like millions have done before?
Thus more are they that drown.
Deep in the sea, life is so hard.
For the value of diamonds, there is no value in life.
Men and women and children flee...
Becoming amputees...refugees...losing families...
All for what I ask?
Will you stand for them who cannot stand for themselves?
And thus the Lord asks,
"Who will go for Me? Speak for Me?"
Paying the price for justice.
Can you see their eyes?
Taste the salt in their tears?
But this is one thing I know...
It is the Lord who cares...for those in the sea.
For I know He weeps with those who weep,
And He laughs with those who laugh,
And He Answers those who cry.
So will you run with Him?!

Chorus:
DEEP IN THE SEA ARE THEY
IN THE SEA OF NOTHINGNESS

What do you do? It is NOT easy. I have been able to speak up on behalf of some locals, i.e. drivers, and managed to help them with bribery dilemmas. They hate the bribes but continue to pay it, which causes the cancer to spread all the more. **Which is worse?**

On the flip side, one driver chased me, took something of mine, then began swinging at me. He had tried taking advantage of a foreigner and charged me more than 10x the regular price. I refused, which brought a problem. **Was it worth it? What is transformation worth? What price does one pay for justice? Transformation for these countries is curtailed by corruption.**

Then you have people like the Ambassador in West Africa who was supporting us with letters and more. He gave us total freedom when the refugees were within the Embassy's compound. There was such favor that I could come to him whenever there was a need. And while we were having great obstacles thrown across every path (at least mine!), he would get all excited, saying, *"You can go right to our country; we will help get you there! You would be able to do great things there. With no hindrances."* He repeated this while the Minister of Foreign Affairs (who had just gotten out of a meeting with the leader of the Rebels and the President of Guinea, along with other ministers) was present, and he was a Muslim!

Now a friend, who pioneered a YWAM base and School of Biblical Studies in India, asked me, *"What do you do if authorities break into your home, demand a bribe and begin to ransack the house or threaten your family? Is it wrong to give them what they want? And how many are there who claim they do not give into bribes, yet have actually paid them without realizing. It just goes through the middle man. For example, you have an accountant. He does your books. But in order for your papers to go through, they have to pay the next clerk ..."* He believes many deny that they give into bribery or turn a blind eye, but more bribery takes place than one cares to believe. The point? As I listened to my friend, it caused me to search deeper into bribery biblically. I have been challenged:

~ It is not black and white at times (not always clear)

~ Not all bribery is sin (I am sure I have your attention now)

These five categories I found in scripture were eye opening:

1. Giving into bribes, as to demand or coerce for what you want taken care of, is selfish. This is obviously wrong. I want what I want, so I offer a bribe (a "gift") to you. My motive is selfish. Self gratifying.

2. Taking bribes in order for service to be given is obvious sin. I refuse to give you electricity, fill out your forms or let you pass unless you give me what I want.

3. Bribery defiles a people and destroys a society. It is clear to see the conditions of countries that run and function daily based on bribery and corruption. There is tremendous lack of trust, integrity, confidence, and security, plus a lack of character and dignity within its walls. Investments one desires to make into or within the country are hindered, denied or even avoided at times because of this philosophy/disease, holding back a nation from prosperity and security. The testimony of a people and nation are lowered greatly due to this lifestyle.

4. God opposes those who impose a bribe. God clearly states His opposition to those who impose bribes on others for service, etc.

5. There is no guilt or sin imparted to the victim who pays without choice. God seems to be silent toward the victim of bribery. When a person is genuine and true in character and is forced to give into a bribe, I do not see evidence that they are held accountable and are in sin or committing an evil.

Having said that, I will wait for you to pick your jaw from off of the floor. It is not black or white in every circumstance. We need personal (or corporate, in some cases) conviction and need to look at each situation perhaps differently. So I do not feel I can give a blanket "yes" to every situation you face, whether to give a bribe because you are coerced or because it is just a little too uncomfortable or because it takes just a few minutes too long for you to get where you want to go. Yet, this is not a license to go the easy route either. But when threatened, put into a serious corner, or when a situation is with no alternative with no way out, then I may consider giving what may be demanded by going for the lowest possible amount or with an alternative gift. I will, however, challenge them and speak when possible of God's principles. I will use these opportunities as I am able. Again, it depends on the situation. I am not, by any means, condoning paying into bribes as a victim, but that I believe there should be no self-condemnation or guilt when without a choice.

How Is Bribery Addressed?

~ Exodus 23:8
~ Numbers 22:6
~ Deuteronomy 10:17-18, 16:18-20,27:25
~ Judges 16:5
~ I Samuel 8:1-3, 12:2-3
~ I Kings 15:8-9
~ 2 Kings 16:7-9
~ 2 Chronicles 19:7
~ Psalm 26:9-10

~ Proverbs 17:8, 23, 29:4
~ Isaiah 1:21-23, 5:22-23, 33:15-16
~ Ezekiel 22:12
~ Amos 5:12-13
~ Micah 3:9-12
~ Ecclesiastes 7:7
~ Matthew 28:11-15
~ Acts 24:26
~ I Timothy 6:10

The **victim of bribery** is not the one at risk with the Lord, but the offender, the bribe enforcer or taker. In my former belief system, I thought all forms of bribery or giving into it were sin and one should be accountable for it. In my journey to find what God has to say about this topic, I have realized new insights, though not without challenges! I am not saying I have all the answers for you. It is an individual or organizational conviction at times. But where do we stand locally or universally on this subject?

The Difficult Blessing of Submission

You **will need to know your local mission agency's,** ministry's, and your own ministry or organization's policies and procedures regarding bribery and the giving into, at times, for example with life threatening decisions or the daily challenges of bribery. Submission is necessary to be covered. I recognize, as does the majority, that there is blessing, security and safety when one is submitting to their authorities and accountable partners, i.e. board members or fellow staff. If you are under a structural leadership, look to them for guidance. There is safety in the counsel of others. **The bottom line is to submit to what is required or expected of you.** But I encourage you to express what may be stirring within you if you are without agreement. Often, the leaders over you are at a distance. One moment they can see more clearly than you, yet other times they cannot see from their distant position. But as I have been honest with teams in the past, when I have disagreed with the leaders over me, I still submitted. As long as obvious sin is not present, it is God's best way. As God has ordained the idea, created the idea of leadership since the Fall of Man in Genesis 3, it is obvious that He will endorse one who is working within the stream of keeping some kind of order. Think of the chaos - ah, further chaos - if no one chose to submit to anyone. It would be catastrophic! Yet we ought not forget we are exhorted to submit to one another for the benefit of Christ and others *(Ephesians 5:21)*.

Think if we chose not to submit. Where would the security be? Trust? Confidence? Assurance? Yet, even when we disagree, we ought to discuss why we would not desire to submit to this or that. We ought to consider the following with regards to submitting/decisionmaking:

* Who benefits?
* Who does not benefit?
* Will this hurt my pride?
* Does this benefit the greater good or cause?
* What are the consequences if I/we were to submit or not?
* What are the potential dangers/pitfalls of not submitting?
* What are our motives for submitting or not submitting?
* What message are we passing on to our team or those watching with our decisions or attitude?
* How is unity affected by submitting or not submitting?
* Are relationships possible or maintainable without submitting?
* Is humility possible without submission (if not, neither is unity)?

I have to submit, even at times when I have not agreed. There is blessing there, although difficult. Get counsel - objective counsel - when the need is felt.

Have It in Writing

One big mistake I made was not having our re-acceptance into the refugee camp in writing. I went on a verbal agreement through a friend who knew a particular agent very well. The agent was supposedly going to radio the field leaders - not! There were further complications, and our re-entry was denied. Would things have been different? Hard to say, although God instructs us to use wisdom, which is often gained through an unforgettable experience. It had been apparent that these officials had other excuses up their sleeves. In the case of unforeseen repercussions, it may be in your best interest to document what you may have accomplished in efforts involving refugees, governments, etc. Use your judgment of what is necessary and adds security. **See Appendix.**

With regard to the local churches you may possibly work along-side, it may be satisfying to inquire, with detailed questions, of hierarchy and other foundational structures that "govern" the area. As a team, even with a strong background of Mercy Ships, who trained their pastors, walked alongside their churches, had a good report and invitations of their own government, it was not enough. The church hierarchy still wanted 'papers of per-mission.' Moreover, I had flown in by helicopter via 'Helimission' with the JESUS FILM, which depicts Jesus' life according to Luke, and had spoken with leaders on how to start a church and what is expected of a leader, two years prior. Still not enough.

In our final week of ministry, I had a sensing that all had been going 'too well.' "Do not be naive" was a Word from the Lord, I believe. Sure enough on the second to last Sunday, a group of hierarchal leaders came in and demanded a stop to all further ministry within the church. It was unfortunately obvious they had their own agenda, nursing titles, power and a name. **Did they care about the people?** It was not visible. This meeting seemed to last forever with no leeway or satisfying conclusion. Then, much to my surprise, they approached us with the question, "Could you please provide Bible dictionaries for us?" I was dumbstruck. I did whatever I could to follow principle #468 on maintaining your calm. I took a deep breath and bit my tongue saying, "*I am very sorry, but I do not feel that is an appropriate question to be asking right now.*"

A building and a name is what appeared to be significant to them, not what was really being taught. I asked twice for clarification, "*What you are saying is if we do not conduct any teaching within the church building (of this denomination), we are free to do whatever we see fitting?*" They nodded in agreement. It seemed to be a *Galatians 5:26* concept, like these hierarchal leaders were envious and had not been given precedence or opportunity on what was taking place. They even seemed jealous of what the people were receiving. Even though the local leaders had invited us, we asked for forgiveness for not receiving the city hierarchy's permission. This was because we knew we were covered. Keep in mind, we had a history that backed up who we were as well as our recent time there, yielding much fruit, which was clearly evident.

Following the meeting, the hierarchal leaders from the city had left, and the local leaders gathered around our house. I purposed to clarify and exhort those present. I spoke of the need to:

~ Forgive

~ Not count them as their enemies (people are not the enemy- *Ephesians 6:12*).

~ Bless and pray for them *(Romans 12:14-21)*.

~ Not allow their emotions to cause them to do or say something harsh, hurtful or regrettable (Jesus got emotional - *Matthew 21:12-13*. According to *Ephesians 4:26*, we can be angry, but are not to sin because of our anger. We must deal with the conflict as soon as we are able).

To avoid further damage look at:

Colossians 3:8	*James 1:19-21*
1 Peter 3:13-17	*Proverbs 25:28*

Here we see that through our conflicts, we can walk away from the temptation to slander those who accuse us, malign us, and hurt us. We are to make sure we are suffering for doing good not for evil or by returning evil put upon us with evil. Be careful not to act too quickly against your neighbor. Sort through your conflicts by looking with the heart and concern of Jesus, not your flesh. Attempt to respond in the opposite spirit of those who come against you.

Remember it is not a sin to be angry, but it is what we do with it that makes it sin **(Ephesians 4:26-27)**. Work through it quickly. Be slow to anger, slow to speak and quick to listen. It is more often than not the temptation to let the tongue roll, is it not? Sometimes we just want to express too quickly what we are feeling, which may add fuel to the flame.

~ Do not react in hatred and/or bitterness toward the leaders (Proverbs 14:12, Matthew 5:38-41).

~ Refuse gossiping and talking behind their back. Avoid the temptation.

~ Look inward for what the Lord would like to do through you and in you.

~ Embrace what you can learn.

~ Self control, though not taught much, is a strong weapon of victory when necessary to activate *(Galatians 5:23, Proverbs 29:11).*

~ Love them that come against you. Why? Because it breaks something in the spirit realm. God has more to work with in the situation **(Matthew 5:43-48)**. God is then glorified while the enemy has nothing to use.

Beware of Expectations

Be specific communicating your goals with whomever you encounter. Do not leave room for unfulfilled expectations or say things you may not necessarily be able to deliver. Some cultures expect what is spoken to be lived out. Specifically, in detail, describe what your team is endeavoring to accomplish, even have it in writing. Always cover your tracks, keep your eyes open (this may be more easily accomplished in smaller areas), ask permission when possible, and communicate with contacts.

Express Thanks

It speaks volumes when we express our thankfulness to those we have had as our liaison, main contact(s), hosts or perhaps a government official. Bless them with a card, a gift from your country, photos, etc. Be creative. Offer to pray for them (if permissible and fitting so as not to offend) to be able to carry on in God's name. I am including those who have caused your work to be difficult. I fought with everything in me to thank a particular government official when he had been a thorn in our side...or both sides! Look to the greater good. **See Appendix.**

CHAPTER NINE

Belief Systems, Fatalism and the Like

Building Bridges through Cultural Valleys

Come As A Learner

I am ever reminded of one of the most successful mindsets to have while encircled in another culture of varying tastes, smells, sounds and sights: to be a learner. This is a disciple's heartbeat and defining characteristic. If we are shooting for guaranteed roadblocks in our ministry, which "infect" people's lives, then have a "hop-a-long, be-like-me, we-are-here-to-correct-and-alter attitude." Beginning a mission with these thoughts as your primary focus will trip you up:

'We will start by changing your clothes.'
'That cultural face-paint has got to go.'
'You cannot worship like that.'
'Oh, those children in the street are in the dirt.'
'Why are they carrying things like that?'
'Those men are holding hands!'

Be careful of condemning and tearing apart their culture. Often it is not a matter of right and wrong or morality and immorality, but simply people live differently. Take care where you drive and how you drive your ministry.

Yes, according to what people believe and Who they believe God to be will determine how they live their lives. Biblical Worldview is essential for life and change. As we will see, in part, throughout this chapter, there is a myriad of beliefs that govern people's thoughts and actions (past, present, and future), known as their "worldview." It keeps them still or propels them forward. It spurs development or the lack thereof. One is motivating, the other breeds passivity. When one no longer is teachable, he is askew in his priorities and approach.

Biblical Worldview

The **Biblical Worldview** is set apart by others. The two primary worldviews (Linear and Circular) fall under three categories stated by Darrow Miller, author of Discipling Nations:

    1- Animism

    2- Secularism

    3- Theism

*Linear Worldview:

There is a beginning and an end, i.e. Genesis to Revelation. Yes, there is an end but yet a new beginning, according to one's acceptance of God's work on the cross. It is the understanding that time moves in a line from the center to infinity - in both directions (left and right). There is conviction of the following: action and reaction, cause and effect, sowing and reaping - mainly consequences. God made it clear in the Old Testament when He set up the Law; He allowed zero room for misunderstanding what is good and bad, right and wrong, and what pleased and displeased Himself. We learn His heart behind the laws and covenants that He initiated and remains faithful to implement. Blessed if you obey; cursed if you disobey. Although life in the New Testament functions through God's never-ending grace, the principles remain unchanged.

*Circular Worldview:

Being trapped within a cycle, without knowing, understanding or believing there is a way out and, subsequently, being controlled by whatever outcome - good or bad. "I cannot do anything to change. I am caught in the cycle." It is fatalistic. Ahead, we will look at the effects of one's worldview.

There **is wondrous beauty** in the diversity of the human race. As I said before, I believe God created differences to challenge us in relating and loving one another. In a sense, technically, the idea of cultures probably originated in the mind and heart of God, though the expressions formed through mankind. There is much we can learn. God is smart and clever. His recipe for Mankind is a special mix of so many peoples and flavors, shapes and sizes, colors and cultures, backgrounds and differences so that we would learn to live together, to relate, and to test what is in us. We were created with the desire to relate; it is a basic need. Since "The Fall," you would think we would start getting it right or at least come close. In countries you visit, embrace what may be different but not detrimental, otherwise your ministry will be just like a pre-mature baby, fighting great odds at the start of his life.

Animism

Some believe that all is spiritual without giving much credence to the physical world. Found within folk religions, Hinduism, and Buddhism are varying animistic beliefs, but they are not alone. People of other worldviews could find themselves being affected by this, even some Christians and Muslims. Darrow Miller, author of *Discipling Nations*, states regarding Animism, "In some cases, the physical world may be considered an illusion. Man's highest good and ultimate goal is to return to spiritual oneness while the physical is denigrated." So what is the conclusion? Continual appeasement.

There is also difficulty trying to reach those who are influenced by worshiping the dead, spirits, etc...? When you are faced with a belief system steeped in fear, such as animism, and those who are controlled by spirits and often required to worship dead ancestors, it will be a challenge of praying, teaching and exemplifying how to make life better right now, not in another life.

***Bring in specific examples like: **"Why do humans/animals defecate? Because it is poison and would kill them if it stayed within them, showing, in part, the need to relieve oneself carefully in certain locations.** Or another example: the process one goes through from being healthy to getting infected by a disease because of not washing their hands with soap and [clean] water, i.e. with children: Hand-foot-mouth syndrome (child plays with objects touched by people with unclean hands or dropped on a filthy surface. This object now goes into the child's mouth, and sickness comes). We say disease is caused by evil spirits, but it may be due to lack of self-control, laziness, or lack of attention toward what my children are putting in their mouths. The following may help you when working toward change and development. Without the understanding of value, change will be non-existent and unmotivated.

Secularism

Secularism, in short, is basically the belief in "self" and the disbelief in the spirit world. Only the physical world, what can be seen, is real. There is no belief in God; therefore, there is no guiding purpose for life and living. It is all random. Man comes up with his own answers through science, technology, etc. There is no truth other than what can be proven. Life is mostly based on opinion and is all relative. It is basic Humanism in a broader sense - Rationalism.

Theism

One who is theistic believes in the spirit world and in God. They would also believe in the universe as being personal because they believe God is personal. There is truth, which can be known. This forms our understanding of right and wrong and good and evil. Truth is absolute.

Discern Redemptive Qualities

Embrace and learn to discern "redemptive" qualities or what was once good but turned sour by the devil. One example could be worship. The way another culture worships may not be evil in and of itself, but the object of their worship may be. There is a country in Asia who worships an evil demon goddess. Another example is the

oppression of women. This may be cultural, but it is unbiblical. And more: twin babies who are buried; value determined by money; distinction and value known by the class of people or tribe; distinctions made on skin color, and so on.

Decide what is worth "dying on a hill for." Pick your battles. Ask the Lord. If you are a short-term team (of say two weeks), it is not realistic to crusade against certain issues, which have permeated deeply within their beliefs over the centuries. Always preach the gospel. There may be some obvious areas to address but confront lovingly. Some of these areas take time, coupled with wisdom, sensitivity, and patience. I realize this is quite a simplified explication, though a good jump start. We will not exhaust all belief systems here, but we will journey through the more prevalent levels of beliefs.

KEY: GOD CREATED CULTURES

It is our responsibility to be Spirit led, inquiring of our Father to minister effectively to people's needs. It grieves me when I recognize the burdens that different mission and church organizations have left behind. At times, we appear clueless as to how much we allow culture to permeate our Biblical teaching and attempt to inject it into others. We need to respect cultural beauty and remember that God is the Originator of people. He has given them creative abilities, which is how they have come to express who they are as a people. That being said, there are boundaries overrun in every culture on earth. Man has been given gifts and creativity, but fallen humanity has digressed and has allowed unbiblical, erroneous, and even demonic additions or variables to be interwoven (or permeated) within the fabric of their lives. Major on the majors...minor on the minors.

My friends had a team in a highly Islamic area, but the team before them had built a square church in the area. Yet building the square church had highly offended the local people. Why? This was the community's response:

"God is never-ending. He is continuous, like a circle. A God with corners is weak!"

Oops! Ouch! The unknowing, previous missionaries had caused a set-back, an indication that better communication was necessary. Proper relating takes more diligence, but it is worth your time.

Fatalism

Fatalism is a worldview that gives little (if any) credence to the possibility of change or betterment of life, society, etc. Common statements would be:

" **I**t has always been that way. Our situation is fine. What could possibly change this village, city, people, family? It does not matter in this life. It is like that because it must be the will of God or Allah or Shiva. Whatever the god(s) will. A mere man cannot change the mind of god(s). I believe in fate. Do the gods really care about the millions?"

While venturing into various countries, I have realized that Fatalism is not only a plague devouring developing nations but also courses through the veins of developed (or Western) nations, though more concealed and layered. The common view is that tribal peoples have Fatalistic views, but I challenge that with Western views. For example: how many Christians (or non-believers) do we run across who, all their lives, declare:

"I could never do this particular thing or be a missionary!"
"I have always struggled in that area and probably
will till Heaven comes."
"You do not understand what I have been through.
It will not change."

Hmmm. We take so much "stuff" as our beliefs without ever questioning, wondering, or weighing the consequences, ramifications or relevance to such philosophy. It is necessary to provide opportunities to question so that we may detect other serious, erroneous beliefs wherein we might have unknowingly submitted.

To be effective in any culture, it is of high relevance to research local customs, beliefs and taboos, and investigate, observe, and ask questions (non-confronting questions to simply learn). Dig below the surface; some answers are deceptive or misleading. As best you can, attempt to visualize what the roots look like and move and teach accordingly. There are times where I have chosen not to pray for local people unless local people are praying with us. Other times, I have given a small teaching before ministering through prayer, i.e. how they can hear from God and that they have access to every spiritual blessing in Christ Jesus *(Ephesians 1:3)*.

Working in the jungle, intensely diverse scenarios came across our path. One was between a woman, sick for months, dying, and a young man getting married. We were closely involved with both. We decided to help 23-year-old Sambula with his marriage papers. He loves God without a doubt, and his parents had been leaders in the local church. Sometime after, Sambula came to me asking if we could help him further in his preparations. I asked him a series of questions, which I believed were Holy Spirit inspired. I came to realize that he had already spent about one million Francs ($125-150USD) for a ceremony that would only last for a moment. We had to decline because it would have shown our stamp of approval to their people. The average annual income is about that much. Opposite this situation was Marianette, who lived literally right next door, suffering for months and finally died with no help, and it cost more to bury her than to have saved her life. Another leader in the church named Jacob had been suffering for eight years with a growing medical condition. His pain and discomfort increased daily. His two operations, which we paid for, were about $24USD!

Do you see where I am headed? I asked Sambula, "*Do you realize there is something that is not right here?*" We talked through this for a long time. I prayed that he would see it clearly. His revelation could literally mean life and death and provision or poverty for countless individuals, thus allowing for change and blessing. Cultural pressures, in many cases, cause indebtedness, formulaic tradition, and what is "expected" to dictate your life. The road ends in bondage and poverty. People do the same in America and other lands, but the intensity is covered by credit cards and other plastics. But in a poverty stricken area, the effects are intensified. Privilege is not a common word. Yet, there are times God changes our outcome, like when He asked Jonah to pray for Nineveh and ask the people to repent. You see, He wishes for not one to perish. Those we are reaching must know the Lord is with them, otherwise they can only assume 'what will be will be!'

Truth Without Action Is Useless

Truth is useless <u>unless</u> you are prepared to do something about it. Make a difference. With Godly inspiration, convince people that "this is the truth…walk ye in it." Knowing, alone, does not produce change because it can be in your head and not in your heart. People must witness the value of change. Regretfully, I could share with you innumerable situations of people who "knew" what was "right" yet lived contrarily.

In certain areas, we taught the people that where they relieved themselves would affect their health, yet they continued to relieve themselves in unsanitary places. When they were given something, they continued being greedy without gratitude. They were also taught that cleaning their children or the children's hands (with soap and water) would keep them from sickness or worse, yet they remained dirty. History will take a new turn if they (we) can grasp and live these truths, as in *James 1:22-25; 4:17*. If we learn something and still choose to do nothing about it, we become useless. We would not have unfortunate incidents like the aforementioned woman dying in the village. It is hard when you attempt to help a hurting people and yield no harvest. But maintain balance...remember how easy it is to point the finger while forgetting to look in the mirror to see our own blemish.

Ways of Entry

Be on the lookout for entryways. The Great Wall of China seems ominous, but it is not impenetrable. A classic Western cliché is: "Sticks and stones may break my bones, but names will never hurt me." Nothing could be further from the truth. This fruitless saying impaired me for years. I was born with a cleft palette, and it has served to change the minds of many and has also given people hope in Jesus. While growing up, I could not say my name, and I was commonly teased as "Yon Yurmy" in place of Jon Syrbe. With 12 years of speech therapy, I still could not pronounce my name. Thanks to Dr. Gary Parker of the M/V ANASTASIS, who had completed the last and latest operations on me in 1994 in West Africa, I can pronounce whatever name is out there. So I am a quick candidate to declare the above statement to be rubbish, and that it can cause great damage.

ocate clichés or beliefs that, although commonplace, hinder people rather than help them. Shed light on areas of unawareness. They will be compelled to question beliefs that say they are cursed, possessed and the rest. My testimony has spoken so loudly, loud enough to crack strongholds over them. They can no longer say, 'White man does not have the things that plague us.' We must fully realize the strongholds people adhere to and nurse in the undeveloped and developed world. Some of us are appalled at the knowledge of some burying babies alive because they have birth defects, yet Westerners have millions of good and healthy babies aborted ever year. Whether we are Westerners, Easterners or whomever, we must acknowledge that our culture may offend a person from an opposite culture; someone who sees through different glasses. As we point the finger, three fingers are facing us. All cultures need some form of redemption. It is our job and responsibility to minimize what hinders the Gospel.

Taboos

"You want to build a latrine for/with us? I am sorry. It is evil to dig a hole. We do not believe in digging holes."

Often, we site the Book of Leviticus and Deuteronomy where God taught the Israelites healthy living conditions and how important it was to dig a hole outside of their living area and bury their human waste *(Deuteronomy 23:12)*. But why would anyone think a hole is evil? After searching for the answer, we discovered that a child had died some generations before by falling into a hole. There you have it. Now you see that you must work through the need.

A similar belief connected to *Taboos* is *Superstition*. Many are plagued with them, and some are even affected by them subconsciously - wherever you may live. Here are some examples:

Some believe in good and bad luck: the groom cannot see the bride on their wedding day until the ceremony takes place; you cannot walk under a ladder or have a black cat cross your path; you have to "knock-on-wood" for luck or protection.

*Some fear the infamous Friday the 13th so they take more precautions and are more conscious of evil that day. They may even avoid going certain places and doing certain actions.

*Some throw out their food and clean their hands if you walk by and sneeze.

*Some refuse to eat or drink what you give them (or if they know you touched the vessel) for fear of evil coming over them or bad luck, so they have special vessels for you to use. This is because you are not part of their caste or belief.

*Some are affected if you touch their feet and do not acknowledge them with some action.

*Some cannot have the bride-to-be touch the ground from her home to the ceremony site, so they carry her for fear of evil spirits entering her.

*Some, if born on a certain day or in a specific way, will be sacrificed.

*Some [have to] put on or wear amulets or bracelets around different body parts to fend off or appease evil spirits.

J ust mentioning a few of these taboos or superstitions, you can imagine what drives people to do or not do what they do. But God has set us free from the controls of nature and the [spirit] forces around us. Wondrous freedom! Due to certain beliefs, we become plagued with fear, doubt…and thus controlled. Sometimes the most dangerous are the subtle taboos and superstitions, and it can be more elusive trying to find the root cause.

Good Luck

"G ood luck" is more magical than Biblical, saying, "Well, if it happens, it happens." You become bound by it. It is perhaps linked to fatalism because people believe they win if they are lucky. They have good jobs and families because they are lucky, and those who receive the not-so-good just have bad luck. "I tripped down the stairs, dropped the phone, missed my bus, lost my job, and spilled my ice-cream today. I had bad luck today. I should have stayed in bed!"

L ife with God has its good and not-so-good moments, but the difference is that we are under the protection of a God who cares and guides us if we will listen; Whose character is tried and true…and unchanging; Who is more powerful than the devil and his forces or "chance." As I illustrated before, the devil is this little figure a fraction of the size of God's big toe. Better yet, think of God's big toe being larger than the earth, and the devil is under His big toe. God is THE One in control. All is subject to Him, YET it is essential for us to understand, even though severe circumstances may occur, that God did not and will not slip off of His throne or go on vacation during your crisis. We sleep; God does not! What a great source of relief! God only does what is best, and there is no darkness in Him.

I recently teamed up with a wonderful man named Ajoy from Ravi Zacharias Ministries, and he was talking about how God is not the source of suffering. It is not within His nature. When most people feel suffering or evil takes place, they say, "Where is God?" or "If there was a loving and all powerful God why…?" Like the Bible story of Job, God is the one we usually attack first. Although Job remained sinless, he recognized he was ridiculous and shortsighted so he repents of his thoughts and accusations toward God. God answered Job's questioning with 81 questions listed in Chapter 38ff. There are evils that occur, but be clear that not all things are part of God's will. Suffering happens because:

*My sin against someone.
*The sin of someone against me.
*The devil.
*God allowed.
*That we have been living in a sin-wrecked world for 1000s of years, which are piling up and infecting humanity and at an accelerated rate through technology.

In the end [and through the middle] because God is here, there, and everywhere, we can rest assured and not plagued or fearful of taboos and superstitions. My trust is in God. My life, current and future, is in His hands. In my daily life, I ask Him for wisdom, direction, discernment, etc. for where to go and what to do.

Value of Creation

When one kicks a dog, abuses a child, rapes a woman, takes the life of another, throws trash on the side of the road, or destroys with the tongue, it becomes obvious that **value for life** has been lost or never existed for that individual.

Where does value come from? Why does a shiny rock (diamond) come with a price tag? Why is it that in one country something could have greater value than in another? Are man and woman created from dust? Is there any value in dust? Ever tried selling dust? Where is the value?

There is value according to who, what, where, when, and how something or someone is created. A supreme Power, who is Omniscient, Omnipresent, and Omnipotent, known to us who believe as God Almighty, the Alpha and Omega, the First and Last, the Self-Existent One, Abba Father, Daddy God ("Papa Big Fella" to those of Papa New Guinea) created humanity.

What is His character? The God of the Bible reveals that He is loving, self giving, sovereign, in control, just, caring, faithful, true, holy, without sin, forgiving, life-giving and so much more. Therefore, we can conclude He is valuable and has value, and if so, what God creates has value. So how bought we take care of what He created? How we treat what He has created is directly and indirectly how we treat God and think of Him.

What He does is trustworthy, the best, and is carried out with right motives. Our security is in knowing that what He creates has value:

~ The Universe
~ The World
~ The Animals
~ Man and Woman

How was creation functioning originally? It was 'very good,' He said, 'and without sin.' Once sin entered the world, things changed. There was a severing of relationship between man and God...man and man...man and creation (land and animals).

The Fall

Genesis:
Life before the Fall
1. Man was the highest of God's creation, yet dependent on God **(1:26-31, Ch. 2).**
2. Man was created to rule but not over men **(1:26).**
3. Man was created to work **(1:28, 2:4-5).**
4. Man was created to follow God's commandments **(2:16).**
5. Man was created for fellowship with others **(2:18 & 23).**
6. Man and woman were created to function in harmony-alongside-together **(1:26-28).**
7. Man was created for fellowship with God **(2:19).**
8. Man was a communicator, able to express ideas, intellectually strong, a creative thinker **(2:19 & 23).**
9. Man was created inherently righteous **(2:25).**
10. Man was created for freedom within limits [emphasis is freedom...limits are set by God] **(2:16-17).**
~ How long until the Fall (5:3)? Less than 130 years after Adam!

What happened in the Fall?

1. Beginning of disappointment (3:1ff).
2. Beginning of sin [before Adam and Eve had children] (4:1).
3. Beginning of murder (4:8).
4. Beginning to talk of judgment **(Chapters 3 & 6)**.
5. Adam and Eve doubted where they came from, who they were, and where they were headed.
6. They attacked God's authority with help from the devil.

~ *"As the Devil tempted Eve...he knows He cannot get God, so he gets Him by getting us, going through us!"*
-Rob Morris (Axiom)

What was lost in the Fall:

1. Relationship with God and an unconscious relationship with the devil.
2. Innocence. Being selfish, they now wanted power and control, which is easier than being accountable and loving.
3. Need for dependence. They saw themselves as "god." **The "I can do it myself"** approach.
4. Life, now inverted, is focused on self-preservation, the devil's strategy for not seeing value in others.
5. Truth became relative.
6. Purpose appears lost.
7. Lack of trust, resulting in denial that God knows best and dis-respecting God's authority.
8. Security/Identity is now lost, which has been a pursuit of man to regain/acquire at all costs since the Fall.
9. Sense of contentment. What they had was not enough. They began to focus their attention on what they did not have instead of what they had. God was their most precious gift, yet they were deceived into thinking they were missing out.

Result of the Fall:

1. Responsibility was passed on to others. Adam, Eve, and future humanity have not taken ownership of their faults and weaknesses.

> Adam: *"That woman you gave me..."*
> Eve: *"The serpent tricked me..."*

Who was deceived? Who sinned? Both **(Romans 5:12-14, 1 Corinthians 15:22, 1 Timothy 2:14).**

2. Fear and Pride

~ Man has degenerated to living lower than the animals by committing atrocities worse than that of animals.

God's Response to the Fall:

Was it spitefulness? Anger? Hatred? Fear? Disappointment? Regret? Compassion? Judgment? Cursing? Emotional? Painful? Redemptive?

God knew what Adam and Eve had done, but they needed desperately to see for themselves. **Notice what consequences God spoke to each involved.**

Serpent - ...will crawl low and eat the dust (in the Old Testament, the dust could be actual "flesh," and in the New Testament it can be "flesh" as in the carnal-ungodly part of man. Hence, the devil feeds upon "fleshy Christians." But he has nothing to feed on when one is obediently following Jesus! So, one can feed or starve the devil by his actions/lifestyle. I would go as far as to say the devil is one of God's instruments to reach, wake up, correct, and bring back His children, even to stir those who do not know Him. God also put enmity between the serpent and the woman. The woman's seed, which Jesus would be birthed through, has always been attacked, but the Word says that her offspring (Jesus) would crush the serpent's head.

"The Son of God was revealed for this purpose, to destroy the works of the devil" (1 John 3:8). It is necessary to point out what the devil has done, so many will recognize his pitiful tactics today. God may use the devil, but God also allows things to happen. He does not always cause certain events. **Take a look at Job 1 & 2, Luke 8:12, John 8:44,10:10, Romans 16:20, 2 Corinthians 2:11, 4:4, Ephesians 4:27, James 4:7, 1 Peter 5:8, and Revelation 2:10, 12:10-12, 20:10.**

In the Old Testament, we can see demonic powers working behind and through the enemies of God's people, i.e. Egypt, Philistines. Although this had been happening, it is paramount to recognize and be reminded that God is THE One in control. Things happen not as a result of darkness in God, but because of man's fallibility. God allows things, yet He does not always cause things to happen.

God is the Author of life. We are the ones who bring suffering upon ourselves, and because suffering has entered into our lives, God uses it for good. It is a grand mystery...life comes from suffering. Jesus. Now, suffering is a common part of life due to man's depravation and perceived separateness from God. We should never doubt God's heart as He IMMEDIATELY began to pursue mankind to bring them back to Himself within moments of their fall *(Genesis 3:15)*.

One final point I should mention is Job's situation (during the Post-Adamic Period where sin reigned over grace). What makes Job's situation different is that God declares 10 times in the first two chapters that Job was without sin, blameless, upright or integral. What Job experienced was extreme. Although difficult to see with natural eyes, if we look through God's eyes perhaps we can conclude that it was for the betterment of humanity. (Remember, Job was written during Abraham's time). IF the devil could prove faith only depended on what men have (blessings), he could prove righteousness was a hoax, an impossibility.

The Doctrine of Satan

Many, believers and unbelievers alike, do not believe in the devil while others swing the pendulum to the opposite side. Those in the latter camp believe that everything is of the devil, even to the extreme that under every pillow you will find a demon. Paul brilliantly conveys a balance in Ephesians. What many tend to miss in Chapter 6, where the devil comes into question, is what Paul has been trying to shout aloud previously in Chapters 1-5. Some following insights I learned in SBS Montana through Mark Masucci and Judy Smith.

What is that you ask?
1. Chapter 1-3 refers to our position in Christ, who we are in Him, **Who He is.** There are nearly 100 promises of Who Jesus is, what He has done, and who we are in Him in Ephesians.

2. Chapters 4-5 teaches how we ought to walk. Paul actually describes five walks: walk worthy, walk in truth, walk in love, walk in light, and walk wisely. This implies the Ephesians (and us) are to see their spiritual warfare as a lifestyle.
  - ~ Their battle is spiritual.
  - ~ Knowing their position brings personal victory/defeats the devil.
  - ~ Knowing Who Jesus is and what He has done/does brings personal victory and defeats the devil.
  - ~ Their battle is not against flesh and blood.

Therefore, like the Ephesians, we are to RECEIVE the reality that our neighbors, brothers, sisters, parents, pastors, presidents, prefects, chiefs, witch-doctors are not the enemy. Who or what might be working through them/in them/behind them is the enemy - the devil and his demons. **At all times, remember to love the sinner and hate the sin.** All to often, we attack the people. Someone screams so we scream back, another hits us so we hit back, someone curses us so we curse back. We are living backwards, hating the sinner and their sin. Can you remember a time when you might have been like them? Deceived? This is a question worth asking yourself every so often to keep yourself humble.

How I treat others is spiritual warfare. If I have an attitude against them or gossip about them, etc., it feeds the devil. This affects the heavenlies.

How I speak to another will often determine one of two directions they will go. One direction brings life, by building them up, encouraging them onward. The second brings death by tearing them down, along with their hopes and dreams. What I say can neutralize, even paralyze them from accomplishing all of what Jesus could do within them and through them today, tomorrow and so on. Paul makes it clear that we have to take responsibility. We cannot blame everything on the devil because how we walk/live makes a difference. The devil does use Christians (among others) to derail someone unclear of who they are and their understanding of Jesus to divert their destiny. For example, during the writing of this book, I met with a former leader (and good friend of mine) who told me, "Who is Jon Syrbe? ...I have not met anyone in these 5 years I have been here... that has what it takes to write a book like this..." Well...here is the book. It was apparent they were offended because of my comment, saying, "I am sorry, but I will not receive that...I do not believe that is from God." I was secure in who I was, and what God had spoken to me. I was not diverted from my destiny. Having said that, there had been other times where I felt horrendous, and I believe lost out on what God purposed for me at that given time.

Now for those who DO NOT believe the devil exists ...hmm...that means you believe:
* Not in the inerrancy of Scripture.
* Scripture on the devil is not literal.
* Evil or bad things are just some negative force out there.
* Within God is where evil comes from (as well as others who also think God created the devil since he had been in heaven and cast down to the earth).
* You would not pray against the devil or evil forces.

Eve - Because of the Fall, her pain will increase in childbirth, in pain she will bring forth children, **yet** her desire will be for her husband, and he will rule over her. Does this imply the same under the new covenant? Was it a curse? Or simply a result/consequence of the Fall? [Observe - God did not curse humanity, but the serpent and the land.] **Does this imply sexually and romantically ruling over her?**

The result? She will look to her husband, possibly become dependent on him rather than on the Lord. The result? He will take advantage of her (not to mention the negative results of this physically). So her turning away from the Lord will result in him taking advantage of her. Rearing children, perhaps physically/emotionally/spiritually, will become more challenging because of the sin factor. As I travel the globe, I see in greater measure the reality of women depending on men to an extreme, unhealthy level. Even with fools. It is an interesting, psychological phenomenon to witness a woman, who has experienced trauma in her upbringing, continue to gravitate back to the person causing her pain. Just as humanity has done, women place men in the way of God...with a sense of comfort, perhaps, because of sin or just for the tangible-ness of another human being. Now with the woman being a "weaker vessel," one can see how there may be a dependence on the physically stronger vessel. Is it fair to say that men have been able to dominate and oppress women in greater measure purely due to their physical abilities? I do need to be fair as I am reminded that although women have been exploited, they have also fed into their depravity because of the whole sex, fashion, advertisement and entertainment industry. The devil has taken great delight in this. For example, I was at a local (small) magazine shop in an airport, and there were no less than 53 explicit or semi-explicit photos of women on magazine covers.

Adam - Because he listened to his wife and the devil, which caused him to go against what he was commanded, and ate from the tree (where his wife was), the ground was therefore cursed. Adam, and those to follow, will have to labor to live, eat and sustain themselves. I remember a friend and chaplain of Mercy Ships, Jack Hill, challenging many with why the devil approached Eve first? Maybe it was the woman who was more difficult to convince, but if he got her, getting Adam would be easy. Either way,

Adam fell easily. Did Adam fail in his responsibility? Yes. He knew what was right and chose to cave into peer pressure, known also as "self." He also bailed out on communication...hmm. Is that not seen as a problem of great weight and consequence up until today? According to what we see in Genesis 3, Adam may have not been communicating well or closely with Eve. Bottom line: they exchanged love for power and pride - power now of themselves.

Following these announcements, God makes provision for Adam and Eve by clothing them. Significance? He took care of them in spite of their sin! Did He cover their sin? Forgive them? Well, for one, they became the only creature clothed from without while all other creatures are clothed from within, i.e. fur.

Then they were driven out of His presence, out of Eden. And ever since, God has been intensely pursuing man in love, making every attempt to bring all people back into relationship with Him. Only a few verses after the account of the Fall, we see God's first hint of a redemptive plan (Genesis 3:15). This is the first Messianic prophecy. Later this was fulfilled as Mary, by giving birth to the seed, Jesus, brought her foot upon the head of the serpent -devil (see Romans 16:20; Hebrews 2:14; 1 John 3:8). There could be no doubt in God's love and faithfulness.

Later, in Genesis 6:5-6, God cries out some of the most shocking and piercing words ever recorded in scripture. "The Lord saw that the wickedness of humankind was great in the earth, and that every inclination of the thoughts of their hearts was only evil continually. And the Lord was sorry that he had made humankind on the earth, and it grieved Him to His heart."

It is as though His very breath was taken. As if He were punched with a great blow to His abdomen. Imagine. You have created something with tremendous heart and effort. You have appreciation and value for it, and then some little twerp grabs it, throws it to the ground, and begins to break it apart! That is basically what we have done and continue to do every day and moment we sin against Him and against one another.

There was once a pig messing around in the mud, drunk from wine, who poignantly stated: *"I swear, I'll never play the man again!"* How sad is that?

Conclusion: They ate more than just a piece of fruit!

The Original Intent for Creation
(Genesis 1:26-31)

1. Man was not to take advantage, destroy, or abuse creation.
2. Man was to be a good steward of it.
3. Understand and define dominion, multiply, fill, subdue.
4. Man was to take care of the garden God planted **(1:15)**. Learn the significance of the garden = earth, Kingdom of God **(1:8)**.
5. Man has free will to choose God's will; it is inherently against God's will to rape the land for quick profits or sheer fun. See *Exodus 23:10-11, Leviticus 25:2-7, 26:34-35, Deuteronomy 20:19-20, 22:6-7, Psalm 104:10-23, Jeremiah 12:4, Hosea 41-4, Romans 1:20, 8:18-23, Revelation 4:11.*

ANIMALS

From cities to urban villages globally, one will find the abuse of animals. Is it wrong? What is the big deal? After all, some argue they do not have a spirit. We kill them to eat so why get so uptight about how we treat them?

Sound familiar? I would like to believe there will be animals in heaven. I do not believe they have a spirit, unlike some religions who worship animals. But then again, Jesus cast the spirits into the pigs that drove them off of the cliff...so more food for thought. I suppose my point is why would God only create them to enjoy life on earth. It would not make sense that He would not have them in eternity.

Do animals know what is happening to them?

I was in the Amazon swimming with piranhas who like to eat whatever or whomever may be enjoying the water with them! While swimming, there was a fun-loving dog in the water whose master was Mark Barnes, otherwise known as "Indiana Barnes" - YWAM Director. Now the dog got real excited when others were around so he bolted out of the water like a rocket to greet them. Yet while doing so, he must have caught his paw on a sharp rock. Within the blink of an eye, he began to let out a blood curdling scream as he bit into his paw while limping in circles. Blood had begun to flow enough for concern. For no less than 10 minutes, he yelped and squealed. So, again my question: Was the dog aware of what was happening to him? I say, 'Yes.' He was feeling pain, and he knew he was injured.

Does that mean we do not discipline animals when necessary? Of course we discipline them. It is our responsibility to do so. We discipline children, but we are not meant to beat them. We only use force when dealing with animals who are out of control.

Is eating meat wrong? No. However, before the Fall and Flood, food was eaten and provided from the trees and plants. The killing of animals for food took place later. God then gave instructions on cleanliness of all meat and foods **(Genesis 9:3-4, Acts 10** and **1 Corinthians 10:25-26)**.

Conclusion: to clean, provide for and take care of the animals God has given us, not torture them. Realize they are created and valued by God. God blessed them that He created.

~ Why extinction of animals in our day? Go back to **Genesis 1 and 2** for the worldview. Once animals become extinct, they are 'literally' history. This is not a simple thing we can just shrug off and forget. They are more than just interesting creatures; they are also part of God's marvelous, diverse and complex ecosystem. If you take away this or that animal within the scheme of a balanced system, it now affects the next part down the line, like dominos.

THE LAND

Tony Campolo has written a book on "How to Love Creation without Worshiping It." We are to take care of it as we can and value it for it is not ours to destroy. People are deceived that the earth is at their disposal to do as they wish. There are actually links to health related issues because of the lack of understanding of where, how, and when to clean living areas, walking areas, washing areas, and the like.

For example, we attempted to set an example by not bathing in the river. Instead, we took the water, a massive effort, and did what we had to do on the banks about 15-20 meters away. Value is revealed again here: "Only, you shall not eat flesh with its life, that is, its blood. For your own lifeblood I will surely require a reckoning: from every animal I will require it and human beings, each one for the blood of another, I will require a reckoning for human life. *Whoever sheds the blood of a human, by a human shall that person's blood be shed; for in His own image God made humankind"* *(Genesis 9:4-6).* Here God is declaring the value of life through the sacredness of blood. How do we see the value of life? Innocent animals had their blood shed for men. God made provision for man's sins before Christ, thereby proving He valued us. This is why our Lord is called the Lamb of God.

What to remember? We are created just like the plants and animals, yet humans are the only created beings whom God can communicate with and enjoy fellowship and relationship.

~ God created out of His character...LOVE. So, the question again is: How does He feel and respond when people mess with what He created?

God created us to love Him and enjoy Him forever. He intended to live within everyone until we rebelled. But nonetheless, He created every person, plant and animal, and, if what He created has value, especially other human beings, and we hurt and destroy, it is as though we are hurting God. In actuality, we are doing it to God, not just them.

Why does God not heal everyone "supernaturally?" He chooses to work through one another. He created us to relate with one another, which breaks pride, causes inter-dependence, and fosters love. God is smarter than we think. In this way, those afflicted and reaching out can see God and truly experience Him. He wants us to work together in unison. But love costs. It costs money, effort and time. Sacrifice is necessary at times.

Conclusion: The key to TRANSFORMATION and DEVELOPMENT is for people to realize:

Where they came from, who they are and where
they are going. So knowing what
God is like is paramount to their journey!

Scenarios on Value:

Are we simply passing through this Earth? Are there no physical ramifications, consequences or responses to nature, living, etc.? You may find yourself wondering the following:
* Does it matter whether or not we destroy creation? Does it matter where I throw rubbish?
* What is the point of physical healing or help?
* We are just going to die anyway.
* Why study? Why learn? The world is passing. Is evil temporal?
* Should I be making my life better and progressing?
* Why should I work? Do I treat my house or possessions like people? Like work? The office? The shop?

If what God creates has value, we should thoughtfully consider how we are treating it.

Six Scenarios for Consideration

1. Why the stark contrast between developed nations and developing nations? It is my observation that the developed nations have perhaps been more prepared for conversion and the renewal of their minds while developing nations are more lacking and thus suffer the repercussions of a unhealthy mind and continue in poverty, disease and more.

2. If development is necessary, important and valuable then how should it be carried out?
> ~ Finish what you start
> ~ Clean what becomes dirty/diseased sufficiently, completely
> ~ If something breaks, fix it
> ~ If something is not working, repair it
> ~ If something is lacking, fill the void

People do not like mosquitoes, but they will allow a broken door or screen and spend more money on coils to deter? I am more convinced that the Gospel goes out and comes back with a redeemed heart but without a redeemed mindset or semi-redeemed mind.

3. What and who is born of God should excel, improve, progress.

4. Who is under the authority and life of God's indwelling Spirit ought to be leaving who (recipients and onlookers) and what he has touched, used, spoke into, and experienced in better condition than before.

5. The opposite of the above is:
> ~ Blindness
> ~ Lack of initiative
> ~ Wrong Biblical worldview
> ~ Wrong concept of God, matter, evil
> ~ Lack of good stewardship of God's provision
> ~ Not valuing what the Lord has provided
> ~ Spirituality has a higher value than physical reality
> ~ Physical reality has no value at all
> ~ Super spiritualizing everything so the physical does not have any purpose, meaning or need for improvement

6. Why develop the world (medical system, sewer systems, etc.) if they do not affect people or "the Spirit," making development seem futile?

The Developing Gospel of Developing Nations Develops Salvations - Yet not the Betterment of Man

"Clean hands and a pure heart" (Psalm 24:4)

> ~ Developing Gospel preached (underdeveloped gospel)
> ~ Response made
> ~ Developing the spirit (man)
> ~ Physically I become sick
> ~ Washing/bathing/relieving in river, which is not good, is seen as okay
> ~ Not seeing a change, real value or connection with sickness, thus no urgency to change
> ~ No notice of danger
> ~ Spending money on medicine, ailments, and then missing work, etc.

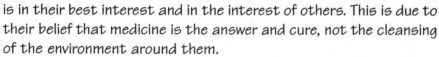

Conclusion: They do not see a need to change the physical and fail to see the connection that taking care of the environment is in their best interest and in the interest of others. This is due to their belief that medicine is the answer and cure, not the cleansing of the environment around them.

Their belief is that the material world is:

> ~ Evil
> ~ Temporal
> ~ Has no value

Thus no need for:

> ~ Commitment (to earthly matters)
> ~ Doing their best at a given "natural" task
> ~ Teaching on environmental betterment
> ~ Taking care of what has been given, being a good steward
> ~ Finishing a task
> ~ Development
> ~ Making living, homes and villages better or more comfortable

For the:

  Animist: Will go to the spirits, make sacrifices to appease, because somehow man has transgressed.

  Secularist: Will go to himself and the sciences, rationalizing his way through.

  Theist: Will go to God, realizing that God is personal, all powerful, caring and involved in His Creation.

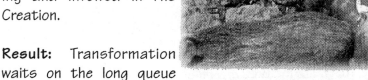

Result: Transformation waits on the long queue toward development with semi redeemed humanity, who are, perhaps, spiritually reached but practically and physically yet to be transformed. A view into Super Structural Belief Systems will more than confirm these findings.

Conclusion: Let us love and respect what God has created...the land, the animals, and you and I by worshiping our Creator, not the created. How we treat what is created could indirectly show how we are treating God. Much like parents who go away and leave you in charge of the house, then you have a party and the house gets wrecked.

How would they feel?
  ~Trust is broken
  ~Taken advantage of
  ~No consideration for what they have done
  ~I provided for you and this was your response?
  ~Angry
  ~Worked hard for what was given
  ~Sacrificed
  ~Dreamed of this provision for you
  ~Wanted you to enjoy it
  ~Betrayed
  ~Disappointed

Always look through God's grid to define and adhere to beliefs that will ultimately guide your life. In some cultures, it is not common to express love to others, i.e. their wives, children. How do their people grow up? Deficiently. It should not be so. Putting this belief through God's grid will shed light on the deception internally. God (and the God in you) always expresses (His) love, embracing His creation. He declares throughout the scriptures that He has loved His people with an everlasting love. Jesus demonstrated God's love even further. Our heavenly Father's emotions and love have never been limited or unseen. This is the model we should follow.

Value is expressed in love, which is in word, deed and truth.

So having a revelation of God's Mandate in Genesis will open one's eyes to the value of all. His Mandate for humanity was intentional - to live for one another, function together as men and women, being "naked" (unashamed, open without covering up, nor passing responsibility), being secure in their identity since BOTH are created in God's image, sharing in dominion over the earth, being responsible stewards of the earth and animals, as well as being fruitful and multiplying God's kingdom on earth, and being extensions and expressions of His love and life. As another Bible School director and friend, Arun, says, **"Not having the Book of Genesis would be like walking into the middle of a movie. You would see all the characters and their actions, but it will have no significance because you do not know what has taken place previously, like where they are from, who they are, why they are there."** Thank God for Genesis! It is great not to have to live clueless, aye?!

Fear

Connected with belief systems, fear would be one of the dominating factors that keeps certain cultures from experiencing the love of Christ. All of us would do well to betray our fears.

"What would the spirits do if we..." (many may ask in some villages)? As far as Africa, researchers conclude:

"Due to the unpredictability of the spirits and the ability of people to curse their enemies, many people in the African traditional religion live in fear. There is fear concerning death because it comes so often in Africa. They believe spirits are much more active and closer to humans when someone in the village or city has died. In the modern world, when many of the traditional ways of dealing with the spirits do not seem to work, fear is heightened. Much of their beliefs breeds hopelessness."

- Africa Missions Research

Ask and keep asking locals about their history, life, family, what is important to them, what does not matter to them, fears, joys, local/tribal proverbs, authority/structure? This builds incredible bridges and insight into their understanding and daily living. Furthermore, it helps incorporate and involve these gems in your teachings.

The Lifestyle Connection

Remember, your actions and daily living speaks volumes. One villager might notice and say, *"For two months these foreigners have not been washing in the river, nor polluting it, and they wash with soap and water in a safe area at a distance from the water source. As we have been living by their instructions, less people have been getting sick! Why?"* "They are doing this and that for the women and children and treating them with respect and value. Why?!" They may be more apt to listen and follow what you have to say because their observation of you has added more weight to what you have been teaching.

One example has been to continually ask and involve various locals (especially leaders) to join in when we pray for others. At times, we will wait to pray until they have prayed, thus giving them encouragement and also re-enforcing that God is THE answer; local leaders are just as capable to hear from Him. This fosters less of a dependence on foreigners.

*** Sometimes it fuels their already-fatalistic view if we were to allow ourselves to do all the praying, initiating, etc.

Situational Ethics

I **realized that there is another belief** that threads throughout nearly the majority of living, breathing human beings, as I listened to my friend and former leader Gary Graham, the Director of the Outreach Department of Mercy Ships. He described how people's situational ethics differ based upon their circumstance(s). Whatever experience is the "special of the day" determines how they will respond. My barometer fluctuates at times like sudden winds out of control, yet I yearn always for the stability of Jesus. There is also a common belief in humanity perhaps more apparent in some cultures than others. I call it the Great Soup of Beliefs.

"Well, today Jesus worked for me but yesterday He did not help with my family member turning against me...so I looked to the Fetish Priest. And the day before, when I looked to the local god of wealth, I got some more work."

A**nd so on.** Thus mixing a bit of Jesus, witchcraft, credit cards, my ancestors and more (whatever substitute works for me today or at this moment), is like making a soup with contradicting beliefs, a soup of deception and sometimes death - certainly spiritual death. Jesus is either the Only soup with all the necessary ingredients for life and wholeness or not.

Cultural Valleys

H**ere are some real belief systems** I gathered from experience that peoples around the globe hold as culturally and sometimes Biblically offensive. As effective ministers of the Gospel, we ought to be in tune where we are and with who we are keeping company so we know how to function within a culture different than our own.

~ Attending certain venues
~ Coming unannounced
~ Smoking, Drinking, Dancing

~ Eating all food/not eating all
~ Laying hands/touching, hugging one another of opposite sex
~ Spitting/Chewing gum
~ Extending your feet/touching feet
~ Giving a chicken to a woman who you do not intend to marry
~ Wearing short shorts/long skirts/short skirts/revealing shoulders
~ Earrings/body piercing
~ Sitting in a seat with the opposite sex
~ Seen talking to the opposite sex
~ Looking at another man or a woman looking at a man
~ Expressing personal feelings to opposite sex
~ Giving address with no intention of corresponding
~ Talking loud or raising your voice (yelling at)
~ Wearing shoes in the house or temple
~ Beginning an effort without contacting the chief
~ Not partaking in what is offered to you
~ Gestures - middle finger or thumb raised, wave, point
~ Eating or touching with the left hand or using it at all
~ Whistling in the house
~ Starting your agenda by asking about their family
      THERE ARE EVEN SOME EXCEPTIONS WITHIN THE CULTURE

So be sensitive. Some cultures believe that if you take a photo, you are taking their soul. While people are praying, preaching or giving their testimony publicly, I have a difficult time allowing photos to be taken. I usually discourage it. If it would be permissible, I would have one person take photos discreetly. It could send negative messages.

Questions to think about...

* Who are the major political and spiritual leaders in this area?
* What has shaped this area, its people and beliefs?
* What is the area's current state politically, economically, socially?
* What is the area's percentage of "solid Christians?"
* What other religions influence the area/country?
* Are there any difficulties in this area because of religion?
* Ask the leaders/people if there are any mistakes you are making or have made that could be changed.

As far as the team goes, we have found it advantageous to become acquainted with the culture before arriving in the country or jumping into ministry. For example, one particular team I was on remained in a capital for four days and on day five we left for the jungle for two months. This helped them transition into the new surroundings, people, and culture. Weigh your team to see what is best. I have done both.

Why do we believe what we believe? Why do we do what we do?

Let us continue thinking the above thoughts, and you and I will move forward in our effectiveness and fruitfulness as learners by discerning cultures, not only for them but also as a challenge for all of us. We will then find ourselves building bridges through cultural valleys and not tearing down potential communication!

CHAPTER TEN

How Does God See Women?

"Women are the cause of evil in the world!"

"A woman should remain in her place - the home!"

"Women are created to serve ME."

"Women are to be silent, listen and obey ME!"

"Barefoot and pregnant is best for them!"

"The reason for the world's turmoil is women leaving the home!"

"Eve was the deceived one; she brought sin."

"Women are subordinate and are to submit to men."

"There is order in creation, and woman is under man."

"Males are leaders and meant for leadership, not women."

"Women are from the devil and are a curse from the Fall."

"A woman has to be covered by a man."

"Women are too emotional to be leaders."

"Women are God's substitute when a man does not follow God's call."

"The man is responsible for the spiritual life and well being of his wife and family."

Come As A Learner

You **(women) can wear** what you want, but you cannot teach (except Sunday school, secular schools, and the home). You do not have to be silent in church, but you must live in full submission at home...**how is that?"**

If **your attention** was drifting, could I make the assumption that you are now wide awake, especially if you are a woman?! Then again, a mirror reaction could be just as painful if you are a man! It is known as the "women issue," but it really seems to be the "male issue!"

This **will prove** to be an emotional chapter and, perhaps, a major stirring may arise because of what you have believed and/or were **taught** throughout your life as women and men. It may cause one of two reactions:

1 - Joy, freedom, relief, searching, and change.
2 - Frustration, anger, passivity (or captivity), hence no relief, no searching, and no change.
Open or closed…your choice

A **sure warning sign** is someone closed to the possibility of change; they cannot imagine that they could be wrong. Once in a Bible study where the focus was a controversial issue, I realized, quickly, that the participants were tweaking and twisting Scripture, forgetting about looking at the context and taking into account the New Covenant of Jesus Christ. Each book of the Bible is to a specific people, and there may have been outside influences, which explains the necessity to view the historical situation and Messianic language used. Yes, the books are God-inspired; nonetheless, the writers are dealing directly with the people of the time. I would or could hardly say that today's people are in a similar society, although our problems are not unique (stoning vs. capital punishment). What is my point? In that study group, not even 100th of a possibility was given that they could be amiss. They argued for a moment, then simply moved on, not even hinting at a possible, "Hmm, I wonder if I could be mistaken?"

Through my national culture and church culture, I had succumbed quite easily on one hand and uneasily on the other. This is because:

* I felt more superior as a male. It was convenient and felt nice (to be honest) to have a sense of power and control over someone else (women, in particular).
* I had taken what was taught as reality and truth.
* I had not taken time to look, think and ask the Lord for myself.
* I was overly influenced by media, family, friends, enemies, and the church as to who women were or were not.
* I felt enormous pressure that "I" would be the (only) one to provide for my potential wife. Furthermore, I believed I had to be her spiritual covering, and I would be judged when I entered Heaven on how my wife and children's spiritual lives were lived. [**Ezekiel** gives a contrary word in **18:1-4ff**, saying that each is responsible for his own sin. In **1 Peter 3:7**, he claims we are heirs together because both have a spiritual capacity.]
* My value was based upon what was in my wallet.
* *I misunderstood what the Bible says about submission, assuming my wife would have to submit to me.*

A lot of things did not make sense to me (apparently), causing me to feel confused and uncomfortable. I had seen women in leadership in my home churches, but I also saw inconsistencies. Eventually, my eyes opened between traveling through 40 countries and inductively studying each book of the Bible at the SBS. I owe them a tremendous amount of thanks for teaching me how to think and ask God for myself without relying on other's theologies and doctrines.

Upon my eyes being opened and also witnessing the world's and women's condition, a passion had risen boldly within me. If others do not agree with me, it is okay. *Where There Is No Leader* should be causing you to think, stimulating your awareness, raising questions, and, hopefully, giving you direction on your beliefs. And through its words, perhaps you may be convinced or become open to the possibility of change.

My passion for addressing who GOD says women are has grown the more I travel and experience life. Unfortunately, on every continent, there has been this disease of pride, fear, ignorance or a wrong perspective when it comes to the female gender. One country has lowered women to just above dogs, yet a man in ministry is not considered respectable if he is not married. Widows are treated disrespectfully. I was on a 24-hour train ride where a woman was quite adamant about letting me sit next to her. However, the Lord saw to it that I would be her companion for the next six hours. I was minding my own business (due to her apparent discontentment) when, all of a sudden, she pulled on my shirt sleeve and exclaimed, **"Excuse me, please. I want to read that"** (I had been studying and highlighting a printed copy of the Book of **James** in preparation for one of my teachings, and it looked like a coloring book). Shocked would be an understatement! Well, she read the entire book. Upon completion, we began to talk whereupon I learned that her husband had "expired" in previous months. It was a phenomenal revelation for her to discover that Christ commanded us to look after the orphans and widows, not to mention **James** speaks against the distinctions between rich and poor - two large, religiously-distorted beliefs in her country.

Another country has been known to kill their women, mothers and female babies because they have laws regarding the number of children they can have. One man, whom I have counseled, began to drink and became more abusive when he realized (after having two girls) that his third child would be a girl. And there are other pitiful excuses for abuse as well. One major religion boasts that millions of their women live in the shadows full of fear, depression, darkness, torment, and the threat of torture. I know of some who, if the slightest bit of their skin is exposed, could face beatings.

While discussing viewpoints in a temple in India, I asked two men, *"Why do women wear black? Why are they completely covered? Why do the men not pray with women? Why are they not allowed inside of the temple?"* I knew why; I just wanted to hear it for myself. *"It is the Law. It is because they are a distraction,"* he replied. So I said, *"How much time do you spend in this temple? 10% of your life? That means 10% of your life is without distractions. What about the 90% living in the world among women? That would mean that 90% of your life is a distraction and unspiritual? Therefore, this all seems very unrealistic? What would it feel like for you if you were commanded to be shrouded in darkness your whole life?"* The only response was *"It's the Law."* *"So does it mean that women are the cause for your sin?*

Distraction? Temptation?" There was no response. *"Is it not the heart and what is in it that is the issue? Can it be blamed on an outside source? Is the war not from within instead of without?"* Passing the buck or blaming someone else for your responsibility retards growth no matter what the situation. God persuades us to change because He does not need changing.

There is a 'Man Church' in California, whom I believe means well, but how different are they from the above story? They are a church comprised **only of men,** who feel they only need each other and that women would only be in the way - a distraction, temptation. But is that reality because it does not really deal with the issue. Even if you are on the moon, lust could still be your neighbor...if it is in your heart.

There was a well-known woman of God who made incredible accomplishments for the Kingdom and humanity, yet she uttered one of the saddest statements I have ever heard as a response to being asked 'who she was and why she had done what she did.' She replied, *"I know that I am, as a woman, not God's first choice, and I have felt guilty and disobedient (to lead or minister the way she did), but I felt so compelled by the needs that were not being met by many."*

Another famous female missionary (and wife of a martyred husband) wrote a foreword speaking out against the **equality of men and women,** which, in my opinion, was disheartening. She made strong comments regarding people who re-write history, psychology, etc., making the Bible more palatable for twentieth century women. She maintained that leadership should only be held by males and indicted the church for conforming to the world. The author said that Christians are trailing the world by opening the doors for women to be leaders. Because Adam named Eve, he has authority over her; male represents the divine side and female, the human side; God is our Father, not our Mother; to be ruled by women is a sign of moral decadence. I could carry on, but I think you see my point.

Some of you may be chomping at the bit waiting for some scriptural evidence of my claim of men and women's equality. **Hold on I am coming...**

Who have been the earth's most oppressed people since the Beginning? Some say Israel (the Jews) while some say the Blacks (African or African descendants) and still others will claim slavery has oppressed people the most. Oppression has, yes, been fierce, gut wrenching and vile to the core, but I would venture to say the greatest oppression has actually been toward half of God's valued creation - women (of all creeds and colors)! Women have been deemed second rate, limited, dependent, immobile, incapable (at least Biblically), prone to sin and seduction, without voice, incompetent to hear God's voice and more.

Am I to see situations and base decisions on my terms and not the Lord's? On what my well-meaning friend, church or society dictates?

Death by Truth?

While teaching in West Africa, there was a pastor from Burkina Faso who raised a significant point: *"If I return to my country and begin teaching this, I could be killed."*

There is never an easy solution. There IS overriding Biblical evidence to firmly stand on without being assumed a heretic, yet there are difficult passages as well. I discussed the following sensitively to the pastor and the class I was teaching:

~ Are we teaching for God or Man?
~ Fear of God vs. fear of man (being a man pleaser).
~ Half (if not more) of God's Creation is a lot of people, and too big a risk to remain silent and do nothing.
~ Often, silence is a sign of agreement.
~ We must lead by example, beginning with family and friends.
~ Are women worth it?

~ You (first) have to be convinced regarding the equality and freedom of/for women. I advise not jumping into the lion's mouth without being able to back up your conclusions.
~ The disciples spoke the truth and look what happened to them. Truth is not always accepted nor appreciated.
~ Wisdom and sensitivity is first and foremost. One would not want to stand in front of the Parliament building to hoot and holler about women's rights.

As a believer or leader, I am often swayed by men's opinions rather than by God's heart because it is difficult to change or challenge what may be a strong current against my culture, traditions and Biblical training. On an Indian train recently, a young woman was raped in front of the other passengers. And what do you think happened? Nothing! They just sat there, turned their heads and were silent. Unthinkable? Unfathomable? Yet how common it is to remain silent. This makes the statement, 'I might as well agree with what is happening!' Scripture tells us, "The fear of others lays a snare, but the one who trust in the Lord is secure" *(Proverbs 29:25)*. Concerning ourselves with what men think over what God thinks is the opposite of wisdom and life. If I believe the Word is from God's heart, then I back up why I believe what I believe, stand as an example, and lead. If I find resistance, I ask the Lord for wisdom and a strategy. I may need to begin with my family and close friends, perhaps have discussions with co-leaders.

Paul and Jesus addressed, empowered, and worked with women, but never incited a riotous revolution on their behalf. A good question is why not? They spoke in similar terms about slavery. Did that make slavery right? Jesus had a unique, internal agenda. Some sections of the Word have clear instructions on how to treat and relate to slaves; some sections refer to women, but primarily it referred to all people, as in **Philemon**: loving a slave as you would love yourself). If you search diligently, you can find obvious comments on the subject of women from Jesus, Paul and others, which were considered radical at that time! **See Appendix.**

Contradictions in the Bible?

There are only **contradictions** in scripture when I, or we, misinterpret scripture. I will be the first to admit guilt. Many of us have often used scripture to manipulate for our own means, whether we realized it or not, all the while forgetting what God wanted to say, but what we wanted conveyed. This happens when we accept one verse or statement and leave or do not accept another. It is almost like choosing a meal: I will have the potatoes but I will pass on the gravy, thank you. Sometimes the gravy compliments the potatoes. We cannot be cafeteria Christians regarding God's Word. After all, the focus is GOD, right?

In general, most people misinterpret scripture because they do not understand God's nature and character in that particular situation or circumstance. It must line up with the rest of His teachings. If it does not – in your opinion – allow it to prompt you to do further study. A brilliant example is **1 Timothy, Chapter 2**.

Church systems say, 'It does not matter how you dress, but you must wear a head covering; you can serve in the church but not be a leader; you cannot teach in the church, but you can in Sunday School, in your family or in the world; you do not have to be silent in church, but you cannot minister; you can have authority in the world (doctor, corporate executive), but not in the church. What does that say about the male gender's opinion of future generations? There is no LITTLE Holy Ghost. Does that make sense to you? In my opinion, if you are going to take one thing in context, whether your interpretation is correct or not, then, at least, see the others in the same context.

I am aware of two things:

1- Be careful you do not separate or combine the Word to suit your needs.

2- Take caution to analyze when scriptures are for the cultural past and what pertains to the NOW so that you will not dismiss valuable teachings. There is always something to be learned from history. Do not assume that everything is written for me now, in this era, or vise versa.

Turn to GENESIS 1:26-31: What actually happened in the Beginning? We will begin after the creation of the Heavens, the earth, and the animals, which the Lord said was good and blessed **(refer back to Chapter 9)**

WHAT DO YOU OBSERVE?

~ Who does He speak of or address?
~ Who are Adam and Eve in relation to God?
~ What is an "image?"
~ Is there an "order?" If so, is it significant?
~ Pay close attention to God's original intent and His mandate.
~ Who is given dominion? Responsibility?

Remember: we are looking from the Adamic point of view through the creation window. Keep this in mind. All was well in the Beginning, yet we are looking back from a fallen position, which causes a fragmented society: countless women left behind with fatherless children; men's tremendous laziness and lack of involvement in their children's lives or around the home; women who have been controlled; women made to feel that there is something wrong with their bodies because of man's heart (lust from the inside); women becoming sex objects rather than people; women tortured, raped and taken advantage of by being "the weaker sex"; women being used by men for their self benefit; women working more than most men and earning less; men not communicating as they ought.

Women also have weaknesses and sin, but for the need at hand we are focusing on an issue that is long overdue. I am excited about more books coming to print about women in ministry, leadership, equality, etc., causing millions of shackles to be unlocked for half of God's creation-task force-laborers-beloved!

What about the feminist movement?

How about a clear distinction of the extremes and motivations, which have been damaging and forceful, often done in anger and intolerance instead of humility and forgiveness, regarding the Feminist Movement, the attempted forging of women's independence? Well, Jesus, Paul, and others were forging INTERDEPENDENCE *(1 Corinthians 11:11-12).*

It is paramount to balance between dependence, independence and interdependence. Ultimately, we are dependent on the Lord and then people (to a degree). We are created for relationships to sharpen each other and to minister grace, truth and love. God deposits bits of His truth to all those who surrender to Him, obey Him and love Him. Yet NONE of us, INCLUDING MAN (as in male), church, family, society, leaders, pastors, prophets, teachers, evangelists or apostles have the corner on truth. The five-fold giftings are for the entire Body of Christ, **which includes WOMEN.**

The Gospel is for ALL people in ALL situations at ALL times!

What does that mean? It means living an exemplary, gospel-filled life, like Jesus, regardless of inward and, in this case, outward circumstances. Paul exhorted the slaves to respond to their masters in love. Mainly, we must realize that all we do is for the Lord, not man *(Colossians 3:22-25; 1 Peter 2:18-21).*

Back to Genesis 1:26-31..."PRONOUNS" are often misinterpreted, and sometimes overlooked as in *Genesis 1* so let me give you an example from Romans. In *Romans Chapter 9-11,* we must look carefully to see whom Paul is addressing: spiritual Israel, physical Israel or the Gentiles. This will determine the correct interpretation of those chapters because Application will follow in one of two ways:

If I am interpreting the passages through pre-conceived ideas [technology of the West, culture, church culture, what I have been taught in the past-only], I will come to the conclusion that "all Israel will be saved." Furthermore, I will consider them more elite and special to God, and feel compelled that I have to get the Jews back to Israel. However, if I interpret without the scenarios previously mentioned, then I will see that it is "Spiritual Israel" who are and will be the saved; that God's heart is for all, not with a higher, special love for "Physical Israel." I realize that I am Israel, a true Jew, if I love Jesus and believe in HIS grace. This can be confirmed by Paul's effort to speak to the Jews and Gentiles separately and collectively throughout the first three chapters, explaining that they are both in need of a Savior. Throughout the book, it was never a physical thing but spiritual (Abraham and his seed are considered God's friends and righteous by their faith, not adherence to the Law or circumcision nor by bloodline).

With this interpretation, I will live totally different. I will focus on God's grace, not my pride; I will focus on God's plan and purposes for me wherever they may be, not spending energy and unnecessary human resources on something that is not part of God's plan for the man's redemption; I would live by calling, not guilt. It is simple: Jesus came to seek and save [whoever] was lost and willing to repent. However, right now, I am referring to the application of scripture regarding the continued enslavement of women to the "will" of man. It is similar here in **Genesis.** We must also observe if something is **"SINGULAR"** or **"PLURAL."**

1:26 - *"Let US make HUMANKIND in OUR IMAGE, according to OUR likeness; and let THEM have dominion over the fish..."*

1:27 - So, God created HUMANKIND in HIS IMAGE, in the IMAGE of God HE created THEM; MALE AND FEMALE HE created THEM.

1:28 - God BLESSED THEM, and God said to THEM, "Be harsh to one another, control each other if YOU can. Let it be known that the man is to rule over YOU woman and dominate YOU?" WAIT! THAT IS NOT WHAT IT SAYS!

1:28 - God said to THEM, "*Be fruitful and multiply, and fill the Earth and subdue IT; and have dominion over the fish...*

And it was so. God saw EVERYTHING that HE made, and indeed it was very good."

What is the excuse for male pride, thinking women were created to serve men? These scriptures refer to man and woman as humankind. **Why?**

~ The job was for BOTH!
~ Repeated pronoun: **"them"**
~ Who has dominion? Both.
~ Who is blessed? Both.

Is there any difference in their responsibilities? Hierarchy? **God created the earth and the animals** before Man. Are the animals more valuable than humanity?

Genesis 1 is an account of how Man arrived on earth, and how they (we-ideally) should function, although there are obvious differences between men and women (not to dismiss God's original and continual intent for humanity - male and female). I told a female friend that I was writing a chapter about women, and, in the blink of an eye, she retorted with a tinge of humor, "And what do you know about women?" My clear response was not to worry; I never assume the understanding of how women think and process! Both genders lean toward certain, God-given expressions, yet they are not exclusive. A woman is generally more nurturing; a man is generally physically stronger. But I am attempting to bring balance where people have crossed the lines on value and hierarchical preferences. I have concluded that it is not a gender issue, but one of calling and gifting.

What is the stuff Adam and Eve are made of?

ADAM=Dust......Eve=ADAM...

Some say that Eve was made from what was closest to Adam's heart.

"Bone of my bones...flesh of my flesh" refers to being second to Adam in time not value. Eve was part of Adam. And remember: Adam was asleep, so he had nothing to do with it! Eve is part of Adam; Adam is a part of Eve. They are, in a sense, each other. So how can there be a difference? **And Adam said it...and recognized it.**

Genesis 2:18-25

If indeed it had been a 24-hour day in the Creation account (according to 2:18, 23), both God and Adam saw a great longing of what was to come -VERY rapidly. It must have taken Adam a long time to name ALL the animals. THAT had to be one long, power-packed day!

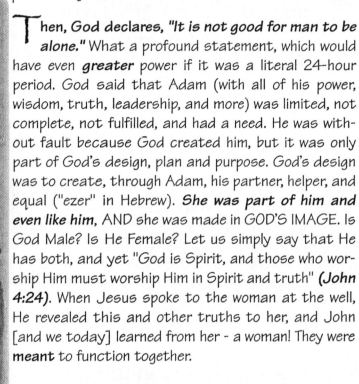

Then, God declares, **"It is not good for man to be alone."** What a profound statement, which would have even **greater** power if it was a literal 24-hour period. God said that Adam (with all of his power, wisdom, truth, leadership, and more) was limited, not complete, not fulfilled, and had a need. He was without fault because God created him, but it was only part of God's design, plan and purpose. God's design was to create, through Adam, his partner, helper, and equal ("ezer" in Hebrew). **She was part of him and even like him,** AND she was made in GOD'S IMAGE. Is God Male? Is He Female? Let us simply say that He has both, and yet "God is Spirit, and those who worship Him must worship Him in Spirit and truth" *(John 4:24)*. When Jesus spoke to the woman at the well, He revealed this and other truths to her, and John [and we today] learned from her - a woman! They were **meant** to function together.

Who's the Boss?

There was a girl in pre-school who asked,
"Daddy, you are the boss, right?"
Father: **"Yes, baby. That is right."**
Girl: **"And mommy put you in charge, right daddy?"**

God gave THEM a mandate for their lives and future, not to control and be dominated by each other. I see where it is not good for "man" to lead alone. As I discussed in *The Value of Creation*, we have to understand who God is and what He is like. If God is like us and vice-versa, would God be involved in the gender separatism of today? Fortunately, we remember daily that God constructed us in His Image...and that He is not made from ours!

ve is a part of Adam as much as Adam is a part of Eve, and BOTH are a part of God. Adam seemed to be pretty secure about the situation with a 'RIGHT ON!' kind of response at his FIRST glance of Eve!
In my words:

"WHOA, FINALLY someone LIKE me but with some nice, beautiful and special differences. I will take care of her like she is me, Lord. THANKS!"

hrough psychology, we know that men and women think, process and reason somewhat differently, yet this only demonstrates their need for one another, to BALANCE and COMPLIMENT each other; they are unique yet equal.

ND: Does God have two images? BOTH were/are created by God and should function in the sobering reality that BOTH are finite and are to be relational and interdependent. What a man can see and express is only part or half of what can be communicated to a needy world (men and women) about God's love and His life-giving message. After all, it takes both for humanity to continue. The point in GENESIS?
    * Take care of what God calls GOOD and BLESSED!

What happened in and after the fall?

PRIDE AND FEAR CREPT INTO ADAM (and the rest of mankind - including women).

think this is the root of the tension and strife found between women and men. Pride is basically "me" calling the shots, stating it is all about "me," everything revolving around "my" (sometimes selfish) wants and demands. "I" am the center of "my" universe. This pretty much blurts abroad to the world:

PRIDE

~ Move over for me.

~ I am right. I have studied enough to know God's word.

~ I do not need to change.

~ I see what I want to see.

~ I push my responsibility on to you.

~ I am very comfortable in the position of myself, my church, and my family.

~ I refuse to think I also have to submit to a woman.

~ I am too comfortable with my husband providing for me, and the pressure he has on his wallet keeps me secure.

Adam did not react negatively with PRIDE or FEAR when God first created the woman, yet today, the pride and strength of man can be sickening and down-right disheartening. Loren Cunningham (founder of YWAM) says, *"The sin of pride is the refusal to accept who you really are. Pride enters in when you think you are better than others...believing a lie about yourself."*

This may also be a deceptive or subconscious pride. Although you do not act prideful, your life is demonstrating your upbringing or theological training and its influences.

FEAR

~ If I am wrong, what will people think of me?

~ If I am wrong, my wife, women, and society will not serve me. There goes the order.

~ If I change and repent that I was wrong about women, will my family and followers still respect me?

~ If I change, it will be uncomfortable.

~ I will lose control (or responsibility) or will not be able to control women any longer.

~ If men change their thinking, I will have to take more responsibility for my personal, spiritual life, and I will not be able to rely upon my husband and the church.

~ If things change, it could be a long uphill battle.

When there is a shifting from a major belief system, which is *"bent"* against God's nature like Ken Paige, my friend and California business executive, defined, there will be challenges, but change is possible.

Which gender does the Bible mainly address?

I have a Bible that is "gender friendly," (saying "brothers and sisters") which I think is going a bit far; however, when the apostle Paul addresses a situation, he is often referring to all people, unless speaking to specific individuals or people, which is seldom in comparison. The Holy Scriptures are more inclusive of both genders than many believe or perceive.

CAUTION: women and men should be sensitive, wise, and cautious when hearing a message like this - be careful how you walk it out and proclaim it! Be aware of others.

Centuries of wrong thinking, depending where live, may take time to be broken. Keep interceding. MEN - use your influence and position to make a difference. Speak the truth. Weigh the value of truth compared to the potential danger or difficulty within your country or country's religion. Influence as you can. Remember (men and women), it is not about a massive, bloodthirsty crusade. At times, it may depend on individual conversations, and your personal, exemplary lives. Live the gospel of Christ in your actions. Furthermore, teach what is Biblical (assuming you have received this as truth). Truth is not easy to swallow at times. **Love well.**

GENESIS 2:24-25 - "Therefore, a man leaves his father and mother and clings to his wife, and they become one flesh. And both were naked, and were not ashamed."

What is that verse saying? If someone is "one," how is he divided? Who is the "greater" half? Is there a "head?" Why did God say that the man would have to leave his father and mother? Is he more passive? Is it also because they are now a separate extension of the family? There are cultures where tremendous pain and frustration exist, not to mention lack of privacy. When the husband and wife do not leave and cleave, they really cannot become one. Instead, they become five, 10 and 15 with the parents, in-laws, siblings, etc. I must acknowledge that there are economic situations that keep extended families together under the same roof or compound, and there are also cultural considerations. I am not disregarding culture in totality. However, if we remain under the same roof, there needs to be clearly defined boundaries, a supporting of the wife to the husband and husband to the wife, a protecting of one another, etc. It is not wrong to hear and receive input from extended family members, and you **MUST** (in humility) communicate to them that you two are a new family and solely-primarily responsible for each other.

In *Why Not Women*, co-author David Hamilton explains, *"We fail to realize how radically revolutionary it [God's intent] was in its original context. In no culture of antiquity did a man give up anything to be married to a woman. Women were not considered worthy of such a sacrifice. On the other hand, a woman had to give up everything on the day of her marriage."*

It is important to see that one of God's intents was for a two-person family. It works only with ONE man and ONE woman...not three, four or five others involved, like multiple wives. If you disagree, research King David's dysfunctional family. He was an amazing man whose life ENCOURAGES me both in what to do and what not to do. He did not have ideal matrimonial relations. How about King Solomon's downfall? Could it have been the influence of multiple wives that God wisely and sternly warned about in **Deuteronomy 17:14-20**, especially in **verse 17**.

And, of course, we cannot forget how, throughout time, the people of God tried to help God out. Abraham and Sarah ring a bell? *'God is not giving us a baby fast enough; we need to help him. Abe, take another wife, my servant.'* And you see the family ripped into sides, with jealousy, fear, rejection, and more. The word "dysfunctional" may be new in our dictionaries, but dysfunctional families are nothing new. That is why polygamy is neither God's original nor continual intent. We have a hard enough time loving one, and yet we are going to have more than one wife?!

The idea was for Adam and Eve to be one and function together. AND we must remember that **pride was not part of the equation** before sin. I believe where there is an absence of humility, there will be an absence of order (as in limited or extended chaos), depending on which male and female buttons get pushed and the situation's severity. The choice: contentment and preference of others or strife, demands and domination. As I said before, it is easier to control and manipulate than to love.

I believe God's original and continual intent works. If He fashioned the idea of two genders, marriage, and reproduction, and He does not make "oopsies" (mistakes), then is it us that are the problem with a bent and twisted perspective?

Spheres of Authority

If your wife has a gifting in finances, by all means release her. You can make decisions with her, but enable her to walk in that area of authority; it is a gift. If your husband is incredible at cooking or with the children, let him walk some of that out. Do not limit each other because of gender and pathetic stereotypes. The same should operate in the church. If there are women with administrative talents and leadership qualities, release them. We will go to the New Testament soon and expound more.

What about decisions?

Many say, 'There has to be ONE who makes the final decisions.' I feel that if BOTH are functioning in humility, and they have determined their "spheres of authority" then hardships and complications will not rear their ugly heads. Arguments that go beyond disagreeing usually occur because one party (maybe both) is not operating in humility at that moment? If there has to be ONE making the decision, let it be the one who has been chosen or mutually agreed to have **authority** in that area? One having all the decision-making power is always a danger and a risk not only to him/herself but to the others involved, as well as placing unnecessary pressure and stress on people. Perhaps take into consideration the deception of sin (or heart), and the husband or wife's current position (meaning their emotions, stress, work, maturity and wisdom [or lack of] in that area, relationship with God and more). At the moment of decision, maybe they may or may not be in a healthy, God-fearing position to make the [final] decision. Trust the Lord together -for each other and for the Lord. May He be glorified. Bottom line.

Can Women Teach?

I bet all of us have heard or asked this question, but it is important to dissect the meaning. What does teaching mean? Basically, it is talking to an individual or group and passing on your knowledge and revelations - what you have seen, heard, and experienced to another.

Who then is responsible for passing along the Word of God? When in India, David Hamilton (assistant to Loren Cunningham, the Co-founder of YWAM and Co-author) spoke on this issue to the SBS and shed light on the question:

"Where have many of the truths, which we know today, come from? And who have they come through?"

When something is very close to you, you can miss it, like a child's mannerisms. Only later do you say, "How did I miss what they were trying to communicate?" Here are some of the truths we know today because God revealed them to a woman.

Old Testament Women Whom God Appointed

Numbers 27 - This is about *Zelophehad's daughters* who, when their father died, approached Moses about their inheritance. The Lord told Moses that the women were correct for demanding their portion...they were entitled to their family's inheritance for themselves and for their future generations.

Judges 4 and 5 - In the dark days of Israel, God entrusted *Deborah*, a prophet, to judge and administrate for the people. It was she who stirred Barak to fight, to war, to take his position, so-to-speak. We learn that God obviously speaks to and through women and empowers them to be people of influence and leaders.

Judges 11 - Here, the mighty warrior *Jephthah* makes a rash vow, which causes his *daughter* to be literally or physically (by separation) sacrificed. She had faith and trusted in the Lord, and her father, despite her father's barbaric decision. She was successful. Why? Because of her faithfulness.

Judges 13 - God reveals to *Samson's mother* the call on her boy's life; her husband Manoah was clueless, never realizing it was an angel speaking with them. She represents a pure heart of sacrifice with right motives. We can say more of Jael who brought victory when she stepped out to destroy an enemy leader instead of simply offering hospitality as was the custom of the day for women.

Ruth- Here is a woman who is NOT a Jew but a Moabite - not of the chosen people - who raises the standard of faithfulness for present and future generations and proves that God loves foreigners as well as Israel. Despite pain and loss, she pressed forward with unwavering determination to be what God desired and designed her to become. Because of her obedience, God placed her in the lineage of the Seed of Christ. Ruth trusted in God, even when the outcome was unseen, and her risks and selfless living, along with *Esther's*, will be read by countless people (including men) and hopefully applied.

1 Samuel 1-2 - Eli, the priest, accused Hannah, Samuel's mother, of drunkenness, yet the Lord spoke through him that He would grant her plea. We glean from her true dedication to the Lord; she dedicated her child! Many parents would renege eventually. Family can be the greatest hindrance to a child (male or female) serving God. Hannah gave Samuel totally to the Lord. Her prayer in **Chapter 2** is loaded with gems.

Esther- Once again God calls His people to learn from the authority and favor given (by God) to a woman. Esther risked her life approaching her husband and king to spare the lives of her people, and God grants divine favor. Without Esther there would be no Israel...no Messiah to come. Yes, God is sovereign, and He chose a woman to accomplish His purpose.

WHAT DOES THE NEW TESTAMENT SAY?

The **New Testament** serves as an interpretation of the Old Testament, and we see repeated accounts of **Genesis** throughout **(Ephesians 5:31; 1 Timothy 2:13-15; 1 Peter 3:5-6; Hebrews 11; and more)**. The New Testament interprets the Old Testament. Since we have recently reviewed **Genesis**, let us look now into the New Testament and see how Jesus, Peter and Paul treated women. Some deem Paul as a male chauvinist. I think the contrary. He and others had women in their ministry and writings. A more careful look may actually unveil obvious evidence of women with a God-given call to ministry and leadership.

The Gospels - WOW! The accounts of Mary, Jesus' mother, are more astonishing than others. God revealed His divine purpose to a woman in **Luke, Chapter 1**, with more truths found in Mary's song. Like David Hamilton says, "**In a male dominated society, imagine what is about to happen and to be written: Luke has to sit with Mary and interview her about things she has seen...because neither he nor any other (male) was around when God spoke to her!**"

John - This is one of my favorites. The disciples (in this account) were **"astonished" (verse 27)** that Jesus spoke with the woman by the well. Jesus was transcending a cultural faux pas by speaking to a woman - a Samaritan woman (there was no mixing with them for they were considered unclean)! He is the Living Water, Spirit and Truth; no one thirsts when they drink of Him. Furthermore, He revealed that He was the Messiah (as revealed to Peter and Martha), and she changed from being an adulteress to the FIRST MISSIONARY in minutes, as Jesus sent her to tell her village! [See more in the Appendix from *Jesus, the Friend of Women*.]

If a donkey spoke (Numbers 22), would that not give further credence to the likelihood that women can speak, teach, and lead? After all, are they not more valuable than an animal? Are women not a part of the BODY OF CHRIST? If you do not agree, explain Ruth, Esther and all of the Bible's women-related occurrences. It is a mind-blowing waste keeping women back - a true tragedy for half of God's beloved Creation. But if they are a part [of the body], what part are they?

"I will pour out My Spirit on ALL flesh; your sons AND your DAUGHTERS will prophesy...EVEN on male and FEMALE slaves..." (Joel 2:28).

Why would the Lord pour out His Spirit on women if they are to remain silent and without influence?

Some say that women cannot be deacons or ministers. What about **Phoebe** from Cenchreae (Corinth)? She was known for delivering Paul's letter to the Romans. Romans is to many like electricity is to a light bulb! This is the book that many would prefer if stranded with nothing else to read. In light of that fact, imagine trusting a woman with one of the most profound teachings on justification, grace, faith, racism and unity! Paul calls Phoebe by three titles in **verses 1 and 2**: our sister, diakonos (servant or minister), and prostatis (helper). She was clearly considered a leader, minister, and supporter of the Gospel, and Paul exhorts the Romans to supply whatever she requires. Imagine someone telling a church to give you whatever YOU require…that is trust and confidence!

Priscilla and Aquila, the dynamic duo, are mentioned in Romans 16:3, Acts 18:2, 18:18, 18:26, 1 Corinthians 16:19, and 2 Timothy 4:19. This married couple risked their necks for the Gospel and were leaders of home churches (together).

They are never mentioned apart, which implies their unity of Spirit. In **Acts 18**, they counsel Apollos, a well-known, powerful advocate of the Gospel, and he listened to a woman. They also traveled with Paul and were recognized by Gentile churches. They were "synergos" to Paul (fellow workers, leaders). This is only scratching the surface of Paul's female co-workers.

Were there female apostles or disciples? More evidence than not declares there to be. Junia (female) and Andronicus, a male, were "prominent" apostles **(Romans 16:7)**, though that is the only specific notation of another apostle outside of Paul and the remaining 11 disciples. In addition, there were female followers [disciples] of Jesus **(Luke 8:1-4)**, though not perhaps known as the "original 12."

What do we do with 1 Timothy, Ephesians (which is where Timothy was when penning 1 Timothy 1:3), and 1 Peter?

In 1 Timothy, **we observe** (these conclusions coming through David Hamilton) that Paul addresses Timothy and the church of Ephesus. Direction can be determined if we pay attention to whom Paul is speaking.

Tim= 1:1-4	Tim = 5:21-23
Church = 1:5-17	Church = 5:24- 6:10
Tim = 1:18-20	Tim = 6:11-16
Church = 2:1-4:5	Church =6:17-19
Tim = 4:6-5:2	Tim = 6:20-21
Church = 5:3-20	

In Chapter 2, take note of the **"singular"** and "plural" gender references (man, woman, men, women). What does this imply in these readings? If we agree that woman can teach, why is it not permissible here? Is that now a contradiction? During that time, women were not taught from Jewish leaders, and, as time passed, the Rabbis added this to the Law. One false addition claimed that teaching a woman [scriptures] was blasphemous!

In the first chapter, Paul has been warning (again) about false teachers. He hands Hymenaeus and Alexander, who shipwrecked their faith and were teaching falsely, over to Satan but not the woman **(1 Timothy 1:19-20)**. Why? Paul later implies that the men should have known better, but that the woman was deceived - not being taught properly perhaps. He instructs them to teach her; they must not give up on her. This was a radical statement. Paul knew not to pin the sin on Eve (the woman) because he mentions Adam being at fault in *1 Corinthians 15:21-22 and Romans 5:12-14.*

I have asked myself, 'What keeps a nation back? What hinders a nation, church, or a family from progressing?' I believe there is a significance in how men relate to women or how much they hold them back. This issue is still a stench within the Church and the world. The Church ought to be leading the world by example, treating women decently, without limiting their functions, giftings and callings. Now, the context of **1 Timothy 2** is with worship-together. Then the following:

* 2:8=men-plural
* 2:9-10=women-plural
* 2:11-15a=woman, man-singular (some debate v.14-15 as being plural)
* 2:15b=women-plural

Since there are passages where women prophesy, that confirms to me that this was a localized situation. My reasoning: I see God moving and speaking through women, Jesus including and raising women, and Paul telling women they can minister and prophesy in the Scriptures, but Paul knew of a woman, in this local church, who had been teaching and leading people astray. She was a false teacher (like Alexander and Hymenaeus). Yet, he had hope for her. He encouraged them to teach her. It is unfortunate that many of us do not realize how radical that was. It was common for women freed from temple prostitution to be loud, out of control, disruptive, and immodestly dressed. This was their acceptable life within occult living, and Paul is exhorting them to live the new life in Christ. First, teach the women. Second, spend time learning and growing. Lastly, be released - what I believe he is intending to say.

As Paul mentioned in *1 Timothy 2:15*, Eve was deceived, but she was not alone. Paul seems to be focusing on Eve (someone they could relate to) because the apparent problem was with woman. Remember, the New Testament writers are primarily addressing a need and a problem.

But if the reference is a woman, why is Paul not using her name? Good question. Perhaps to protect her. And in *1 Timothy 2:15* where it talks about how the woman will be saved through child bearing…it goes without saying that one cannot literally be saved that way, nor more than a barren woman being unable to receive salvation! It simply means that the One [Jesus] coming through the woman will bring salvation, should they believe in Him. And even though both Adam and Eve are both guilty of bringing sin into the world, Eve was the one, by at least a few moments before Adam *(Genesis 3:6)*, to start the ball rolling. YET though she became a transgressor, salvation also came through her lineage (as God [Jesus] came through Mary).

How do we reconcile *1 Timothy 3:1-13*, regarding the elders' and deacons' qualifications? It seems as though Paul is communicating in order of male-female-male. But is he really? Was Paul's intent inclusive? In the Greek language, there is no distinction of gender. (Yet, if *Chapter 2* is a permanent, universal truth, then women are not qualified to be overseers and deacons). In my opinion, many of these conclusions can be readily understood without knowing the Greek interpretation! What does it say? "Whoever aspires to be a bishop…" Well, if you are a "whoever" raise your hand! Then he goes on to address deacons. *In 3:11*, women are included (note the word "likewise").

"Married only once" or "Husband of one wife…" *(1 Timothy 3:12)* - Meaning? You can see in your footnote that the Greek is "husband of one wife." The male is to be faithful to his wife. If his wife dies, it does not mean that he cannot re-marry. What if he gets a divorce? How many of us have considered a divorced person "2nd class?" The Church has declared boldly (yet silently) that divorce is unforgivable. Sometimes we even forgive murderers and other heinous offenders before forgiving a divorced person. I am not trying to justify divorce. As a victim of it, I realize how evil and destructive it is. But when there is genuine repentance, God forgives and forgets...so why are you and I bearing the grudge? With sins, such as divorce, there are consequences that may be greater than other sins, but let us not continue elevating some sins more than others. In an upcoming book, I hope to expound on this more.

Now, there is no command for a woman to be the wife of one husband because it was illegal and unheard of for a woman to have more than one husband. [I feel it necessary to stress, once again, what Jesus is saying and to whom He is addressing about divorce and re-marriage. Jesus was revealing men's false motives and lusts, and, sometimes, He was addressing the Pharisees - a dead give away.]

The context of 1 Peter reveals new insights as well. The Book is about the suffering of the righteous. In Chapter 3:1-7, keep the theme in mind. Notice the repeated phrase "in the same way" or "likewise," which implies a connection to the previous statement. The first statement regards submitting to the government's authority, and continues with other areas of life such as slaves, wives, and husbands, and Peter's reasoning is "the sake of Christ." The challenge was to submit in the hopes of winning them over to Jesus. So do not berate your unbelieving husband and drive him away (this would be couples who were born again after marriage - I do not encourage marrying unbelievers at all). Peter realizes that there are people who come to Jesus after marrying and, thus, he addresses accordingly.

Does he say for the husband to rule over her? Be master? What about suffering under an abusive husband? Should they remain in that situation? Is the woman inferior? Is her spiritual nurturing dependent on her husband? Is it because she is the weaker sex, as some say?

Look at Genesis 21:11-12 where Abraham was asked to obey Sarah. Sarah also called him "Lord" and

"Master" when he was absent, which implies respect; it was her choice to call him thus because he respected her. So when Sarah was asked, she listened to Abe out of love and respect. If men and women would learn to love properly, submission (respect) would follow suit.

Is submission still today's mission?

Ron Smith, co-founder of the SBS, said, **"In a woman's quiet time, what if today's verse read in 1 Peter 2:19: 'For it is a credit to you if being aware of God, you endure pain while suffering unjustly,' and she had been praying about leaving her abusive husband - and this abuse had been for ages. How will she interpret this passage?"**

This **woman is likely** to think that God is asking her to grin and bear it. When you are talking about women (or men) in a submissive, oppressive culture where there is no other option, then more endurance is certainly necessary, but it is my estimation that we need to let God out of the box and be free of absolute formulas. I am not referring to an easy way out when there is ONE blow out in the home. We ought to persevere; however, after ages of continual battering with no sign of change, I do not believe it would be sin to leave that situation. There is nothing about abuse that is Godly. For a divorce or separation, compare your circumstances to God's Word, including when and why you married the person. Here's another thought: Why is it that the focus is always (or all too often) on the woman 'this' and the woman 'that.' Where is the focus on the man??

Some may say, **"What about my difficult life with my husband. I live in a country where women are not accepted if they leave their husband?"** How challenging this is! Pray, endure, get counsel, and possible aid or protection. God will bless your attempts of continual reciprocating love to the unlovable. Yet, I do not believe in remaining within the situation blindly. I know a woman in India who had been beaten for years, nearly every day. Since the Lord brought her family and I together, the abuse has dropped dramatically. She, and one of her daughters, had come to know Jesus personally during my time there counseling her and her husband. I admire her greatly for persevering over the years. She was walking true, sacrificial love whereas her husband, who thought he did nothing wrong, deserved nothing. What a testament to Christ dying for you and me, but I do not see the scriptural basis for living with abuse until the day you die.

Should Men Submit?

Men, **do not get comfortable just yet!** While conducting seminars or speaking on this subject, I have asked hundreds this scenario: "**Turn to Ephesians 5:22?** What does it say? Wives submit to your husbands...amen! Okay, everyone close your Bibles. I am holding 10,000CFA, or 1,000 pesos, or $10US and would like to give it to anyone who can tell me what 5:21 says!" I have had very few people know. Why do so few people know? Because it is not taught! We (men) have **Ephesians 5:22** memorized, often times before we even come to Christ! Again, we often approach scripture with pre-conceived ideas and ways to support current conclusions. In the Greek language, the two verses were together, but in some versions of the Bible they are in separate paragraphs (remember verses and chapters were added in the 1500s). Sadly, many believe the Bible was written in this fashion. All the more reason to act like detectives and search for clues.

10% of Christians worldwide read the WHOLE Bible - a fraction of those actually study the WHOLE Bible (even if I were generous and added another 20%, it would still be small).

The point? One cannot draw conclusions and support convictions without having studied the Bible (or at least in context the whole particular book or letter).

There are even others whose theology is based upon what others tell them, and why not? It is easier to listen to others than **examining the scriptures** for ourselves, like the Beroeans in **Acts 17:10-11**. Is it any wonder why societies, churches, families and leadership structures are so out of whack? The church has remained illiterate, on a whole, even thought it has a precious **33,322 verse, 72**-hours-to-read (**17** hours for New Testament), God inspired book. Challenge and discipline yourselves to cut back a bit on outside stuff and spend more time with the Holy Spirit, our Teacher, who will lead us in all truth.

Just for an exercise, I would like the men to count how many times they have submitted (in various ways) to a woman or their wife throughout the week. Perhaps they may be pleasantly surprised. Even the Christian literature used in Bible studies may have been written or influenced by a woman. **Uh-oh!**

Mutual Submission

In Ephesians "5:18-23, there originally was no break, but one of Paul's long sentences. In this section, the only imperative or command is to 'be filled with the Spirit.' ...being filled with the Spirit must carry over into our relationships. The statements are commands to men, not women. Husbands love (laying down type of love). Wives submit (lay down life, voluntary submission). Paul fully redefined household relationships."
-Loren Cunningham

I **believe the scripture teaches** mutual submission. For women, it is not a command given, but a voluntary (automatic - if you will) response to a man's love. One would certainly long to submit when love and other qualities are present.

Life in the Spirit is:
1 - Speaking to one another in psalms (not p-slams).
2 - Singing and making melody to the Lord.
3 - Always giving thanks.
4 - Submitting to one another out of reverence for Christ.

David Hamilton states that in Ephesians 40 words (in Greek) were addressing wives, 150 words were directed to husbands, and 15 words concerned fathers. There is clear evidence that Paul's main concern was the male mindset of the time.

Author Thomas Finger says, "When everyone operates out of patience, forbearance, tenderheartedness, and forgiveness ...where I only consider the needs of others and give myself to others, and they do the same for me, that is walking in the Spirit, submitting to one another. And when such a way of life, energized by God's own Spirit, is really working, it is no wonder it produces spontaneous singing and thanksgiving!"

The men of Paul's day (and even today) are commanded to love their wives because they have yet to master Jesus' undying (yet dying) love. Remember: Paul's writings address a need and a problem. Men, here is the punch...if you have a doubt about mutual submission, remember what Jesus asks of you...to be like Him. What did He exemplify? Laying down His life, which includes serving, humility, selflessness, loving without limits, sacrificing, and, yes, submitting, i.e. Jesus submitted to the Father, but He was still God). Whether it is a marriage or for the Body of Christ at large, the same would apply. Hope it does not shock some of you too hard, but that is the Word of our Father. Perhaps look at Ephesians 5:18-33. Do I need to submit to women? Paul is defining spirit-filled living. Men and women, are we passing bondage or freedom on to our children? Yes, I believe in order. God's order of business is men and women working together, supporting each other.

Anyone know where the head went?

So, what is the head? Is there a head? As Judy Smith, co-founder of the SBS defined it as the beginning of a river, or the "source." There is another word for it: head. We in the 21st Century hit auto mode as soon as we hear the word "head" as reference to authority. In 1st Century Greek, it was not intended as authority. It would make sense, as there is nothing that describes authority (as in "power-over") in this section. If anything, it gives attributes of Jesus surrendering and laying down His life.

Definition of Submission:
= a yielding from my own wants or needs for others' benefit, like Jesus; a willfulness to follow the other's decision in humility (with the exception as known sin); letting go of my rights and trusting the bigger picture (this does not mean that I agree with what is done or said); considering my direction physically, spiritually and verbally; bringing strength under control (healthily) by voluntary surrendering. The motive is Christ.

But wait! Does 1 Peter 3:7 say that men can demand submission? Remember Peter first says **"husbands in the same way..."** or **"likewise husbands..."** implying a connection to the previous advice or command. They are to do the same as Peter instructed the women or with what Peter stated in **2:13ff.**

How are they to honor the women?
* By helping them and giving consideration to their gender.
* By responding to their needs and realizing they are co-heirs.
* Include them and show value, not dominate them by manliness.

Look at the repeated statement "since they, TOO, are ALSO HEIRS." The significance is they are together spiritually.

Conclusion: "Marriage was meant to serve namely our relationship with God."- Cranfield
* Peter is talking about duties, not rights!
* Men are instructed in what they should give, not claim!

God does not say, 'Wives, your husbands owe you honor because you are weaker...' nor 'Husbands your wives ought to be in your subjection.' He does not say marriage succeeds because of demands and obsessions to rights. The challenge is to love according to value not behavior.

If we hold on to previous beliefs:

~ The man is responsible for the home's spiritual condition (and God help the home if he is disobedient or not a believer). I know of an American family who believed that the negative results in their home were a result of there not being a functioning "priest" or "head!" Who are priests? Peter says all believers (*1 Peter 2:5, 9*). My Dutchie friend Ingrid Mazzola said, "It is about loving and learning. That is the best way to describe [my] marriage." Whether it is relationships in marriage or within the church, this is the heart we ought to have. I remember someone saying that family is meant to be an extension and expression of God's love to this world. How true. How does that happen?

Yet, **the devil can work** through many situations, especially when we are uninformed. BUT scripture is INCLUSIVE of women; it teaches about our personal accountability of sin and relationship with God (so we cannot blame it on our parents or anyone else). Ephesians offers about 44 promises of who we are in Jesus, and 57 promises of Who Jesus is and what He has done for us. The first three chapters of Ephesians reveal this clearly!

The Responsibility?

* Release one another
* Be supportive of one another
* Be builders, not breakers
* Submit to one another for the sake of Jesus, His word, and trust in one another

Free Way Ends

You know, it is much like two signs I saw while in Australia: **"Form One Lane - Freeway Ends."** That is Christianity in a nutshell, and the key to lasting relationships. True Christianity is motivated by love, not for gaining control and forcing ourselves on each other. The world often just shakes its head declaring (often truthfully) that Christians are hypocrites. They lord over each other, control, manipulate, prefer themselves, keep each other 'in their place,' and more. What an indictment on the Church.

1 Corinthians, Chapters 11-14

In Chapter 14:33b-36, Paul addresses the Corinthian church concerning women. What I missed for years was Paul's tone of voice and the cultural and societal atmosphere? Paul was emphatically implying something in **verse 36**. The RSV Bible has exclamation points behind his statements; NSRV has question marks. So what did he mean when he wrote, "As in all the churches of the saints, women should be silent in the churches. For they are not permitted to speak, but should be subordinate, as the law also says. If there is anything they desire to know, let them ask their husbands at home. For it is shameful for a woman to speak in church. Or did the word of God originate with you? Or are you the only ones it has reached?"

Look at the questions or statements again. Is he not addressing the Corinthians' problematic lifestyle? The context of the letter is paramount. I know this to be true by what is spoken in the next paragraph and the three preceding chapters teaching Corinthian Christians how to function in the Spirit. Not to mention, they are having evident sexuality and gender issues. Most of all, Paul permits women to prophesy in **11:5**! Is Paul contradicting himself? No, but many miss what he is communicating to the original audience. **1 Corinthians 7:4** is the one and only place where authority is used regarding relationships, and it is in reference to the mutual giving of their bodies to one another in marriage. And throughout Chapter 11 there is no call for women to submit. Authority is used; however, he was describing her personal authority. Much of the context is referring to cultural conditions, i.e. **11:6, 13-16**. In **Chapter 11**, there is further talk of headship. Paul's order reads as:

Christ - husband - wife - God - Christ. It begins and ends with Christ. They were to recognize that Christ is the source of man, man is the source of woman, and God is the source of Christ (look at **v. 11-12**).

I have chosen not to go into detail regarding **1 Corinthians 11 and 14** but here are some initial thoughts to chew: Paul was probably stating what they believed and used it like a mirror to challenge them. If someone asked you those two questions: Did the word of God originate with you or are you the only ones it has reached, how would you feel? Are they positive questions? Or are they challenging you in what you believe? I think it is obvious because he allows women to prophesy in **Chapter 11**; therefore, he must have had another agenda in mind!

The more I process God's original and continual intent for women (from the Beginning to Jesus redeeming what had been lost, including women's value), it becomes more relevant to proclaim this message loudly on behalf of those who make up half of God's creation - women. Just take a look at how early reformers and religions denounced women in their ignorance of God's scriptures.

"Woman must neither begin nor complete anything without a man: where he is, there she must be, and bend before him as a master, whom she shall fear and to whom she shall be subject and obedient." - Martin Luther.

Are we any different than Islam or the pagan religions of Jesus' day? Even from the Jewish writings come heinous, unbiblical accusations.

"Out of respect for the congregation, a woman should not herself read in the law. It is a shame for a woman to let her voice be heard among men. The voice of a woman is filthy nakedness." - The Jewish Talmud

What will our response be? First, as men (if not already by now), we ought to lower our face to the floor and weep in repentance for what we have done in the name of God against women, our wives, sisters, mothers, relatives, and neighbors. As men, shall we raise the bar, make a stand, and further the cause of women's freedom that they might be lifted up, supported, mobilized, encouraged and enabled to run with their God-birthed destiny? If we want to really see God's Spirit move more powerfully across this planet, release your partner and the women who are created in God's image.

Dr. Yonggi Cho, pastor of the world's largest church, has had countless leaders wondering HOW IN THE WORLD his church could have become nearly 1,000,000 people, only to retreat in disappointment that one of three key factors has been his release of women! Dr. Cho has mentioned that out of 50,000 cell group leaders, 47,000 are women. Ladies and gentlemen of the church, the evidence speaks for itself.

It is pathetic and depressing to see and hear of highly underqualified men taking the place of highly qualified women in leadership roles strictly because of pride and cultural (church) baggage. Several leaders have been quite vocal to accuse Mercy Ships of functioning in rebellion or disobedience (400 aboard and hundreds elsewhere serving, including the thousands who support us) because we had a female CEO (Chief Executive Officer)! Actually, according to a 1990s United Nations survey, 80% of the world's manual labor is accomplished through WOMEN. Hmm... Whether these conditions are good or bad, it certainly says a lot about females.

Let us all practice walking more like Jesus. He destroyed the double standard placed upon the woman caught in adultery when He embraced her, forgave her, and, more importantly, proclaimed her equality and value to those who sneered and jeered at her and not the man involved (as if a woman can be caught in adultery alone!). Jesus saw to it that women were involved in His ministry, and He revealed major truths to women that were not revealed to men. Why? So that they could share that aspect of the Lord with us (men). Have you enjoyed truths that you have learned from women? Reach out, thank, and appreciate a woman today, and, in doing so, realize that God is pleased. From this point on, read the scriptures with new glasses, new insight, and expect the promise of new revelation!

CHAPTER ELEVEN

Further Pitfalls

Someone has been known to declare:

There are two points about leadership:

1. The leader is always right.

2. When the leader is wrong, refer back to number one.

Pitfalls of Leadership

Interesting, yet many consider this to be true (consciously or subconsciously). Like a mosquito that will not go away, when something goes wrong, all eyes glance at the leader. It is a sacrifice of leadership. You get to clean up the spills and lick the wounds. Do not try to be a leader in your own strength, but, in humility, support others with God's Word.

My favorite video game growing up was Pitfall! Maybe that was prophetic? Maybe pathetic? That was my life for years - one pitfall after another. The object of the game was to run through the jungle while swinging and running over crocodiles, scorpions, holes, fires and the like. It was exciting. It kept me on the edge of my seat, and it was a bummer when I fell! Fortunately, I think I am running, swinging, and avoiding more pitfalls as I journey on this long and still wonderful road of serving in ministry.

Once again Ron Smith, co-founder of the SBS, taught me valuable words of wisdom. One gem was his teaching on the big picture of the Book of Jeremiah: stand encouraged. Always summon from the depths of your being that it is God who calls you to ministry - not people, organizations, nobody. Whether or not elders and organizations affirm your call, God is still your lifeline. If darts come your way without warning, just like Jeremiah and Paul, you will stand secure. If He called you to ministry, He can keep you. If man does, the ground will drop from beneath you by surprise. I have grabbed on to this truth in times of discouragement and less enjoyable moments of leadership.

The Unexpected

After stepping off of the M/V Anastasis in the Port of East London, South Africa, I was walking along as the train, which seldom frequents the tracks throughout the port, passed. Suddenly, I was able to draw a parallel to what we just discussed. Many towns have train tracks that are no longer in use, and when you are accustomed to not having trains around, you drive over the old tracks constantly, never fearing an oncoming train. Your ministry may be exactly like that. Without warning - whammo! You had not been accustomed to experiencing the real thing.

One of the greatest wake up calls and surprises I ever had was in 1990 while driving in the wee hours. The traffic was as thick as smog (New York, of course), and I was still deliriously pushing through the new day when I heard **THUMP!** *'Oh, it is just someone's car door,'* I thought. Then to my horror, enough for one to jump out of their skin, I realized **I was sitting in the middle of the railroad tracks.** If I had stayed there, a lot more than my body would have been jumping through my skin! I put two and two together and ascertained that it was the railway arm and signal light that hit the roof of my car. In a split second I gunned it. Two or three seconds later, the train raced behind me! Take a guess how I approach railroad tracks now? I keep my eyes open for trains and signal lights!

Obstacles may catch you by surprise when you least expect it because you may have become numb or conditioned in certain areas of your life. The point? Watch out for those trains: ministry problems, challenges or doubts. You are okay if you have your head up, eyes peeled and know it is Him Who has called you. In addition, many of these upcoming examples and principles could be pertinent and beneficial not only for you but for the team in general.

The Graceless

A grace-less leader is walking down a lonely road without God's blessing and is not extending to others what he/she has been freely given...something they do not deserve. It is called unmerited favor, the receiving of something good that we did not earn. Another definition of grace is the God-given empowerment to live as we ought by His Spirit.

We are glad to have God's grace, yet people say, "Come on, you mean I am supposed to be merciful after what they did? I am expected to do this for them? I have to let this issue go?" If King David received it from God even though his transgressions rose to the level they did, then surely we can. His life encourages me. His heart was continually drawn to the Lord; he desired God more than anything.

Okay, face it. It is a lot easier and worthy (in our minds) to receive it, but to extend it to others, whoa... that is a chore and a half. So gritting out teeth with our backs against the wall, we try to gratefully lavish on others this blessing called grace. This gives others ample occasions to pour out grace upon you. After all, any leader in their right mind would hope for grace toward him or herself. But the truth is...you cannot give what do you do not have...do you believe you have God's grace? Oh, that is a whole other issue!

We are no longer who we once were. *"Jacob, the deceiver, becomes Israel, the deliverer. Simon, the pebble, becomes Peter, the rock. Saul, the persecutor, becomes Paul, the persecuted. Grace calls us and asks us to act in ways we otherwise would not; it beckons us to become better individuals; it asks us to think thoughts we are afraid to think; it charges us to become more than the flesh, which is ever before us and all around us."*
- Andrea Gancarz, Stop the Cycle Ministries

Initiative

Lack of initiative may be simply due to the inexperience of the team and/or individuals. They may be clueless as to what options and opportunities are available. Yet excuses are commonly found as sure as there are mountains in Switzerland and heat in Africa:

    ~ I do not know the language (#1 on the charts).
    ~ I do not feel well...
    ~ I did that yesterday...
    ~ It is not my responsibility...
    ~ Tomorrow I will do that...
    ~ Oh, I did not know it was for then and there...
    ~ It is too hot, too cold, too windy, too rainy...
    ~ There is not enough people; there is too many people...
    ~ It is too late, too early, too much, too far, too big,
      too long...

This is the song that never ends. And the larger the team, the more potential fires you will need to light and put out. Is your excitement building? You are probably saying at this point, "Can I get a refund on my plane ticket?" My friend Dave Savas, a carpenter who would make one of the best politicians, says, "Don't you worreh-bout it; evereh-thangs' gonna be ole-right!" Where God guides, He provides. In that case, He is with you as your Enabler.

What is the answer? A great benefit to any team (as I spoke of in Chapter 3) is having (team) vision, purpose, and a motivating leader, likewise having some of the skills previously written and the ones to come shortly on your tool belt. It may be as challenging as slaloming behind the speed boat of ministry with unseen waves, but hang in there! Though you might have to swallow some water, by His grace you can do all things.

Humble Servant Leadership

If one is not following Jesus' style of servant leadership, those involved might be experiencing hiccups and bumping along without a map through the treacherous gullies of day-to-day life.

An intriguing discovery, which may have caught your attention long before I, is that the further **Jesus progressed in ministry and leadership, the more He displayed humility and serving (John 13; Mark 10:45)**. Of course, He lived this way all the time; however, there is a gem that I believe He wills for us to see, and it is paramount to leadership.

The difference between Him and us? Very simple. The more popularity, stature, miracle services, speaking engagements, outreaches, recognition, pats on the back, persecutions, betrayals, and misunderstandings that Jesus received, the further Jesus exemplified humility and servant leadership. And us? We tend to pad the scale on the opposite side, thus the fall, the crash, the hardships, the frustrations, the deserts, the dismay, the disillusionments. But we say, "We have made it past that stuff. That is for them [followers] to do. I have arrived (whether we feel this way or not, our actions surely reveal it). I am right."

We become proud, independent (perhaps more so from God), over-confident, and above the team. Been there. Guilty. I sure am. Gosh, if we had a dollar for every one of those mistakes, we would be rich, huh? Then again, if some of us had the riches, more challenges would be waiting at our doorstep, like a faithful dog with a paper in his mouth called The Defeated Times. Ouch!

Assuring Another Will Not Have Potential and Discouraging Potential Leaders

All *of us are leaders,* although not all are in "formal" leadership. But when we watch a leader in action, a conscious or sub-conscious thought(s) travels through our mind at space shuttle speed. And what is that? Glad you asked. Simply this:

Do I want to be like him/her? Do I desire to follow in their footsteps? Do I want to react that way? Is this the best way to work through this situation?

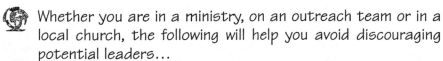

This chapter applies to us all, as we all set an example for someone, but it will be especially useful for those who are "called" leaders. Remember, we have NO idea what extent our influence may have on others and who else is a potential leader. So let us be ever so careful to not step in the way of what God desires and CAN do in those behind us, around us and under us. Followers are just as important as leaders...and the wheel goes around and around...

Whether you are in a ministry, on an outreach team or in a local church, the following will help you avoid discouraging potential leaders...

Be willing to release people. Do not hold them back. Pray for them to surpass you. Work yourself out of a job, so to speak.

Do not assume that their innovative ideas are irrelevant, or that they have no right to make such a suggestion and discourage them from doing so again.

Do not assume that their new ideas or dissatisfaction with the status quo are a form of independence or disobedience and force them to submit to what has already been decided without some discussion.

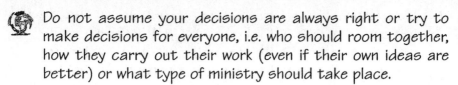 Do not assume your decisions are always right or try to make decisions for everyone, i.e. who should room together, how they carry out their work (even if their own ideas are better) or what type of ministry should take place.

Do not fill up their hours so that they do not have any free time or leave them so exhausted that they only have time to do laundry and sleep.

Try not to constantly refer them to others for all their questions about the mission, lecture material, and their ministry vision, especially if their small group leader (or other leaders) is not a visionary, does not have skill in discussing the lecture material, and/or is not a good communicator about the ministry or mission.

Do not discourage access to those with information that is valuable.

Do not discourage their participation through prayer and discussion about major decisions concerning outreaches, policies and new directions.

Never assume that God has brought everybody to your school, outreach or ministry to do spiritual surgery on them and discover you are looking for their weaknesses or for the moment when they will receive a "breakthrough." God may have just taken a person through a time of breaking or what is worse...they have only seen God as harsh, and God may want this to be a time of encouragement and support plus an opportunity for challenge and responsibility.

Take them seriously when they are struggling with rooming situations, work duties, or other related areas. Do not assume that God wants to use their tough situation to work character in their lives, hence becoming a self-appointed judge of what God wants to do in their lives.

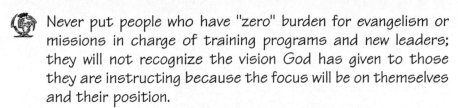 Never put people who have "zero" burden for evangelism or missions in charge of training programs and new leaders; they will not recognize the vision God has given to those they are instructing because the focus will be on themselves and their position.

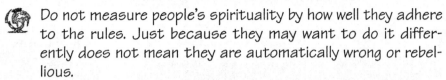 Do not measure people's spirituality by how well they adhere to the rules. Just because they may want to do it differently does not mean they are automatically wrong or rebellious.

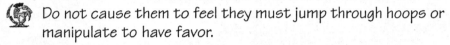 Do not cause them to feel they must jump through hoops or manipulate to have favor.

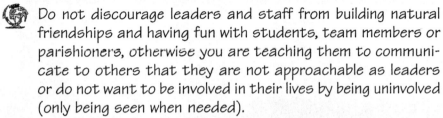 Do not discourage leaders and staff from building natural friendships and having fun with students, team members or parishioners, otherwise you are teaching them to communicate to others that they are not approachable as leaders or do not want to be involved in their lives by being uninvolved (only being seen when needed).

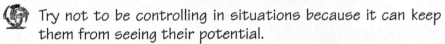 Try not to be controlling in situations because it can keep them from seeing their potential.

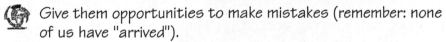 Give them opportunities to make mistakes (remember: none of us have "arrived").

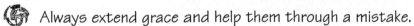 Always extend grace and help them through a mistake.

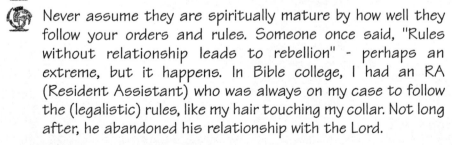 Never assume they are spiritually mature by how well they follow your orders and rules. Someone once said, "Rules without relationship leads to rebellion" - perhaps an extreme, but it happens. In Bible college, I had an RA (Resident Assistant) who was always on my case to follow the (legalistic) rules, like my hair touching my collar. Not long after, he abandoned his relationship with the Lord.

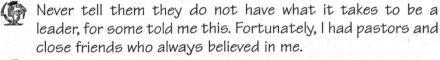 Never tell them they do not have what it takes to be a leader, for some told me this. Fortunately, I had pastors and close friends who always believed in me.

Support them in decisions, directions, etc. when appropriate.

Do not subscribe to the mentality that it is your way or the highway or that if you want something done right, you have to do it yourself.

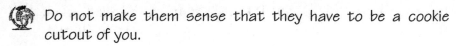 Do not make them sense that they have to be a cookie cutout of you.

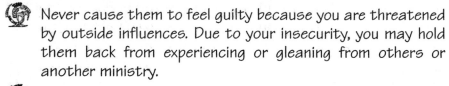 Never cause them to feel guilty because you are threatened by outside influences. Due to your insecurity, you may hold them back from experiencing or gleaning from others or another ministry.

Be led to give them responsibilities. Stop thinking you know better because they are inexperienced ("They have only been a Christian for two years - what could they know?!").

Do not cut them off when they do something incorrectly, like exercising a spiritual gift. The Corinthian church was abusing life in the Spirit or rather in the flesh, yet Paul never cut them off, never stopped them. He exhorted them in "just" the right way. Do not discourage them by going for their jugular vein and severing all life in the person. If you do, they will retreat into a corner, never wanting to step out again for the fear of rejection.

Contrary to popular belief, it is okay to express or let them see your faults. But, whatever you do, never cover up your mistakes or make poor excuses; this truly sets a bad example, and people are not foolish. They know you are not perfect anyway!

Do not be a taskmaster, making projects of higher importance than people and relationships.

Conveniently never have all the answers (sometimes you really do not) for this could intimidate them and breed insecurity.

Be a listener. Talk and interrupt less. Do not command more than you listen.

Attend to others' needs as best you can and do not deny your need for others.

Never show favoritism to a select few or pay attention only to those you favor, for whatever reason.

Show that you are open to being wrong, corrected or questioned.

Never cause them to suffer guilt if they do not pray, read or reach out to the lost enough - at least not as much as you yourself!

*** Remember: What are we producing?! ***

ere is **further advice** to help you avoid pitfalls, not only for you, but also for those alongside you in ministry and life. Some may seem repetitive, but they bear repeating:

 Depend on your Father and His Son Jesus *(John 14:10, 15:1-17)*.

Be willing to express emotion *(John 11:35...Jesus weeping)*.

Be willing to be wrong *(Romans 7:14-25; Psalm 51...Paul's* struggles and David's confession of his sin).

Be willing to admit when you do not know something or how to do it.

Be willing to ask or extend forgiveness.

Be willing to express what God is doing in your life (discern how much to reveal).

Make decisions with your team on how you want to handle potential relationships that may arise during the infant phase. At times, it could be a real distraction, especially if there is tension between the two, exclusivity, or a break-up. These can affect the team's momentum or strength. Sometimes relationships are great and something to support. Ponder priorities, timing, motives, etc. Be aware. For I know of a team who had some real problems in this area, yet some good came from it (this would include a relationship begun with a local). If you are one that strongly opposes any relationships, I would ask, "Are you living in reality?" Of course, this would not apply nearly as much with a 10-day team but for a group that are going to be spending months together. Turning off potential attractions or hormones is not necessarily healthy either. What I mentioned above (motives, timing, priorities, could it wait until the second month or fifth month) still applies to each individual situation. Include God and do not rely solely on formulas.

Accept help when needed.

Learn and exhibit self-control.

Delegate. The temptation is to do everything yourself so it will be done properly. One sign of a secure leader is he/she can delegate responsibilities to others. Have faith in your discernment of other people.

 Be open for advice and change.

 Protect your teammates if erroneous claims are made against them or anything hurtful and destructive is spoken upon them.

 Be real.

 Be a learner. You can and WILL learn from your team members.

 Check your motives.

 Take sufficient time for fun and learn to relax.

 Remember how you were once dragged from the pit.

 Avoid promises that you are not in a position to fulfill, as well as declaring, "We will be finished at 9pm for sure" then continue until 10pm.

 Do not squelch people's gifts. Paul guided the Corinthians through all of their mistakes by reminding them of who they were in Christ. He never hindered them; he simply encouraged them.

 Accept prayer from others. Many times, Christians are afraid of things "jumping" on to them, but do not let fear rule in your life as a leader. Yes, you are a moving target for the enemy, but greater is He who is in you, than he who is in the world. Trust your discernment and God-given power.

 When you need something, especially prayer, ask. It furthers humility.

 Be accountable. This helps us remain constant to our words and actions and keeps others, who are looking unto us, secure and confident.

 Be an encourager. How do you speak to people? What is your response (or reaction) when a task is completed? Do you focus first on the mistake(s) and then encourage? Make sure your encouragement is not flattery, but something true and real.

 Encourage those around you to think, find and see for themselves. They can find answers to questions, the Bible, life scenarios, and more. The Holy Spirit dwells within them, too. Explain how He has operated in your life until they are more sure-footed.

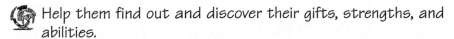 Help them find out and discover their gifts, strengths, and abilities.

Make sure you and your co-leader have (and are given) time away with Jesus, even though you get to see Jesus in the people everyday. There is nothing like your personal time with God.

Demonstrate your dependence on Jesus; He is the One that you trust.

Integrity: your word is your word. If not, what is it worth?

Be responsible, not passive. Look ahead as much as you can and anticipate.

An advantage to you and your teammates would be holding individual meetings to ask them:

> * What are your goals for this time?

> * What would you like to see Jesus do in you through this time?

> * How could we help and encourage you while you are here?

> * What are your expectations for this time?

Let them make mistakes. Know when to step in or wait.

DO NOT do, act, or say what you would not want for yourself or are not willing to do yourself.

Legalism kills life. It controls through insecurity. It takes people back to "the law." Legalism believes that God is only big enough to save...not sanctify. It will make you put extra rules on people due to your fear, thus squeezing the life out of them.

Decide not to control people and situations. This is a sure sign of a leader's insecurity.

Be decisive.

Always begin with trust and work from there. If you give a responsibility to someone, release them - no strings. Do not get in the way mid-stream and say, **"This way is more efficient or better."** They will stop growing if you keep stepping in and interrupting God's process. Only step in if it is harmful or going to cause a major problem. Give room for mistakes. If it is not your way, it does not always mean it is wrong.

Love the difficult and unlovable. I have been SO challenged with this and convicted of preferring those who I related better with or by their appearance. Not good.

Be willing to respond, correct and confront, but do so always in love. **"Out of all the ways you could respond (anger, silence), why not respond in love."** - Ron Smith

Do not gossip. Basically, do not talk about what you should not talk about to the one you should not talk to about it. Got it? - ha, ha.

Desire to please God, as you can never make everyone totally happy. Avoid being a man pleaser.

Do not take advantage of your position or abuse it.

Allow for others' ideas, vision, and creativity.

Expectations should equal experience. On this one particular team, I lectured a team member for something I "thought" was important, wondering why they did not follow through with what was expected of them. It was simply their lack of experience. They went to the city from the jungle for the weekend to see some friends. We got a note from them two days later, brought in by a local, stating they would not make it back for another day. Long story short, they did not anticipate the travel time, which to me was obvious. That is when I realized, **'Jon, how many teams have you led? You have been to 30+ countries, involved in missions, and leading for 10 years, blah, blah, blah. And she is 19. Maybe your expectations were too high?'** So try to set expectations accordingly and remember grace.

Learn to listen.

Beware of being too defensive and critical.

The Pre-Judging Dilemma is judging without the facts or without knowing what is truly in a person's heart. Not understanding words or actions can be hurtful. Do not assume. Anticipate the best. Judge them up. We jump the gun at times (I know I have). Horrifyingly enough, we actually see our weak points in others, and we cannot wait to "nail 'em." Why? Because it bugs us! It gives us an outlet. We get to pick it out of someone else while we pet our own weaknesses. Ugly!

 Do not tell a person, "You did this wrong," and walk away. Explain. Helping them to see "why" is as much or more important as what they did wrong. - my friend, Marta Siczek

 Beware of three major leadership pitfalls, particularly for males. My friend Ken Paige reminded me of this group of startling temptations, the 3Gs: Gold, Glory and Girls. Yes, it is fairly self-explanatory - lust of the eyes, the pride of life and lust of the flesh.

Remember, you had your first day skiing, first day ice skating, first bicycle ride, first swim so give others opportunities to take "first steps." Risk knowing when. I was given many chances, and I am where I am because people believed in me or at least showed it! God uses people to build up people.

Bottom Line

The message from the beginning: that you LOVE one another (*1 John 3:11*).

It is all encompassed within the beauty, power, magnitude, yet simplicity of the above words. As the dew within a desert, life with air, a poet with words, a map with a traveler, a computer with memory, and a jumper with a parachute, so is love to be with humans. That is it. What it was all meant to be from Beginning to End, Genesis to Revelation...LOVE.

"After all, He loves us to death."
- my friend, Brian Hogan

What to Do When We Think Our Leaders Could Be Wrong

What do you do when it seems that your leader or a person in an authoritative position is wrong either in attitude or actions? As we enter this section, a forewarning is necessary. I need to weigh out the situation. Am I to approach the person(s) in the apparent wrong? If so, it should be with sensitivity, love, and the right motives. Search your heart because the tendency is to be like a child - if I do not get what I want, then I will whine and pout. After pouting, I may find myself whining to other people, thus possible backbiting and slandering may begin leaking out.

I thought of beginning the SFC Church (Shoppers for Christ), as there are so many who continue attending a church until they do not like what they get, or if they are confronted with something that offends them, they begin shopping for another church. Or how about the CFC Church (Complainers for Christ) or KFC Church (Kentucky Fried Christians)? Hmm…

The problem is that they carry their diseases with them wherever they go. Use precaution when problems arise with leaders. It does not necessarily mean you should leave so quickly. Reconciliation, restoration and resolve should be your primary thoughts and actions. There are different ways of looking into a leader's potential wrongs. One question to ask is whether it has it been a personal wrong or public a wrong.

Personal Wrongs

When there are personal wrongs with a leader, the process of resolving should be the same as with the general populace. You may need to confront certain issues or bring them to the attention of other leaders that you or the leader in question is connected with, should it be a concern of well being for you or others.

Leaders have greater influence, thus greater ability to harm through testimony or example to the watching world as well as within the Body of Christ. An example could be repeated offenses toward or against you. Once again, I must reemphasize the need to be careful with judging leaders and whom you speak to about the offense.

Remember **David and Saul?** Even though Saul threatened David's life numerous times, David was angered when others attempted to bring Saul harm (1 Samuel 26). David respected God's choice of leadership and would not harm a man that the Lord had anointed. Take the gentle road [prayerfully] in confronting and correcting leaders, trusting the Lord and not taking things into your own hands, and the Lord will bless and vindicate you. Let both good and bad situations be opportunities to develop your Christian living.

Public Wrongs

While in a **West African country** holding leadership training classes, a pastor asked me a question. Here is the scenario: A leader came into this pastor's church one day with two chickens in his pockets. He was wearing the traditional garb, a big, flowing robe. The visiting speaker was preaching on Moses, and, as destiny would have it, the pastor with the chickens was also named Moses! Well, during the message, the speaker suddenly says, "Moses, what is it that in your hands?" With a puzzled countenance, the pastor slowly takes out his two, smuggled chickens. It was a sovereign act of mercy on God's part to expose what the pastor had been doing. Those of you who are African (or experienced within Africa) know where I am going with this. The pastor had intended to go to the Juju priest after the service!

The pastor, who mentioned this scenario, asked what was the right way to confront the other leader. First, I asked him what he thought (always wise to do when you do not know what to say yourself...ha, ha). He said his church elders would talk to him alone to work out the situation without letting the congregation know, as it could divide the church and cause great turmoil.

My response was somewhat different. First, I suggested he ask him, without a judgmental tone, why he was carrying those chickens (into the service). Next, according to his reaction or response, would be to confront him on his answer, talk through why he thought it was no issue to be go to a Juju priest, since he is a Christian [leader], and give him opportunity to repent. If he could not see the error in being a pastor and also worshipping false gods, then a period of time should be determined for him to be released from his leadership responsibilities. But I would also take it one step further by giving him the option to stand before the church and repent, with another standing with him for support. Or I would bring it before the church myself. My feeling is that it was a public event, making it a public wrong, and it should be addressed publicly. We owe it to the people who trust us as leaders with their lives, their spiritual well-being and more.

I believe that the accused leader would gain more respect and honor from people through his act of humility. After all, how many of us sit in our churches hiding our own shortcomings. Furthermore, how much more will God make a way for restoration and transformation. But if we keep it hidden and refuse an open door for change, your authority will be taken...if not now...eventually. I feel we all have a responsibility to care for one another - leader or follower. Confronting in love and humility means you have sincere compassion.

Fear and reasoning can stop you from approaching them. The prophet Nathan confronted King David (2 Samuel 12); Jonah threw words as sharp as swords toward the leaders and the city of Nineveh, yet, beforehand, he ran quickly in the opposite direction, thus being swallowed up! I am sure joy was not in his diet that day. But we learn not to succumb to the lying thoughts of "Who am I to speak to _____?!" And furthermore, "What about my skin? I will get into trouble."

Confide in the Lord, and He will carry your words. Simply do your part and leave the rest up to the Leader. That is the beauty of trusting the Lord. As you obey your call to declare, speak, and relay, you can wash your hands of the matter because the rest is up to Him. You are not the answer, although part of what God desires to accomplish could be and possibly is through you. Yeah, I know...exciting! The below thoughts are taken from a handout in DTS - author unknown

Be cautious in how you approach the leader, always bearing in mind that they, too, are a child of God and do make mistakes. How you walk into and address the situation will make the difference between a positive or a negative experience. The following guidelines may be helpful:

- Make sure the facts are correct. Do not judge a person wrongly and/or accept a charge against a person on the word of just one other person (Proverbs 18:17; Deuteronomy 13:12-15; 1 Timothy 5:19). It is very important to hear all sides of a conflict before passing a judgment.

- Pray for the leader and make sure you do not have a critical spirit or a root of bitterness in your heart toward them. If you have been hurt or disappointed, make sure that you keep forgiving until your heart is free of hurt.

- Allow love to have its perfect work since sincere love covers a multitude of sins (1 Peter 4:8). In some situations, it is possible to lose your objectivity when you accidentally take on the hurts of others.

- What are your motives? Why do you want to bring this wrong into the open? Make sure you have a genuine motive of care and concern and not malicious intent.

- If you counsel with people who have been hurt by an authority figure, and you take on their pain, you can take sides in the conflict and lose an opportunity to both offer sound Biblical counsel to one who is hurt (to forgive and pray for the ones who hurt them) and to be a minister of reconciliation in healing the broken relationship.

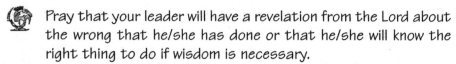 Pray that your leader will have a revelation from the Lord about the wrong that he/she has done or that he/she will know the right thing to do if wisdom is necessary.

If the leader has done something wrong, and there is no change, seek God in humility about speaking to them.

If it is an obvious wrong (such as stealing, being involved in sexual sin, being dishonest), and you have gone to them and they do not repent, then go to another godly person and ask them to go with you to talk to the person again (*Matthew 18:15-18; Luke 17:4*).

If your leader does not respond or show repentance after you have approached them in humility, consider whether the matter is one of serious disobedience to obvious moral principles before you go to others in the Body of Christ. Criticism and false gossip could erupt from the situation.

The Bible speaks strongly about unity and forgiveness in the Body of Christ. It is the key to keeping and building relationships. Confronting others because you disagree with a decision could land you in a worse position. Always consult the Holy Spirit. The scriptures warn about taking matters into our own hands and trying to correct them. Even David would not attack Saul, in spite of his great sin, because God had put Saul in that position of leadership. David trusted God to rectify the situation (*1 Samuel 24:6; Numbers 14; Ephesians 4:26, 29-32*).

If the leader is authoritarian, immature or unwise, you have one of two options: you can stay under their authority and continue to pray for them after you have expressed your concern or you can leave the group. Do not stay and become a source of division.

If you do stay, have faith that God is going to bring change to the situation and that He wants you there as a blessing to others and for your personal growth. God will vindicate you if you keep your heart right and continue to pray and believe the Lord. If the matter is of moral impurity or the compromise of orthodox doctrines (the inspiration of scriptures, Christ's divinity, Jesus' death and resurrection, His atonement on the cross) then, after bringing due notice to the person, you should leave the group. To stay where there is moral impurity or doctrinal heresy could lead to compromise in your own life, i.e. going into a cult.

 If you are not sure what to do, seek the counsel of godly people outside the group. Go to a mature pastor or leader in another organization. Every believer has that right.

Nothing is easy about these matters, and there are many fine lines, but this should guide you if you find yourself in the challenge. Exposing sin is necessary, in the right way, time and place and to the right people.

The reality is some will not see that they are wrong.

CHAPTER TWELVE

Team or Ministry Debriefing

Whew, We Made It...Now What?

The pressure has definitely surpassed all other experiences in your life, right? There is always an issue with something, like the bank (is there money?), the travel agents, ministry and ministry contacts, the team, ideas that work, messages, immunizations, buying this and that, phone lines, e-mail not zooming through space and time correctly or quickly...this list is endless sometimes. Oh, but for the grace of God!

And you might think to yourself: 'God definitely injected suffi-cient grace when and where we needed it. What the Lord showed us, did through us, poured down on us, helped us get through, made us invisible, got us off that edge, brought the one with cancer to Himself, kept us together through thick and thin, allowed us to be honored guests at a wedding, gave us a word when we needed it, healed a little baby, touched a girl's leg, revealed Himself to a Muslim in a dream, brought vision to that church, encouraged

those believers, protect-ed us through troubles with authorities, hid the Bibles we had, moved in spite of our mistakes, brought hope to the hopeless, allowed us to be vessels for the refugees, gave us favor as the first foreigners to go there and the first Christians to speak in that school, opened doors to proclaim Him for the first time to this per-son, that village, on and on... He brought us through moments of frustration and conflicts within and without, to be channels of the ONE thing that cuts through anything and brings life and change...HIS LOVE. WOW! Whew! Wonderful!'

But What Now?

It is important to reflect upon your time as a team in possibly a group setting; a leader should always gather feedback and encourage the team members onward. Those of you who are following have responsibility as well; you are part of the body of life. You are a valuable asset, able to see into situations and to give significant input as well as others.

Each of you has a tremendous opportunity to bring your team, friends, leaders, and followers words of encouragement, exhortation, healing, restoration, and closure. The danger is leaving it solely to others. Seize the moment. You may not have another time, moment or season. Be one that causes this time to be uplifting and a place of safety. The challenge is to be part of the solution, not part of the problem. Be a listener as well. Do not remain silent because of fear or sit on the fence and be only an observer.

Here are some brainstorming concepts, questions and ideas for leaders and followers that may save you from having to storm your brain since you all may be a little "spent." With the possibility of a lot happening upstairs in your minds, this will help you glide through with a bit less stress.

 Take time to thank God.

 Worship Him, regardless of what has happened or not and as difficult as it may be. He is always worthy, and there are always blessings from Him and ways to thank Him. There is never a moment in which God is not good.

 How has your relationship with Jesus changed/increased while here? There?

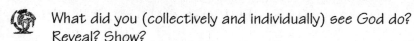 What did you (collectively and individually) see God do? Reveal? Show?

What has God worked out IN you? Worked out OF you?

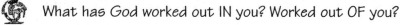 How can you see God utilizing you (add a story of someone you touched).

What area(s) in your life has been transformed into Jesus' image?

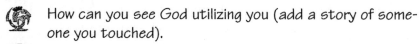 Where have you gained victory? Overcome a weakness?

What strategy did the team have and employ?
Was it successful? How?

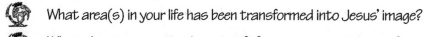 Is there anything the team could do differently next time?

Is there anything you would do differently (personally)?

Any regrets?

Highlights?

Disappointments?

Where did we see Jesus touch and transform people's lives?

How did you witness God's faithfulness?

What advice could be helpful for anyone else returning to the country where you were, anyone stepping into leadership or going there with another team?

Culturally speaking, what have you learned?

Working as part of the team is vitally important. Give one example of how you believe you contributed to the team running smoothly.

Give one example of how you had to change and adjust to be a better team member? To aid in the unity of the team?

What is your favorite/worst memory?

Describe your experience, expectations, unmet desires, or fulfillment etc. Or ask each other to describe in one word what they feel.

Remember, never will all of you (potentially) be together again. Choose to leave "regret free." Be clean and unburdened.

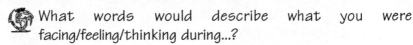 What words would describe what you were facing/feeling/thinking during...?

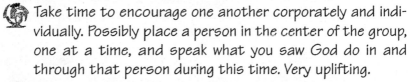 Take time to encourage one another corporately and individually. Possibly place a person in the center of the group, one at a time, and speak what you saw God do in and through that person during this time. Very uplifting.

Listen to each other. Pray for each other.

Commit to pray for someone after you leave the team? A teammate? Someone from the city? The village?

Talk about the positive and negative aspects of criticism.

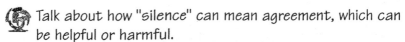 You may need to address the suffering of the righteous *(1 Peter)*. For example, what if you were on a team, like one of mine, where there was individual or team suffering because of being arrested for helping refugees? What if one in your ministry or the country's ministry had a tragic or unjust circumstance occur? This is significant as there may be several unspoken or unanswered questions within your ministry or outreach team. 1 Peter is all about the reality of suffering, yet the challenge to do right and trust God. Why? Because we are in a 'win-win' situation with God. There are some who have the theology that we are to be blessed, and if we suffer something is wrong. Well, how much did Paul suffer?! What would that make him? What he not blessed? So it is good to talk about a balance.

Talk about how "silence" can mean agreement, which can be helpful or harmful.

Meet one-on-one with each team member.

Talk about the ill effects of boasting and exaggerating what really happened.

Think beforehand and come ready to express your thanks and appreciation for what you saw in each person.

Forgiveness

Honesty and integrity are crucial. Be keepers of your word. This is what your team will remember about you. What they have received and proceed to impart could be healing, refreshing, and life-giving or cancerous, dividing and murderous to those with whom they live and interact.

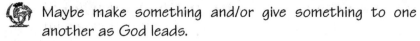 Maybe make something and/or give something to one another as God leads.

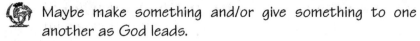 They need to know this is just one part of the journey; God is not finished with them.

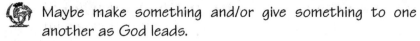 Openness and vulnerability (within boundaries) is what liberates and helps others get free.

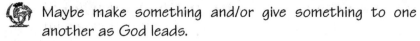 They could help compose "Helpful Hints for Future Teams."

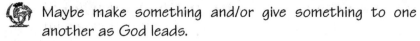 Encourage time with one another.

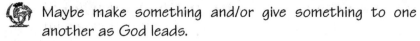 Be careful not to spend too much time on the negative.

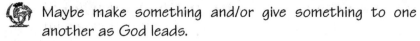 What has this time been worth to you (a heavenly perspective)?

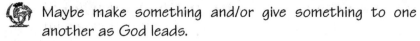 Reflect upon the team's expectations at the beginning and the differences/similarities now.

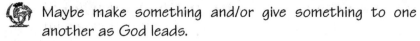 Write on big paper for all to see: What God Has Done, Desires, etc... Visuals are helpful to see the big picture. Some can always see what we have not seen ourselves. When fighting in the trenches, each view is limited; everyone has their own perspective.

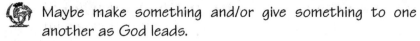 Read from the team journal (assuming one is kept and should be). Read the team's desires. Were they met? Which were or were not?

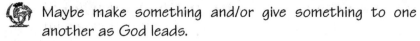 What did it feel like in the airport when you were first together? The trip? First impressions on where you were going to live? How did you find the culture? The people? The language? Your roommate(s)? What about the rats? The food? What were you feeling when you bid farewell to the people? The village? The town? The country? How was it ministering together? On your own?

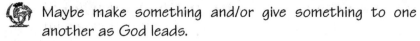 How can you be better prepared next time?

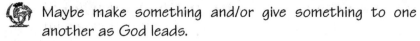 Everyone should write down any disappointments they may have had or still have, then gather the papers together and burn them (or individually burn them). Let it symbolize a release to God, choosing to trust in Him

despite what did or did not transpire. Decide not to let any matter or person have a hold on you and let the Lord shoulder your burden.

 How do you feel about leaving the team? What are your future expectations?

 There will always be some who see only the negative, critical aspects of anything. For their sake, focus on whether Jesus' cup is half full or half empty. They may say things like, "It was a bad trip." "Where was God." "I cannot believe this happened."

 Discuss discipleship, i.e. picking up an overturned bottle in the house. The simple things in life are unfortunately overlooked too often. We tend to focus and sway over what we consider the significant stuff in life, like not lying, showing up for a meeting, stepping out to preach, not talking about others, and more.

 According to YOUR outreach or ministry, there may be specific questions or doubts, so be prepared. Hopefully, these occurrences worked themselves out before the trip's end.

 Let everyone know what they say is protected within the group and is valuable.

 Remember: it is okay not to know an answer. Too many Christians place undue pressure and hurtful expectations upon one another to know all the answers, causing some to make it appear as though they do. Express your doubts, struggles and questions. It is obvious but missed at times so be real.

 If you had difficulties with a country's authorities, contacts, people, corruption and the like, you might want to discuss this before you embark on another outing.

 If the Israelites could forget about one of the greatest miracles in humankind's history, namely the Red Sea, then it is possible that we can forget Red Sea-type experiences that God has done for us. No one is infallible. You may see more of God's hand throughout your experience with the team, so it may be good to pour out what YOUR eyes have seen (after you have given them a chance to share). [An encouragement for critical types.]

 People do not know your past and what you have been through before, and even after, you came to know the Lord. And currently, people still have no idea what you have been thinking, praying and sorting through during their time knowing you. As a result, they have neglected to value you as a leader like they should. ***"You see me as I am, but God knows where I have been"***.

 It is a good idea to raise this up in humility and gentleness. Often we are unfairly judged because a) we only see what we want to; b) we do not consider what another may have experienced; c) we do not ask them what they meant by such and such; d) we see/saw an action and immediately attack their character; e) we assume why they said this or did not do that, like why they did not help in ministry that night...how lazy...blah, blah, blah. Take into consideration that the other might have worked all night or had someone become sick, die...or other extenuating circumstances.

 Often others do not consider the leadership experience: all the hours of prayer, work, effort, sacrifice, studying, and further prep. They are quick to look at a speck on the table instead of the beautiful arrangement of food, the shining cutlery, the candles, the décor, etc. People are unfortunately prone to be critical and negative about small issues, turning them into giants.

 Choose to "rehearse" or "release" your struggles. Remind them that they are overcomers!

 Have communion.

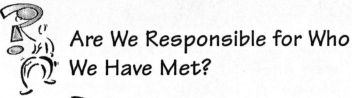

Are We Responsible for Who We Have Met?

Do **we have** a responsibility as we leave people or situations, maybe feeling, *"Well, we did what we could,"* or *"Whew! They are there, and I am here."* There are strong debates. Some believe that unless we stay connected, they will die spiritually. Others declare, *"God is big enough to keep them. After all, Jesus called and kept walking."* Is follow up really Biblical? Did Paul always stay where he evangelized?

You **need to decide.** I have tried when possible to follow up, send letters, return, and pray for the Lord to send laborers into their surroundings. I think each of us should seek the Lord in regard to this rightfully challenging area. Lord, give us courage and the capacity to hear and recognize Your direction. One way I have responded is by continuing to send help, long after I have gone, to those who are genuine, truly in need, and trustworthy with what I have given them, like the Kingsley family and their daughter, Rebecca, who at the time of this writing was suffering within Refugee Camp confines. I am continually praying for the appropriate action. Perhaps there is no one, in particular, on your heart. That is okay, but leave your heart open. No matter what, always ask Jesus what you should do. Do not regress back to certain belief systems by default.

I trust you will do well. Trust in His directives. Move as He moves. Wait when He asks you to wait. Speak out what you sense He is longing to say. One step of obedience is worth years of study. Risk is worth it. Yes, I still struggle with this as well...do not think you are alone! Hopefully, you will be left with vigor and strength to hear Him whisper, **"Well done, good and faithful servant."**

The Grand Finale

"**If you are not living on the edge, you are taking up too much space.**" I suppose this has been your life to some degree! You have given up much. You have walked the extra mile...or has it been two? The hours drift on before sleep overtakes you and before the roosters awake you to yet another day!

You may be in the ministry, on a team or attending a church, and you have questioned why your leader(s) or followers did this or that, but, after reading this book, I trust you will say, "*I have learned to submit in what they have asked of me, and I am looking at the bigger picture. I have gained an initiative to approach them when I have a need or a concern about their character. I have grown to appreciate what my leader(s) and fellow followers have had to endure. In addition, I have come to a place where I can see the blessing in supporting my leaders with my time, effort, and prayers. I am aware of their needs and the needs of* others more than my own now. God has shown me, through them, how to be more of a team player and how to set an example, even when things are not going my way. I now have a better view of how to function in the Body of Christ."

Remember, especially if in a leadership capacity: you are not "spending" yourself for yourself. Instead you are expending yourself on the behalf of others. Because of what the Lord has seen you do in secret (in the "after hours" where others cannot see or feel the weight of your responsibilities), He will reward you and take care of you. Besides, you are not home yet, as Eric Dennie professes, **"We are all homesick for Eden."** Until then, be faithful and live worthy of respect and honor. While you are here, and with great opportunity ahead of you, ask God to "bring it on" as Jon, my former teammate, poignantly stated with passion.

Can leadership be perfect? Well, we have yet to perfect it. Not much in this life is perfect (in the human sense). I ponder how many times I have tripped, choked on food, spilled liquid on my shirt, bit my cheek, and more. I have been (and you) walking, eating, drinking and breathing for years, and I still have not perfected it! Yeesh! Intriguing, huh? But that is okay. Just keep on trucking, hopefully with less choking, tripping and the like!

There is a huge possibility that certain contents of this book rattled your cage…good. Again, as my Pastor Dennis Bambino has always said, **"Sometimes you need a good negative to make a good positive."** That is how pictures are made, you know. I pray my writings will forever leave a permanent picture, a Godly impression, on your hearts and minds.

My desire is to live the way Jesus died. He died forgiving. He died obeying. He died believing. He died loving. It looks like we are leagues ahead, thanks to our Lord and Savior. Perhaps this will give us impetus to carry on with His message. May you pass on the great fruits of understanding, humility, truth, compassion, reality, love, and experience, enabling multitudes to plow through the Millennium. You are part of the solution rather than part of the problem, bringing and leading more of the lost into God's Kingdom. For others, witnessing the life you live is like catching a glimpse of Heaven. Is it worth it? You bet!

God's Best to You...

Because of him,
Jon Syrbe

About the Author

Jon Syrbe has been following Jesus since 1987. Through what he endured and poor choices he made over 19 years, Jon has developed a heart and passion for walking alongside youth (in the day-to-day battles and struggles in which they find themselves) as a Youth Director in New York, USA. In 1990, Colin Fullilove, founder of People for Missions (PFM) came to Christ for the Nations as a keynote speaker. It was the beginning of the end of ordinary life for Jon! Though he had lost his job the very day he registered for CFNI, Jon was determined that God was leading him to step out on new waters of faith. Soon after, he met a man named Bert who told his son, "Justin, go get my checkbook...we're sending Jon to Mexico!" Once Jon placed his eyes back in their sockets and reeled up his jaw from the floor, he has from then covered over 40 countries in 14 years and never ceased to live in astonishment at God's provision - in more ways than one.

Part of Jon died in Central America, yet new life emerged, and he was never to be the same. Through his pastors Randy and Leslie Paige, Dennis and Jackie Bambino, the Fulliloves, and Mercy Ships, he accredits much in the way of confidence, experience and accomplishment from their love, wisdom, support and continual belief in him.

From North America to Central America, South America to Africa, Europe to Russia, and India to Australia...among the asphalt jungles to the remote jungles, he has led teams, taught the Bible, ministered in prisons, helicoptered in the Jesus Film, helped begin churches, led and trained drama evangelism teams, worked with Discipleship Training Schools of Youth with A Mission (YWAM) aboard the Mercy Ship M/V Anastasis, and more.

He counts it a privilege to have helped save the lives of refugees, hold children in cancer hospitals and orphans, be held at gunpoint, be threatened, experience teetering on the edge of cliffs and especially to have expressed who Jesus is - the Pinnacle of Life, the Only Life Giver - and express life with God through the pages of scripture.

Jon continues in his 15th year in missions as a traveling teacher globally, having begun BridgeStones International in 2002 with the passion of restoring value to life.

ENDORSEMENTS

"Jon Syrbe is the living, breathing representation of II Corinthians 5:17-"If anyone is in Christ, he is a new creation..." Jon is taking the living Jesus all over the world to connect with people who have never seen a real Christian or heard the life-changing message of Jesus Christ. This book contains the real life lessons learned through suffering and joy in the farthest corners of this world. Jon keeps it simple and clear so everyone can know and love Jesus. Enjoy each lesson and experience. Don't be surprised when you find yourself growing more deeply committed to the God Jon trusts with his whole life."

> **Jack Crabtree**
> **Director of Youth For Christ (YFC), NY - USA**

Where There Is No Leader, TAG - You're It! is a very practical, helpful and easy to read book on leadership, especially for short-term outreach leadership. It is full of real life illustrations and gives hope to the potential and practicing leader to 'go for it.'

> **Elisabeth Cochrane**
> **YWAM South and Central Asia Co-Director**

"Missionary, Teacher, Preacher, Friend of outcasts, Champion for the marginalized, Hero to thousands of children in developing nations, Servant of the poor...These are the phrases we hear from Guatemala, Mexico, Brazil, Africa, India, China...

Jon Syrbe heard the call of God on his life at age 19 and later enrolled in Christ for the Nations Bible School. Within months he was in Latin America and a few years later on the West Coast of Africa aboard the YWAM Mercy Ship M/V Anastasis. For the last 13 years, Jon has traveled the world as a full time Missionary. He has written a book not only for leaders of Mission Teams but for every believer with a heart for evangelism. His stories are real and from the heart. His photographs capture the urgent, crying needs of the two-thirds world. His experience is real.

As Jeremiah speaks of the fire of God burning within, Jon's heart for missions ignites a passion for reaching the lost with the great news of Jesus Christ!"

> **Pastor Randy Paige**
> **Christ Church United Methodist, NY - USA**

"Jon Syrbe has compiled a very useful handbook for inexperienced leaders who find themselves in non-formal settings. The material is humorously presented, designed to be practical rather than theory, and easily read. It will be an asset to many involved in short-term outreach. Every short-term local church mission's team should have at least one copy."

Don Stephens
Founder of Mercy Ships

Discovering an author who can convey their experiences and make them ours is like finding a needle in a haystack. *Where There Is No Leader - Tag! You're It!* is such a tour de force, which was uncovered in a New York haystack. While maintaining his whimsical sense of style, Jon Syrbe paints a written picture of human behavior worldwide and touches on relevant topics where each of us can improve our interpersonal relations. He calls us to live higher and not settle for mediocrity no matter what our line of work. Working on this book taught me about character, integrity, servant hood, the requirements for quality leadership, and the discernment to know if situations and people are right for my life. I have no doubt that this personal memorandum will be a huge success.

Elizabeth Foster
Editor-in-Chief
Powerful Publishing, LLC
New Orleans, LA - USA
powerful@airmail.net

APPENDIX

CHRISTIANS FOR BIBLICAL EQUALITY

The Bible teaches the full equality of men and women in creation and in redemption (Genesis 1:26-28; 2:23; 5:1-2; 1 Corinthians 11: 11-12; Galatians 3:13, 28; 5:1). God has revealed Himself in the totality of Scripture as the authoritative Word of God (Matthew 5:18; John 10:35; 2 Timothy 3:16; 2 Peter 1:20-21). We believe that Scripture is to be interpreted holistically and thematically. We also recognize the necessity of making a distinction between inspiration and interpretation: inspiration relates to the divine impulse and control whereby the whole canonical Scripture is the Word of God; inspiration relates to the human activity whereby we seek to apprehend revealed truth in harmony with the totality of Scripture and under the guidance of the Holy Spirit. To be truly biblical, Christians must continually examine their faith and practice under the searchlight of Scripture.

Biblical Truths

Creation

1. The Bible teaches that both man and woman were created in God's image, had a direct relationship with God, and jointly shared the responsibilities of bearing and rearing children and having dominion over the created order (Genesis 1:26-28).

2. The Bible teaches that woman and man were created for full and equal partnership. The word "helper" (ezer), used to designate woman in Genesis 2:18, refers to God in most instances of the Old Testament usage (e.g. I Samuel 7:12; Psalm 121:1-2). Consequently, the word conveys no implication whatsoever of female subordination or inferiority.

3. The Bible teaches that the forming of woman from man demonstrates the fundamental unity and equality of human beings

(Genesis 2:21-23). In Genesis 2:18 and 20, the word "suitable" (kenegdo) denotes equality and adequacy.

4. The Bible teaches that man and woman were co-participants in the Fall: Adam was no less culpable than Eve (Genesis 3:6; Romans 5:12; I Corinthians 15:21-22).

5. The Bible teaches that the rulership of Adam over Eve resulted from the Fall and was not a part of the original created order. Genesis 3:16 is a prediction of the Fall's effects rather than a prescription of God's ideal order.

Redemption

6. The Bible teaches that Jesus Christ came to redeem women as well as men. Through faith in Christ, we all become children of God, one in Christ, and heirs to the blessings of salvation without reference to racial, social, or gender distinction (John 1:12-13; Romans 8:14-17; 2 Corinthians 5:17; Galatians 3:26-28).

Community

7. The Bible teaches that at Pentecost the Holy Spirit descended upon men and women alike. Without distinction, the Holy Spirit dwells in women and men and sovereignly distributes gifts without preference as to gender (Acts 2:1-21; 1 Corinthians 12:7, 11; 14:31).

8. The Bible teaches that both women and men are called to develop their spiritual gifts and to use them as stewards of God's grace (I Peter 4:10-11). Both men and women are divinely gifted and empowered to minister to the whole Body of Christ under His authority (Acts 1:14; 18:26; 21:9; Romans 16:1-7; 12-13; 15; Philippians 4:2-3; Col 4:15; Mark 15:40-41; 16:1-7; Luke 8:1-3; John 20:17-18; compare also Old Testament examples: Judges 4:4-14; 5:7;2 Chronicles 34:22-28; Proverbs 31:30-31; Micah 6:4).

9. The Bible teaches that New Testament economy showed women as well as men exercising the prophetic, priestly and royal functions (Acts 2:17-18; 21:9; 1 Corinthians 11:5; 1 Peter 2:9-10; Revelations 1:6; 5:10). The few isolated texts that appear to restrict the full

redemptive freedom of women must not be interpreted simplistically and in contradiction to the rest of Scripture, but their interpretation must take into account their relation to the broader teaching of Scripture and their total context (1 Corinthians 11:2-16; 14:33-36; 1 Timothy 2:9-15).

10. The Bible defines the function of leadership as the empowerment of others for service rather than the exercise of power over them (Matthew 20:25-28; 23:8; Mark 10:42-45; John 13:13-17; Galatians 5:13; 1 Peter 5:2-3).

Family

11. The Bible teaches that husbands and wives are heirs together, and that they are bound together in a relationship of mutual submission and responsibility (1 Corinthians 7:3-5; Ephesians 5:21; 1 Peter 3:1-7; Genesis 21:12). The husband's function as "head" (kephale) is to be understood as self-giving love and service within this relationship of mutual submission (Ephesians 5:21-33; Colossians 3:19; 1 Peter 3:7).

12. The Bible teaches that both mothers and fathers are to exercise leadership in the nurture, training, discipline and teaching of their children (Exodus 20:12; Leviticus 19:3; Deuteronomy 6:6-9; 21:18-21; 27:16; Proverbs 1:8; 6:20; Ephesians 6:1-4; Colossians 3:20; 2 Timothy 1:5; Luke 2:51).

Application

Community

1. In the church, men and women's spiritual gifts should be recognized, developed and used in serving and teaching ministries at all levels of involvement: as small groups leaders, counselors, facilitators, administrators, ushers, communion servers, board members, and pastoral care, teaching, preaching, and worship.

In so doing, the church will honor God as the source of spiritual gifts and will fulfill God's mandate of stewardship. God's kingdom suffers when half of the church's members are excluded from positions of responsibility.

2. In the church, public recognition is to be given to both women and men who exercise ministries of service and leadership.

In so doing, the church will model the unity and harmony that should characterize the community of believers. In a world fractured by discrimination and segregation, the church will dissociate from the worldly or pagan devices designed to make women feel inferior for being female. It will prevent their departure from the church or their rejection of the Christian faith.

Family

3. In the Christian home, husband and wife are to defer to each other in seeking to fulfill each other's preferences, desires and aspirations. Neither spouse is to seek to dominate the other, but each is to act as a servant of the other, in humility considering the other as better than oneself. In case of decisional deadlock, they should seek resolution through biblical methods of conflict resolution rather than by one spouse imposing a decision upon the other.

In so doing, husband and wife will help the Christian home stand against improper use of power and authority by spouses and will protect the home from wife and child abuse that sometimes tragically follows hierarchical interpretation of the husband's headship.

4. In the Christian home, spouses are to learn to share the responsibilities of leadership on the bases of gifts, expertise, and availability with due regard for the partner most affected by the decision under consideration.

In so doing, spouses will learn to respect their competencies and their complementarity. This will prevent one spouse from becoming the perennial loser, often forced to practice ingratiating or deceitful manipulation to protect self-esteem. By establishing their marriage on a partnership basis, the couple will protect it from joining the tide of dead or broken marriages resulting from marriage inequalities.

5. In the Christian home, couples who share a lifestyle characterized by the freedom they find in Christ will do so without experiencing feelings of guilt or resorting to hypocrisy. They are freed to emerge from an unbiblical "traditionalism" and can rejoice in their mutual accountability in Christ.

In so doing, they will openly express their obedience to Scripture, will model an example for the other couples in quest of freedom in Christ, and will stand against patterns of domination and inequality sometimes imposed upon church and family.

We believe the biblical equality as reflected in this document is true Scripture. We stand united in our conviction that the Bible, in its totality, is the liberating Word that provides the most effective way for women and men to exercise the gifts distributed by the Holy Spirit and thus to serve God.

Copyright, 1989, Christians For Biblical Equality.
P.O. Box 7115, Saint Paul, MN 55107-0155.

Traditionalism
(Held by Christians)

A. The male (man) is the leader in the church and home due to God given qualities.

    1. In the church, men hold leadership positions.

    2. In the home (family), the husband (male) is the leader of the family. Men are urged to "take the lead" in the family.

        a. The husband (male) is the sole financial provider.

        b. The husband (male) is God's representative in the family.

            1. high priest

            2. covering

            3. chain of command

B. Men and women's differences are greater than their similarities. From creation, they've had God ordained roles that include more than reproductive and marital relationships. These roles are seen as morally obligating, morally correct, and one cannot deviate from these roles. There are strict guidelines.

    1. Man's role (male) - leadership in church and home - sole provider for family.

    2. Woman's role (female) - subordinate, support role, dependent - full time mother (women are to raise the children and if this is not done by them the social order will collapse).

C. Men and women are spiritually equal (both are saved), but equality is not functional or practical.

    1. man (male) leads, has authority

    2. woman (female) is subordinate

D. Biblical morality is upheld: against abortion and homosexuality.

E. States a need to separate "evil" from modern culture.

F. States that their position is Biblical, orthodox, holds a high view of Scripture (inerrancy).

    1. Sees the Bible as a blueprint for life-proof texts.

G. States that their position is God's ideal; it is the model and has been so since forever.

Evangelical Feminism

(Held by Christians)

A. Equality: men and women are equal. Gender does not limit or determine ministry opportunities. The gospel upholds full partnership.

    1. The Bible does not teach male authority.

    2. God is not male; He is spirit.

    3. Mutual submission Is modeled in marriage.

B. Male and females are different. This is not denied, but the emphasis is on their common humanity.

    1. The differences affect marital and reproductive relationships.

    2. Interdependence of the sexes according to 1 Corinthians Chapter 11 and verse 11 is especially upheld.

    3. Stereotyped slots, roles and rules are not upheld.

C. Spiritually but the equality goes beyond just one's worth. It is equality functionally and practically.

D. Morality is upheld against abortion and homosexuality.

E. Culture (all culture: past and present) needs to be evaluated in the light of Scripture.

F. Evangelical feminism states that their position is Biblical. They hold to inerrancy. They hold to principles of interpretation, not just proof texts. The clear is used to interpret the unclear passages, and historical background is taken into consideration, etc.

G. Equality (spiritually and functionally) is rooted in Genesis 1:26-28. They also trace their roots to the Christian reform movements that were a result of the 2nd Great Awakening.

Modern Secular Feminism

A. Men and women are equal and should have equal opportunities in vocational options.

    1. Angry in the 1960s because the view of men as primary and women as secondary still prevailed.

    2. From equal opportunities to quotas.

    3. "Victim" response.

    4. Self-fulfillment

    5. Radical individualism: the individual has the rights and these rights are absolute and cannot be constrained. Personal choice is god. Humanistic.

B. Men and women are different. Men will never change. Male traits such as: violence, aggression, abusiveness, and competitiveness are inferior, and the female traits of gentleness, cooperativeness and motherliness are superior. These vast differences will never be reconciled, and the newest thought in modern secular feminism is to create a female superior society. They do not want to be like men. Only women can relate to women and give a real sense of self.

C. Do not hold to Christian morals: pro-abortion and not against homosexuality.

D. Western civilization, which is based on patriarchy, must be abolished in its legal, social and cultural structures, which means the family, the church, and the educational structures must go.

E. Modern Secular Feminism is against the Bible because they say it upholds patriarchy and male authority over women. They are now moving into feminine goddess worship.

OLD TESTAMENT CONSIDERATIONS OF WOMEN:

Creation of man and woman: Genesis 1 and 2

Woman made in God's image: Genesis 1: 26-27.

Do not imagine God as either male or female: Deuteronomy 4: 16.

Feminine imagery for God: Deuteronomy 32:11, 18; Psalms 131:2-3; Isaiah 42:13-14; 49: 15; 66:9-13; Hosea 13:8.

"Man" means "humanity": Genesis 5:1-2.

The Fall: Genesis 3.

GREAT WOMEN LEADERS

Miriam, the prophet: Exodus 15:20; Micah 6:4; Exodus 2:1-10; 15:20-21; Numbers 12:1-15; 20:1; 26:59; I Chronicles 6:3.
(Financing the Exodus - Exodus 3:22; 11:2).
Deborah, the judge and prophet: Judges 4 and 5.
(Judges raised up by God: Judges 2:16; Nehemiah 9:27).
Hulda, the prophet: 2 Kings 22:8-23; 2 Chronicles 34:14-28.
(Her preaching triggered a great revival; the results are enumerated in 2 Kings 23:4-27; 2 Chronicles 34:29-35:19).
Other women in ministry: Exodus 33:7-9; 38:8; I Samuel 12:22; I Chronicles 25:5-7; Psalms 68:25-26; Nehemiah 7:67.
Female Prophets: Nehemiah 6:7,14; Isaiah 8:3; Joel 2:28-29.
Does God simply use women when men are not available? Esther 4:14; Matthew 3:9.

Wise Women:
Attendants to the mother of Sisera - Judges 5:29.
To reprove David: 2 Samuel 14:22.
Of Abel-beth-maacah: 2 Samuel 20:14-22.
Abigail: I Samuel 25:1-44; Proverbs 14:1; 19:14; 31:10-31.
Women as Construction Engineers: Nehemiah 3:12.

LESSONS TO BE LEARNED FROM SARAH
Abraham commanded to heed his wife's advice - Genesis 21:12 (Compare with I Peter 3: 1- 7).
Sarah's compliance with Abraham's wishes makes him less than "a blessing to all nations."
Genesis 12:10-20, esp. 17-19; 20:2-18. Note v. 18. (Cf. Genesis 26:6-11).

LESSONS FROM QUEEN ESTHER
Esther 1:16-22; 8:17; 9:11-12; 9:29,32.
Affirmations of wives and mothers: Leviticus 19:3; Deuteronomy 5:16; Proverbs 5:18- 19;12:4, 18:22; 19:14; Malachi 2:14-15.

Stories of Women's Rights

Genesis 38; Exodus 2:16-19; Joshua 17:3-6.

"The Lord giveth the Word: the women that publish the tidings are a great host." Psalm 68:11.

"Oh woman that bringest good tidings to Zion. Get thee up into the high mountain; O woman, that bringest good tidings to Jerusalem, lift it up. Be not afraid: say unto the cities of Judah, 'Behold your God.'" Isaiah 40:9.

Jesus, the Friend of Women

Women in the genealogy of Jesus -
Matthew 1:3, 5. Note Galatians 4:4.
Women in the birth narrative -
Elizabeth - Luke 1:5-7; 13-18, 24-25, 40-45, 57-61.
Anna, the prophet - Luke 2:36-38.
Mary, the mother of Jesus -
Matthew 1:18-25; 2:11-14; 12:46-50; Mark 3:31-15; Luke 1:26-56; 2:4-51; 8:19-21; John 2:1-12; 19:25-27; Acts 1:14.
Miracles involving women -
Matthew 9:18-26; Luke 4:38-39; 8:43-48; 13:10-17.
Jesus gives a lesson in assertiveness training -
 Matthew 15:21-28; Mark 7:24-30.
Jesus rejects the double standard -
John 8:3-11; Luke 7:36-50.
Concern for widows -
Mark 12:40-43; Luke 7:12-15; 18:3-5; 20:47; 21:3.
Women accepted as learners -
Luke 10:38-42; John 4; Luke 8:1-3.
Parables using women -
Matthew 13:33; Luke 13:20-21; 15:8-10; 18:1-8.
Women as spiritual examples -
Matthew 15:21-18; Mark 7:24-30;12:41-44; 14:3-10; Luke 7:36-50.
Jesus' Use of Women in Public Ministry -
John 4:28-39; Luke 8:43-48; Luke 8:1-3 (cf. Acts 1:13-14 and 22); (cf. Mark 3:14); John 11:27; Matthew 26: 6-13; Mark 14: 3-9 (cf. John 12:1-8).

His acknowledgement of the ministry of women -
Luke 4:25-26; John 4:34-39.
The sole voice raised in defense of Jesus at His trial -
Matthew 27:19.
Women as prepared witnesses -
Luke 1:1-4 (cf. I John 1:1-4); Luke 24:6-8; John 19:25; Matthew 27:55-56; Mark 15:40-41 (note progression in Luke 23:27-31, 49, 55-56).
Women at the burial -
Matthew 27:61; Mark 15:47; Luke 23:55-56.
Women proclaim their risen Lord -
Matthew 28:1-10, esp. 7-10; Mark 16:1-11, esp. 7-11; Luke 24:1-12, 22-24; John 20:11-18, esp. 17 (cf. John 8:17; 19:35; 21:24; 3 John 12; Acts 1:3; 2 Peter 1:16-19; Deuteronomy 19:15; Matthew 18:16; Mark 3:14).

BIBLICAL RECORDS OF WOMEN IN THE EARLY CHURCH

Participation in decision-making in the upper room -
Acts 1:13- 26.
Equal recipients of the Holy Spirit -
Acts 2:1-4,17-18.
Full recognition as hearers and bearers of the Gospel -
Acts 8:3; 9:1- 2; 22:4; - persecuted by Paul as subversive evangelists. converted to Christ - Acts 5:14; 8: 12.
A disciple engaged in social service -
Acts 9:36-43.
Women prophets -
Acts 2:17-18; 21:8-9; I Corinthians 11:5 (Cf. I Corinthians 14:3-4, 26, 31).
Women as leaders of house churches -
Acts 12:12;16:13-15,40; Colossians 4:15; I Corinthians 1:11; 16:19; Romans 16:3-5; 11 John.
Women teachers -
Acts 18:26; 2 Timothy 1:5; 1 Corinthians 14:26,31; Colossians 3:16; 2 Timothy 2:2; Titus 2:2 (kafodidaskafos = good teacher or teacher of good things).
Business women -
Acts 16:14; 18:2-3; Romans 16:1-2.
Women deacons -
Romans 16:1-2; I Timothy 3:11.

Office of bishop -
1 Timothy 3:1-7: note that Jewish men were permitted more than one wife, hence the restriction about the number of wives applies only to men.
Office of widow -
1 Timothy 5: 9-10.
Women elders -
Philippians 1: 1-5; I Timothy 5: 1-2; Titus 2:3-5 (hieroprepreis = worthy of the priesthood).
A women apostle -
Romans 16:7.
A woman overseer -
Romans 16:3-4.
The understanding of "prostates" occurs in Romans 12:8; 1 Timothy 3:4; 5:17; 1 Thessalonians 5:12. "Genesthai," used for ordination or appointment to office, is 1 Corinthians 1:30; Ephesians 3:7; Colossians 1:23, 25; Hebrews 5:5.
Paul's ministry to women -
Acts 16:12-40; 17:1-4, 10, 34.
Paul's ministry shared with women -
Acts 18:1-4; 18-28; I Corinthians 16:19; Romans 16:3-4; 2 Timothy 4:19 - a missionary associate: Philippians 4:2-3; Romans 16:3-4; fellow laborers (Cf. I Corinthians 16:16).
Shared labors in the Gospel -
Romans 16:1-16.
Paul in trouble with well-behaved upper class women -
Acts 13:14-50.
Paul given a new perspective on integrating gentiles into the church -
Acts 14:26; 15:29,36; 21:25.
Paul's principles of adaptation -
Romans 14:1;15:3; 1 Corinthians 8:1-13; 9:1-10; 10:23-33.
Paul well received by well-behaved upper class women -
Acts 16:1; 13-15; 17:4, 12; 18:1; 24:24; 25:13, 23; 26:30.

Information contained on pages 264-270 courtesy of YWAM SBS Montana.

Report for Refugee Work in _____ and _____.

January 27, _____

To the Minister of Interior,

It is our endeavor to write a brief report of our work in _____ and _____ from the time of _____ to _____, _____. We know that you are aware of the goodwill efforts, relief and development of _____. And we thank you for all of your assistance with our work.

As a part of _____, we have another program or arm if you will, that seeks to train and work on location in a given area of need within neighboring countries or within the country that the vessel is currently functioning out of , for example; in _____. The concentration of this team of 15 _____ was originally going to be within _____ for a period of eight weeks: _____ to _____, _____. However, due to the unfortunate circumstances and danger that _____ is facing, we have not been able to render our services there.

During the month of _____ while acquiring visas at the _____ Embassy, I was approached by a father, Komba _____ - a refugee from _____, who's eight-year-old daughter Rebecah was dying of an internal infection of some kind. I felt compelled to help him as I saw tears streaming down his face. Soon we were off to a local hospital. I spent several hours with them driving to several pharmacies to find syringes, anti-vomiting solutions, and other medications. In a few days time, she was showing much improvement. In the week following, I assisted a few other girls in a similar way.

In these weeks, there had been up to a suggested number of _____ refugees in the _____Embassy compound by evening. Our team, after becoming well acquainted with Mr. _____, the Head Chancellor and the Ambassador to _____, became more directly involved at the Embassy for nearly a week. We purchased enough food for feeding over four days while assisting and observing directly. In addition, we gave Health Teaching (Worms, Malaria, Diarrhea, and Scabies), helped some to receive treatment locally, listened to their recent afflictions and hardships that they endured, and played with the children.

Before long an estimated _____ plus were transport-ed to _____ Camp. This is in part how we came to understand and know of _____. I , _____, took a day trip to observe and meet with people we had gotten to know to see about the possibil-ity of continuing our efforts there, for we understand the gra-ciousness of the Government of _____ to open its borders for its unfortunate neighbors. We feel that extending help to the Refugees is indeed helping _____ and its people. We realize with a team of _____ it is on a smaller scale; however, it lessens some degree of the strain, brings comfort and meets immediate needs one-by-one. We are aiding the economy of the town of _____through the things we buy and transport, communications, our daily interaction with the local people, and help with any needs that arise through that interaction.

I met with the governing people within the Camp, _____, the president, and others. I asked who would be the specific author-ities that I should rightfully contact. They mentioned the Superfer and the Prefect, UNHCR and GTZ, when we come. I asked if there was anything else we ought to do. I regret the need to confess that perhaps we were not informed about the procedures commonly understood. It has certainly been our desire to follow the correct channels of authority. We met with the Superfer and UNHCR. We had not understood, until sometime later, that there was a Prefect whom we should have met. Upon working thru UNHCR (or attempt-ing to) and _____ (having received a letter of partnership with them), and the _____church, and having gone to the Superfer, we had the understanding that we were in accordance with local authorities. And furthermore having been given Visas and Protocol of invitation by the _____ Government, we had understanding of the freedom to work within the nation. We are aware of the differ-ence of working within the Camps and now know it is best to have written documentation for this specifically. However, when residing in the town of _____ and working locally outside _____ Camp, there seemed to be confusion to permission granted or withheld.

We have had several meetings with UNHCR that proved to be difficult in the pursuit of bringing aid in various forms. We had met on _____morning, _____, _____, having arrived at

_____ Camp the night before. The 3rd in command met with us and assured us that everything was fine and to come back for a meeting on Monday. We resided in the Camp until Monday afternoon, followed by our meeting, when requested to leave the Camp. We had not held any public meeting within the Camp other than a church service. We began to establish relationships with the people and re-establish prior ones. We had intended to initiate programs for the people from Health teaching to counseling, etc.

Following the meeting, we were asked to leave the Camp immediately by _____, a volunteer, 2nd in command. We responded to their request and found temporary residence in town with local missionaries until we were able to resume our initiatives. I , _____, traveled back to _____ and met with _____ and _____ at the main UNHCR office. In two meetings held, they gave permission for us to resume our goodwill there. Though upon returning to _____ expecting to resume, UNHCR there denied our team...once again. Then upon having another meeting, _____, the new acting Head, met in _____. I was not able to have another meeting with them to negotiate. They simply gave no opportunity for us.

We decided then to just work within _____ and, if any Refugees came to us, we extended our help to them. On _____the ___ of _____, a few of our team members were abducted by the local military and questioned. _____, our teammate, came to find me. I went to the office of the Prefect to find _____ there with the Mayor and other officials. Our one translator had gone to _____ that day, thus we were at the mercy of _____ translating. He spoke no less than 25 minutes. Another man, understanding English, declared that he was speaking against us and later on was not translating correctly on our behalf.

The Prefect had spoken for a few minutes. I apologized, expressed that we are here only to do good and that we intended to do what we thought or understood necessary and best for all involved, and expressed my respect for those whom we were in contact. He mentioned the Minister of Interior was not informed of our presence there. Our Protocol covers a greater area of freedom then solely for _____. _____ apparently translated falsely about that fact. We were asked to leave the town of _____ immediately, yet, if we went to _____ to retrieve a signed letter from the Minister of Interior, we were welcome back.

Following the meeting, we were escorted by the Military back to our residence, whereupon they searched our house and all of our belongings. We were given one hour to pack everything to depart. I was denied exit from our compound to speak with _____, of Mission _____, for assistance and translation. We were given instructions that no one was to leave the compound until we were with transport to depart. Daytime had been coming to an end thus making it more difficult. After some time, the Military had left saying they'd return in 20 minutes. _____ came by and then went to meet with the Prefect. We had not found transport that night so we left early the next morning. As we were driving through town, the Military had one of its leaders lead in front by motor bike, until the first checkpoint.

In closing we would like to thank you for your travailing work here in this nation and its people. And if there is any possibility of reconvening for discussion and negotiating with regards to Refugee work here, that would greatly be appreciated.

Best regards, _____

Dear Mr. Prefect, Mr. Mayor and officials of _____,

February 4, _____

We wish to extend our thanks and appreciation for enabling us to reside within _____ up to the _____ weeks given, _____ to _____, _____. Endeavoring to work and partner with local agencies and authorities has been our desire as being part of _____. We look forward to collaborating together in the future should our efforts seem of need and would be seen to benefit existing assistance.

We do apologize for any inconveniences and possible misunderstandings that may have occurred during our stay. A mistake perhaps was not understanding fully the complete, local authoritative channels to work through in this particular region. There had been some confusion as to which were the proper authorities, between the Superfer and the Prefect. We had understood that our presence was known in the area. If it had not been known, it seems inconsistent because we were residing within _____ for ____ weeks without any difficulties, other than UNHCR. The local people, _____, _____, _____ Church, local missionaries, refugees and the Superfer of _____ embraced who we were and the assistance being given.

It is unfortunate for the need to have retreated from having access in _____ and to the refugees for we understand the graciousness of the Government of _____ to open its borders for its unfortunate neighbors, and we feel that by extending help to the Refugees, it is indeed helping _____ and its people. We realize with a team of _____ it is on a smaller scale; however, it lessens some degree of the strain, brings comfort and meets immediate needs one-by-one. We are aiding the economy of the town of _____ through the things we buy and transport, communications, our daily interaction with the local people, and helping with any needs that arise through that interaction.

We look forward to another opportunity to extend our efforts in _____ and the local Camp in _____, should that be possible. Thank you once again.

Best regards, _____

_____ Refugee Report

_____of _____, _____
(For personal files, security and accountability to your leaders should any problems arise).

 We felt from the Lord to pursue efforts toward the refugees at the _____. As I have spoken with _____ and _____, they are aware of the needs. _____ has been there. When he and I met, we discussed the possibilities of bringing some aid (_____ as well). We are aware that the _____ Government wants the ship to be focused on their people not refugees, but we think it is due to the nature of the school. This could be further defense should there be any negative feedback from varying sources. I phoned _____ the day before (_____) so they were aware of our strategy and plans.

 We had a time of prayer and devotion before heading out to the Embassy. We arrived at the Embassy by _____am/pm. Soon after, there was a lot of commotion. This had been because of a group of Muslims who had formed a committee for refugees and who wanted to take control of the food stuffs and do as they wished. I had heard nothing of this group...neither _____ nor _____. I asked them to please step aside and not hinder our work and plans. They were greatly disturbed, and let me know it. I mentioned to them that if _____ would have informed us we could have moved accordingly.

 We continued on until _____ came. Then we had to have several meetings and discussions for hours. I told _____, "You know, this is supposed to be easy."
He repeated that statement. He was in agreement with nearly everything I said. There was a journalist and wanted to do a story and take photos of us, but I repeated many times we did not wish to have our name (_____) be used or photos.

Specifically, $ _____USD has been used - personally from team members and another $ _____ USD from the team budget to buy:
 1.) 5 - 50 kg bags of rice
 2.) Boxes of Maggi (seasoning)

3.) Bags of Salt
4.) Big cooking pots
5.) Charcoal / wood
6.) Bags of onions
7.) Bags of tomatoes
8.) Bags of Fish
9.) Carbolium (antiseptic cleansers)
10.) Cases of soap
11.) Oranges for all

And we also had given the _____ family gifts of clothes. This is the family that I helped by taking their daughter _____ to the hospital.

These provisions were projected to last _____ days according to _____. They had wanted us there during the cooking times and distribution of the food to see that it was handled correctly and justly. They continued as normal by doing a role call by family or individual.

I met with the Ambassador for _____ on _____ the _____ of _____, along with his deputy, the president of the rescue committee , _____, _____, a doctor and the chief guard. The meeting took place at his residence. The Ambassador expressed tremendous gratitude for our taking part in bringing some relief, health teaching and life principles to their people. They dialogued for a while between _____ and English about the rescue committee attempting to control the food stuffs, etc. He was very clear that the authority should remain in the hands of _____, _____ and _____. In addition, they discussed their concerns about the increase of refugees. At this point, they turned to me for input. _____ felt the refugees should do as they do. I expressed my concern and disagreement .

I said, 'This is not equipped for refugees...it is a _____. The reality is (the Ambassador echoed in agreement) we have people there that are becoming sick and are dying so whether you are here at the Ambassador's residence or at _____ or a Refugee Camp, it is of great value and importance to know what makes one sick and to remain healthy. To be aware of what is right and what is not.' I mentioned some practical points and explained the value of them. They seemed to be in full agreement. They plan to put a few ideas I had into action.

The Ambassador thanked me again and apologized for the disturbance the day previous. It is good to note that he is aware that we are apart from the work of _____; team that has come from there but is not functioning directly with them, and that we are still currently planning to continue on to _____.

The health teaching and closure went very well. _____-RN, _____ and _____ had taught on Diarrhea, Scabies and Worms. I (_____) closed at the end, teaching the importance of individual and corporate assistance. They are not to be selfish and hold to themselves what they know to be right and good while watching others urinate on the open ground, children continually being dirty/unkempt, putting contaminated objects or fingers in their mouths, becoming sick unnecessarily. They are not to wait for one to get sick and then say, 'Oh help, can you do something?' To take preventative measures so the discomfort and suffering can be reduced. Understanding and knowledge is of no value if not lived out. Furthermore, they are not to be lazy and expect and expect...but to be pro-active. For example, if I see garbage spreading - deal with it. Take initiative. Because I realize if it remains, it brings greater likelihood of illness.

Finally, I took a few moments to explain why we had left our homes and countries. "We have come to know the value of human life and that has been because of Jesus Christ - God coming down in human form to show us the way and changing and working in our lives. We are aware of your pain, fear and discomfort and have been here to attempt to gain understanding of how you must be feeling. Know that God is still God. He is the One you can always put your total trust in..." We felt there was a positive response. Time will tell. A spokesman for the people arose to speak of their gratitude for our time there, thanking us and asking us to pray and pray for them.

Final note: The overall atmosphere was calm and the people were receptive. It could be helpful in providing anti-malarials, worm pills, and other antibiotics.

Blessings,_____.

Tips for Speaking

The more professional your presentation, the more your audience will respect you and listen. This is especially important as you share your testimony and ask for support. Below are some principles that will help you communicate. Often people must practice to be effective because it may not come naturally. Look below and try to focus on one or a few items a day, or weekly, that could aid in improving your communicating and presentation.

1- Establish good eye contact. This will serve to hold people's attention and will be more personal.

2- Look at different people as you speak. A person will begin to feel uncomfortable if you speak only to them. Other people may feel left out, as though they are not there, because you may only be looking at one section of people.

3- Maintain eye contact even during distractions. Do not bring attention to the distraction by looking at it.

4- As you speak, focus toward the back of your group. This will cause you to speak at the right volume for everyone to hear.

5- Do not look at your watch while speaking. It shows you must have something other than your group on your mind, and it makes them time conscious (it may be good to have a way at looking at the time to honor the time given - a clock on the wall or your watch set on your notes).

6- Smile! Imagine you are speaking to close friends. If you are speaking about "life"- as in Jesus - remind your face! Or at least the right facial expression connected with what you are saying in that moment.

7- Be aware of your posture and stand up straight. Carry yourself with confidence.

8- Avoid a monotone pitch in your voice. Let variations in your voice convey interest.

9- Pause in order to recapture people's attention or emphasize a point. Also, if you ask for questions or comments, give people a moment to respond. Do not be afraid of a pause. Your pause usually feels much longer than what they feel -within reason (up to a few seconds perhaps).

10- Try not to use the word "uh," "you know," "totally," "like," "only," too much. It would be different depending on your language, country, culture, and audience.

11- Always repeat questions so the group will know what was asked.

12- Answer questions with more than a one word (yes-no) answer when applicable.

13- When interacting (a question or discussion arises), do not be drawn into long conversations. It is not polite to ignore the rest of your group. Instead, let them know you will be glad to talk after the meeting or during a break.

14- If you do not know an answer to a question, do not guess. Just say you do not know. If opportunity allows, let them know you could try to find an answer to the question later.

15- Chewing gum or sucking on a candy is not acceptable during public speaking (there are some mints that are small enough not to affect your speaking or be noticed).

16- When praying or taking with people after the meeting, use breath mints when possible. It can be very offensive in some countries to have bad breath. You want them to be overcome by the Spirit of God - not your breath!

17- Within reason, present a good appearance and performance (if doing drama or puppets, etc.). Excellence should be our desire. This should be balanced with grace and exceptions from time to time. You are perhaps their first impression of a believer, or they have judged other Christians in the past at how sloppy or disorganized they were. It is paramount to rekindle in your memory that people's time is valuable and should be used the best way possible.

18- Depending on the nation, culture or audience, you will want to present yourself appropriately. We ought to be presenting ourselves not for people but for the Lord, yet there are different standards depending where you go.

PREPARING YOUR TESTIMONY

(some of the following is from my friend and former director of the DTS on the M/V Anastasis, Ginger Cash-Etcheson)

The reason for giving your testimony is that people see in another way the reality of God. It lets people know why and how the changes that have happened in your life are beyond what you could have done. People are drawn in by real life stuff. In addition, it is humbling. There are times when people will be very moved at how someone could express their the pitfalls, troubles, hurts, and sicknesses.

Look at Paul's boldness with King Agrippa in Acts 26:0-11 and Acts 26:19-20. If a testimony is genuine, there is great confidence and boldness that can be felt in humility. Remember to focus on Jesus, the cross, His resurrection, and what HE has done.

1- Ask the Lord for wisdom (James 1:5-6).

2- Outline

      a. Explain life before Jesus.

      b. How you became a believer (they should know how you were born again by the time you finish).

      c. Life after (changes after Jesus).

3- Emphasize point "c" above. Do not focus too much on your past sin.

4- Begin whole testimony with a bold statement or attention getter (a question to grab interest).

5- End the testimony with a good conclusion or question, wrapping up where you started as a reminder perhaps.

6- Make sure it is written or said so they can identify!

7- Give enough details, yet not too many. Make them specific enough to peak their interest. If you are too vague, you will not hold their attention, i.e. "I had a tough time for 20 years." "I have had a good life."- Well, what was good about it?

8- Use at least one scripture (no more than a few is best).

9- Edit and re-write the testimony if it helps to clarify and refine.

10- Make a tract from your life and journey with God.

11- Keep to about three minutes, depending on the location, audience and the time allotted to you.

12- Do not use "christianeze," Christian language that sounds foreign to the audience.

13- Do not be too wordy.

14- Do not add to it. A friend of mine asked me forgiveness because he said he was caught with a gram of cocaine when actually it had been much less, but it sounded better. What lies can God use?

15- It is best (usually) not to mention denominations or speak against them. You can mention cults, etc., but be sensitive and have a relative need or point in mentioning them.

16- Do not speak critically of others. Honor and respect.

17- Speak with enthusiasm. This should not have to even be mentioned! But some people look like and speak like they just came out of a funeral or had a bitter-lemon!

18- Do not give the (false) impression that Christianity is a bed of roses. That life is always so wonderful and void of problems.

19- Speak loud and clear. It is only as good as the people can hear you.

20- Do not argue and make others share or force them.

21- Avoid preaching at them (it is not a "preachimony").

22- It is best to express your testimony in a personal, first-person way.

23- Memorize, if need be, until it becomes natural. Expressing a testimony loses its real touch when it is not coming from your mind and heart.

24- It would not hurt to smile!

25- PRAY before and after sharing your testimony. Remember Revelation 12:10-11: their is tremendous power in our testimonies. It cannot be questioned. You and I are the Bibles that unbelievers read!

PRAY FOR LEADERS AND PEOPLE OF INFLUENCE

1-Pray that they be God-fearing and accountable - Proverbs 9:10.

2-Pray for wisdom, knowledge and understanding - James. 1:5.

3-Pray that they be presented with the gospel - Romans 10:14.

4-Pray that they be drawn to a saving encounter with Jesus - 1 Timothy 2:4.

5-Pray that they recognize their own inadequacies and pray and seek the will of God - Proverbs 3:5-8; Luke 11:9-13.

6-Pray that they be convicted - Psalm 51:17; John 8:9.

7-Pray that they heed their conscience, confess their sin and repent - Proverbs 28:13; James 4:8.

8-Pray that they read the Bible - Psalm 119:11; Colossians 3:2.

9-Pray that they value the teachings of Christ and the Word.

10-Pray that they respect and honor their parents - Ephesians 6:2, 3.

11-Pray they respect authority and practice accountability - Romans 13:1-7.

12-Pray that they be given godly counsel and advisors - Proverbs 24:6.

13-Pray that they be faithful to their spouses and children - Malachi 2:15, 16.

14-Pray that they desire purity and avoid impurity - 1 Corinthians 6:9-20; 2 Timothy 2:12.

15-Pray that they be timely, reliable and dependable - Matthew 21:28-31.

16-Pray that they be honest in all matters - 1 Corinthians 6:10.

17-Pray that they seek pastoral care and counsel when needed.

18-Pray that they seek out and nurture godly friendships - Psalm 1:1-3.

19-Pray that they have thankful and teachable spirits - Romans 1:21.

20-Pray that they be generous and have compassionate hearts for the poor and needy - Psalm 112:9.

21-Pray that they redeem the time and know priorities - Ephesians 5:15.

22-Pray that they desire honesty, integrity and loyalty.

PRAYING FOR OUR CITIES AND COUNTRIES

1-Stand in the gap for our cities and countries - Ezekiel 22:30.

2-Recognize that failure to pray is sin - 1 Samuel 12:23.

3-Persist in prayer for all leaders in authority - 1 Timothy 2:1-4.

4-Acknowledge that leaders are in authority by God - Romans 13:1.

5-Pray that leaders will know God and His involvement - Daniel 9:22.

6-Pray for the election of godly leaders - Job 34:30.

7-Pray that unrighteousness will be exposed - Psalm 5:10.

8-Pray that corrupt leaders will repent - 2 Peter 3:9; 2 Chronicles 32.

9-Pray that authorities will have a pure heart, good conscience and faith in Christ - 1 Timothy 15-6.

10-Pray for just leaders to rule in the fear of God - 2 Samuel 23:3.

11-Pray that leaders will find wisdom and direction in God's Word - Proverbs 21:1; 2:10-11.

12-Pray that decisions will be made according to God's truth - Psalm 109:29.

13-Pray that your city and country will rely on God - Psalm 20:7; 60:11,12; 127:1.

14- Pray that God will be Lord of this city and nation - Psalm 33:12.

15-Pray that this city and nation will practice righteousness - Proverbs 14:34; Psalm 119:29-30; Proverbs 29:2.

16-Pray for God to protect the city and nation - Psalm 108:3-6, 11-13.

17-Pray for revival in the church and spiritual awakening in the nation - 2 Chronicles 7:14.

Information contained on pages 282-284 courtesy of my friend and leader on the M/V Anastasis Susan Parker.

PHOTO CREDITS

Page	Photo Description	Photographer
1	Jonny Skydiver-New York	LI Skydive/Loreto Mazzola
9	M/V Anastasis DTS July 1998	Kristy Layton
11	Shaking Hands-Holland	Unknown
14	Lion Roaring	Unknown
21	Working through Prayer-West Africa	Mercy Ships
21	Clock in Chicago	Jon Syrbe
23	Hitting the Piñata-Montana	Jon Syrbe
26-27	The Tree-South Africa	Jon Syrbe
29	Baby Ryan Syrbe-South Carolina	Shannon & Bobby Syrbe
33	Cockroach	Jon Syrbe
34	Kangaroos Dancing	Unknown
34	Tiger Roaring	Unknown
39	Jonny Tree Climber-New York	Jon Syrbe
40	Rolls of Film	Jon Syrbe
40	Jonny Shooter-Montana	Noe Gomez
41	Boukrans' Bridge-South Africa	Jon Syrbe
43	Baboon Attack-South Africa	Robert Gable
45	Train Approaching-New York	Jon Syrbe
46-47	Broken Down Walls-Ireland	Jack & Joan Meade
50	Rebellious Ostrich-Mexico	Jon Syrbe
53	Walking to Escalators-South Africa	Teresa Wallace/Jon Syrbe
64	Shaking Hands-Holland	Joy & Ann Hartman
65	Couple Under Tree	Unknown
66	Jesus in the Slum-Brooklyn	Jon Syrbe
67	Jesus Washing Peter's Feet-Texas	Jon Syrbe
68	Polar Bear Enjoying Water Spray-Mexico	Jon Syrbe
69	Riding Elephant	People For Missions
69	Tiger Roaring	Unknown
70	Guys Jumping	Kristy Layton

Page	Photo Description	Photographer
71	Overlooking Outreach Teams-Senegal	Mercy Ships
72	Team Hiking in Madagascar	Jon Syrbe
73	YWAM Rio Praying-Brazil	Jon Syrbe
74	Yield Sign-New York	Jon Syrbe
74	Watching the Amazon-Brazil	Jon Syrbe
77	Team Working-West Africa	Mercy Ships
79	Mouth Full of Balls-Hong Kong	Jon Syrbe
81	High in the Fjords-Norway	Jon Syrbe
82-83	Clocks	Unknown
84	Jonny Hiking in Guatemala	Jon Syrbe
87	Mountain View-Sierra Leone	Mercy Ships
89	Jonny Cliff Jumping-Caribbean	Tommy Henderson
90	Sierra Leonean refugee-Guinea	Mercy Ships
91	Mouth Full of Balls-Hong Kong	Jon Syrbe
91	Stairs of Confusion-Chicago	Jon Syrbe
93	Friend laying in Coffin Dramatized-Germany	Jon Syrbe
94	Moscow-Russia	Jon Syrbe
95	Passport	Teresa Wallace/Jon Syrbe
96	The Stamper-New York	Jon Syrbe
99	Collage of Ideas for Helping	Jon Syrbe/People For Missions
100-101	Overlooking Market-West Africa	Mercy Ships
100	Christi Kambs & Refugees-Guinea	Jon Syrbe
101	Keith Krueger & Kids-West Africa	Mercy Ships
101	Lisa Burke-Schwind Teaching	Mercy Ships
102	Dr. Gary Parker Operating-M/V Anastasis	Mercy Ships
102	Savaka with Team-Madagascar	Jon Syrbe
104	Colin Fullilove Preaching-India	People For Missions
105	Crosstide Drama Team-France	Mercy Ships
106	Skyline-Chicago	Unknown
109	Colin Fullilove Jr. Tree Resting	People For Missions
110	YWAM Rio Hospitality-Brazil	Jon Syrbe
112	Fighter Plane	Jon Syrbe
112	Villagers Carrying Supplies-Madagascar	Jon Syrbe

Page	Photo Description	Photographer
113	Overloaded Vehicle-Ghana	Jon Syrbe
114	Local African Salesman-West Africa	Mercy Ships
117	Loreto Mazzola Walking?-M/V Anastasis	Teresa Wallace/Jon Syrbe
118-119	Wall of Chaos-Hong Kong	Jon Syrbe
120-121	Street Performer-Holland	Jon Syrbe
122	Tom & Linda Nolan Praying-Nicaragua	Nolans
124	Monk in the Ball-Brazil	Jon Syrbe
125	Father reading to Daughter-New York City	Jon Syrbe
127	Collage of Giving	People For Missions/Jon Syrbe
129	Team Giving to Villagers-Madagascar	Jon Syrbe
130	Team Carrying equipment-Madagascar	Mercy Ships
133	Man Asking for a Hand	Jon Syrbe
134	Overlooking Port-West Africa	Mercy Ships
137	Collage of Leaders	Jon Syrbe/Mercy Ships/PFM
140	Life Injustice Drawing	Jon Syrbe
141	Refugee Suffering in Quarantine-Guinea	Jon Syrbe/Teresa Wallace
142	Ocean Waters	Unknown
143	African Ambassador	Jon Syrbe
147	Chinese Writing-Hong Kong	Jon Syrbe
147	Jonny Helicoptering-Madagascar	Monika Lindas
148	Anchored Church-Germany	Jon Syrbe
149	Monkey's cleaning each other-India	Jon Syrbe
151	Collage of thoughts with Ryan Syrbe	Teresa W./Shannon Syrbe/Unknowns
152	Driving on Cliffs-Guatemala	People For Missions
155	Soldiers-New York City	Jon Syrbe
156-157	Hanna Collins and friend-Madagascar	Mercy Ships
158-159	Crowd-West Africa	Mercy Ships
159	Collage of cultures	Jon Syrbe
160	Great Wall of China	Jon Syrbe
164	Collage of Animals-Africa	Jon Syrbe/Kreig Ecklund
164	Adam & Eve-New York City	Jon Syrbe
165	Boy Carrying Bucket-Africa	Mercy Ships

Page	Photo Description	Photographer
165	Cannon-India	Jon Syrbe
166	Ant	Jon Syrbe
166	Boy being Bathed-Africa	Mercy Ships
167	Carrying Wounded Soldier-Ireland	Jack & Joan Meade
167	Cobra-India	Wayne & Becky Phillips
170	"Eve" (lil China Girl) and Cobra-China/India	Wayne & Becky Phillips /Jon Syrbe
171	"Adam" and Cobra-India	Wayne & Becky Phillips
173	Collage of Tulasi and Animals-India	Jon Syrbe
175	Mountains and Skies-USA/ South Africa/Amazon/Holland	Jon Syrbe
178	Children Swimming in River-West Africa	Mercy Ships
178	Children Going toilet on Street-West Africa	Mercy Ships
179	Pigs Enjoying the Pipe Meals-India	Jon Syrbe
181	Woman-Latvia	Mercy Ships
184	Frame and Bridge-Madagascar/ New Zealand	Jon Syrbe
185	Collage of Women	Jon Syrbe
189	Muslim Women Walking Outside Mosque-India	Jon Syrbe
190	Mary Pondering-India	Jon Syrbe
192	The Bible	Jon Syrbe
193	Adam and Eve and Walls-NYC/Ireland	Jon Syrbe/Meades
194	Woman Warrior-Ukraine	Jon Syrbe
195	Adam and Eve-New York City	Jon Syrbe
196	Jesus Washing Women's Feet-Texas/India	Jon Syrbe
202	Flags of United Nations- New York City	Jon Syrbe
203	Collage of Women	Jon Syrbe/Mercy Ships
206	Man Carrying Donkey-Holland	Jon Syrbe
206	Dyana Dreaming-Belgium	Jon Syrbe
208	Muslim Women Walking in the Shadows-India	Jon Syrbe
210-211	Women and Submission	Jon Syrbe

Page	Photo Description	Photographer
212	Jason Reading the Bible in the Dark-India	Jon Syrbe
213	Danger Sign-with 'women' added-Australia	Jon Syrbe
214	Iram and Daughter-Mexico	Jon Syrbe
214	Collage-Ideal Head-New York/ Brazil/Africa	Jon Syrbe
216	Free Way Ends Sign	Jon Syrbe
219	Joki-Mexico	Jon Syrbe
221	Dave Witbeck Jumping-South Africa	Ian Christmann/ Teresa Wallace
222	Man Holding Globe-New York City	Jon Syrbe
223	Train Approaching-New York	Jon Syrbe
225	Randy Paige Water Skiing-New York	Leslie Paige/Jon Syrbe
226	Ian Washing Bride Carolyn's Feet	Jon Syrbe
227	Ryan and Mark Paige-New York	Leslie Paige
228	Do Not Enter Through Door-M/V Anastasis	Jon Syrbe
230	Children Following Scott Knight-Canary Isles	Jon Syrbe
235	Cross and Apartment-Connecticut/Holland	Jon Syrbe
237	Stairs of Confusion-Chicago	Jon Syrbe
243	Kyle Strickland Resting Well-North Carolina	Jon Syrbe
244	Kids Shining-Guatemala	People For Missions
244	Beauties of the Streets-India	Jon Syrbe
245	Woman and Baby-Madagascar	Jon Syrbe
251	Joshua Bauman and Train-Chicago/New York	Jon Syrbe
252	Collage of Espinosa and Friends-Mexico	Jon Syrbe
253	Living on the Edge-Norway	Jon Syrbe
255	Collage of Vision and Planning	Jon Syrbe/ Teresa Wallace

Jon Syrbe is available for speaking engagements and personal appearances. For more information contact Jon at:

BridgeStones International
434 Broadway
Port Jefferson Station, NY 11776

www.bridgestones.com

To order additional copies of this book or to see a complete list of all ADVANTAGE BOOKS™ visit our online bookstore at:

www.advbookstore.com

or

call our toll free order number at: 1-888-383-3110

Longwood, Florida, USA

"we bring dreams to life"™
www.advbooks.com

Printed in the United States
38856LVS00003B/22-39

9 781597 550062